FOUNDATIONS OF MENTAL HEALTH PRACTICE

The Foundations of Mental Health Practice series offers a fresh approach to the field of mental health by exploring key areas and issues in mental health from a social, psychological and a biological perspective. Taking a multidisciplinary approach, the series is aimed at students and practitioners across the people professions, including student nurses, social workers, occupational therapists, psychiatrists, counsellors and psychologists.

Series editors:

Thurstine Basset worked as a community worker and social worker before becoming involved in mental health training and education in the 1980s. He is Director of Basset Consultancy Ltd and has experience of working with a number of universities, statutory and voluntary mental health organisations, service user and carer groups. He has published widely across the fields of mental health training and education. In collaboration with Theo Stickley, he is a co-editor of *Learning about Mental Health Practice* (2008). He is also an editor of the *Journal of Mental Health Training, Education and Practice*.

Theo Stickley is Associate Professor of Mental Health Nursing at the University of Nottingham. He has authored and edited many books and journal articles about mental health. Each represents his interest in promoting a fair, just and genuinely caring way in which to think about and deliver mental health care. His area of research is promoting mental health through participatory arts and he advocates a creative approach to care delivery.

Available now:

Working with Dual Diagnosis: A Psychosocial Perspective by Darren Hill, William J Penson and Divine Charura
From Psychiatric Patient to Citizen Revisited by Liz Sayce
Models of Mental Health by Gavin Davidson, Jim Campbell, Ciarán Shannon and Ciaran Mulholland
Values and Ethics in Mental Health: An Exploration for Practice by Alastair Morgan, Anne Felton, Bill Fulford, Jayasree Kalathil and Gemma Stacey

WORKING WITH DUAL DIAGNOSIS

A Psychosocial Perspective

DARREN HILL
WILLIAM J. PENSON
AND
DIVINE CHARURA

 macmillan education palgrave

First published 2016 by
PALGRAVE

Palgrave in the UK is an imprint of Macmillan Publishers Limited, registered in England, company number 785998, of 4 Crinan Street, London N1 9XW.

Palgrave Macmillan in the US is a division of St Martin's Press LLC, 175 Fifth Avenue, New York, NY 10010.

Palgrave is a global imprint of the above companies and is represented throughout the world.

Palgrave® and Macmillan® are registered trademarks in the United States, the United Kingdom, Europe and other countries.

ISBN 978–1–137–33766–5

This book is printed on paper suitable for recycling and made from fully managed and sustained forest sources. Logging, pulping and manufacturing processes are expected to conform to the environmental regulations of the country of origin.

A catalogue record for this book is available from the British Library.

A catalog record for this book is available from the Library of Congress.

Printed in China

Contents

List of Tables and Figures

TABLES

FIGURES

Introduction

> Hallucinogenic drugs have been used by humans for as long as we can determine
> to provide novel insights into the mind and enhance social bonding. For moral
> reasons, hidden behind spurious concerns about health harms, modern day society
> has attempted to deny the value and importance of the use of these drugs and
> the study of this altered state of consciousness.
>
> (David Nutt, Professor of Neuropsychopharmacology at Imperial College, London, and
> former British Government advisor, in a special issue of *The Psychologist* devoted to
> hallucinogenic drugs (Nutt, 2014:658))

This textbook takes a bold position on dual diagnosis, and by doing so it embraces the ideas that this is a challenging area of practice and 'dual diagnosis' is a much-contested term and concept. Despite this, and in acknowledging that critical positions may not always feel very helpful to the practitioner in contemporary services, this text will also give some clear practice and clinical guidance. So it is a book of two halves – the first being a social, political and historical critique of dual diagnosis, and the second a practice guide based on our own practice 'wisdom' and experience, current best practice guidance and evidence. As David Nutt (2014) suggests in the quote above, concerns and thinking about substance use is as much driven by non-clinical issues such as politics and morals, as it is by health concerns.

As a starting point, we need to have at least a provisional definition of 'dual diagnosis'. There are different definitions which include 'severe mental illness' with either substance misuse, alcohol problems and/or learning difficulty. The Department of Health (DoH) (2002) suggests the relationship between mental illness and substance misuse is complex, and may include:

- a primary mental health problem leading to substance misuse;
- substance misuse worsening, perhaps altering the course of a mental health problem;
- intoxication/substance dependence leading to psychological problems;
- substance misuse/withdrawal leading to mental health symptoms/illness.

The DoH goes on to provide a chart (see below) showing the relationship between mental ill-health and substance use, and it notes the upper right quadrant as being of greatest concern. These are likely to be familiar terms and ideas to the practitioner, but with a little critical thinking we begin to entertain the idea that even a simple chart has within it ideas of normal substance use, rationing of services, risk management and risk aversion, and given that it is a graph, the user experience can be located in any of the quadrants to varying degrees. This implies a broad norming of the user experience because we are invited to locate the person in the quadrant.

In this text we will see 'dual diagnosis' as a term that can have a number of definitions, and at least some defining characteristics will be about its function as a term. So, dual diagnosis can be:

- a descriptor of the service user who has a diagnosable mental health problem and who uses non-prescribed psychoactive substances;
- a statement of whether the service user has concurrent problems in a number of diagnosable areas defined by clinical models;
- a tag that locates the service user within service provision and care pathways.

But equally 'dual diagnosis' has become a term that can be understood in relation to class, ethnicity, gender and sexuality (who ends up dually diagnosed?), a statement of hopelessness or comment on the potential for recovery, and a political tool for service organization. Test this out by checking how many service users who smoke and have a mental health diagnosis are dually diagnosed. We know tobacco is very bad for people and that it is addictive, but it is broadly normed along the lines of legality and class. This is not a point in favour of having a more inclusive term, but to note that 'dual diagnosis' is a term constructed with functions, and with edges, that vary based on the terms of the construction.

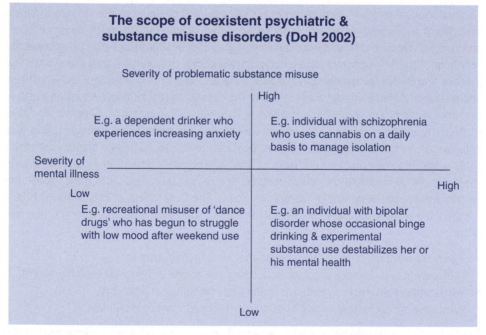

Figure I.1 The Scope of Coexistent Psychiatric & Substance Misuse Disorders

Source: DoH (2002)

In the first half of this book we tackle the idea that while 'dual diagnosis' is a relatively recent term, the relationship between the human sciences and vocational, clinical professions in substance use and mental health/psychiatry is well established and is perhaps best conceptualized as related, sometimes very closely and at other times less so. There are points wherein the relationship (and practice) converge, and likewise, points when they drift apart and diverge. In fact, this typifies the push and pull of support and care for those people that have concurrent distress that results in a psychiatric diagnosis and those that also use substances for whatever purpose.

There is also a possibility that this relationship between practice and clinical discourses, and all the complexities that seem to go with dual diagnosis, is not one of 'natural' clinical category(ies), but is rather a perfect storm of 'madness' and 'badness' that comes into view when the human sciences pass their clinical gaze in that direction. A curious clinical phenomenon has emerged that suggests, in the first place, that there are a number of distinct clinical entities that are separable and subsequently identifiable in combination. This is in the face of knowing also that we have little to consistently draw upon about the 'chicken and egg' of dual diagnosis; that is, the interactions between substances and distress, and the life outcomes for the range of people that may have dual diagnoses. We will see that what constitutes distress, poor mental health and problematic substance use, and indeed what constitutes a problematic substance, is as much to do with social and moral mores of the time as it is to do with human sciences or easily definable positions. We also argue that what it means to function and be whole in the modern, technologically advanced Western democracy is not a given, nor are the social, political and economic contexts simply neutral backdrops. The very real problems that people experience are in conjunction with the demands and expectations made of them; dual diagnosis problems are situated problems that reference the expectations, life position, resources and connections that a person has. Thus, we take a thoroughly social perspective of dual diagnosis and see that problematic behaviour is a situated problem, with tolerance of such problems extended to some people and not to others, depending on functioning, demographic, type of usage, kinds of diagnosis, social capital and social position. We will speculate on why that might be so.

So, we establish that a psychosocial perspective, as the book title suggests, goes beyond the usual parameters of attending to the psychological and immediate social needs of the client and family in a way that sees such needs arising out of a presumed psychopathology. There are concentric rings of influence on the individual which may be felt intensely but seem distant, for instance professional discourse and welfare policy. Neither do we neglect the 'bio'; we are just less certain, given some very well-articulated arguments, that distress being embodied is the same as distress as an indicator of an underlying illness. Clearly, all clients have bodies, and so all distress and altered states are physiologically mediated. But we might also note that embodiment of distress is a means to exercise power over the client, which is why clinicians often require that people meet them; they may detain, delay, examine and, certainly, medicate them. Our aim is to not lose sight of the person materially and to in fact dwell mainly on the social and psychological conditions under which substance use, altered states and distress become problematic.

As mentioned above, having exercised our need to critique current perspectives on dual diagnosis, we take a firm position back in practice. We understand that the practitioner may be left with few options in terms of social change, but they will still need to do the upmost for the people they are helping. The second half of the text reviews and presents practice guidance and explains the models most often used in the dual diagnosis field. We do note that there is something of a hybrid in action, often drawing on clinical guidance and know-how from two historically (and some would argue still) separate fields. The message we give to practitioners in this position is to make the most of their relationship skills, optimize their practice tool box and retain their optimism and belief in the possibility of recovery. While there are practical skills from a range of approaches, and some relevant treatment protocols, it is essential not to lose sight of the individual, their family and their community. And, if the reader accepts some of the positions advanced in the first half of the text, they will also entertain the possibility that what has brought dually diagnosed people to their point of needing help is not personal failings but contextual effects. It is all too easy to suggest that because some people do not experience, or end up with, dual diagnoses, that it is fair to conclude it is a personal predisposition or lack of something, without then looking at the demographics and data that may show curious regularities and what can happen in recovery terms, and prevention, for those with 'capital'.

Key therapeutic models and approaches are motivational ones: strengths-based practice, cognitive behavioural therapies, group therapy, peer support, harm reduction and physical treatments for withdrawal and distress. We review these and give the reader a clear process of how these models can be applied in practice. Additionally we would recommend that caregivers and practitioners invest in their continuing professional development, including effective supervision. Given that the field of practice in this area is evolving, we are also keen to speculate on what may be just ahead for practice guidance, such as the current use of technologically assisted support with 'apps' available for mobile devices to monitor substance usage and mood. We purposefully do not reference medical interventions because these are already established in other texts.

However, there remains a staggering mismatch that we are unable to resolve in this text. If in Part I we are suggesting that a social perspective posits that there is a social and political milieu that is an essential context within which dual diagnosis problems arise, in Part II we are suggesting that the interventions, following current evidence and guidance, focus on remediating individuals. This is not a neutral clinical convention but rather we believe this is a symptom of individualizing and dividing practices that locate social problems back into individuals. It is essential that readers understand that we recommend these interventions to be important to reducing distress, burdens and misery, but we are pessimistic about such clinical approaches in their effectiveness at addressing social and health inequalities. We might suggest to readers that one of the interventions, currently without compelling clinical evidence, that may be anticipated to help people is to become politically active within their communities and to demand and lobby for the kinds of living conditions that reduce the likelihood of the problems arising from dual diagnoses and support communities towards a generally healthier disposition.

Guide to the chapters

Below is a brief synopsis of each of the chapters in the book. On reading you will see that the chapters are somewhat interdependent, and so the argument that builds in Part I does so against the backdrop of previous chapters. Similarly, the issues for practice in Part II build from some important bedrock recommendations in Chapter 4 onwards. Despite this, we think the chapters can also be fruitfully read as standalone documents. A note on the language: we heartily believe that the choice of language conveys the underlying beliefs and values in a given piece of writing or discourse. As such, while it is necessary to use clinical terminology and to engage with clinical and human scientific concepts at times, we hope that it is evident we see people as people first and see them wholly within their community. As far as possible we have used language that is non-stigmatizing and non-pathologizing. The choice of the word 'client' is the one we can get closest to across the range of interests, but we know this may not suit some readers. The problems with evidence in pathological, biomedical models notwithstanding, we do not believe that such patholo-gizing language improves the lives of people affected by stigma and the problems faced in dual diagnosis.

We hope that the whole text is of interest to those people engaged in the world of dual diagnosis, but broadly speaking, Part I will be of interest to those people wishing to gather an account of the socio-political factors and contexts that lead us to the notion of treating a dual diagnosis in contemporary contexts. In effect, it also sets out the rationale for why we believe that a psychosocial perspective is the one that will yield the best results for people with distress and substance use issues. Part II aims to cover the main best practices from both our own perspective and the theoretical and research literature. Throughout the book we make use of case studies to illustrate the points, practices or principles; there are also moments of reflection with prompts and a glossary of terms for reference.

Part I: History, politics and concepts

Chapter 1: The historical context of substance use, mental health and dual diagnosis

This chapter traces the historical roots of some of the concepts, laws and practices that are evident in understanding dual diagnosis today. The chapter starts to provide a definition of dual diagnosis while always noting the fluidity and problems of such definitions.

Chapter 2: The socio-politics of dual diagnosis: psychiatry, law and economics

This chapter argues that the rise of dual diagnosis is intimately tied to a number of institutional interests broadly within an industrializing (and post-industrial) capitalist democracy. Throughout this chapter links are made between allegiances in institutions and how they come to form a variety of powerful outlooks and discourses on madness, substance use and dual diagnosis.

Chapter 3: Key models for understanding dual diagnosis

Picking up from Chapter 2, this chapter concentrates on the main models that are used in practice and clinical areas, as well as key critiques and tensions in the models. Whereas many texts begin with an outline of the main models, this chapter begins with the critical and marginal views so that the reader can have these in mind as they read on.

Part II: Working in practice

Chapter 4: Working with individuals: the broader picture and getting started

Most services working with dual diagnosis start by working with the individual, and so does this chapter. It maps out and explains the main ingredients of a contemporary psycho-social practice, including the therapeutic relationship, case management, risk, assessment and formulation.

Chapter 5: Psychosocial interventions

Having set out the conditions we believe are necessary to successful dual diagnosis practice in Chapter 4, we outline the major psychological models and what they have to say about understanding dual diagnosis.

Chapter 6: Working with groups and families

While not as prevalent and routine as individual work, group and family work is a potent area of activity in supporting people with problems of dual diagnosis. We draw not only on best practice for group work but also the literature and practice of family work both in substance use and mental health contexts.

Chapter 7: Working in communities: dual diagnosis and the recovery movement in a community context

This is a shorter chapter, which to an extent indicates that while most practices are individual, they are often not about community engagement and development in dual diagnosis services. We discuss recovery and the community-based practitioner before outlining the social model of disability that can be a useful orientation to gaining resources and access for clients.

Conclusion

Here we briefly review the main points outlined in the rest of the text with some suggestions for what may come next. In broad terms we suggest that a blend of clear value-based practice, which is in turn supportive of sound psychosocial assessment, and evidence-based interventions is best practice. Even with such approaches in mind, the practitioner should not lose sight of the socio-political and economic drivers and concerns that influence dual diagnosis practice.

PART I

History, Politics and Concepts

1 | The Historical Context of Substance Use, Mental Health and Dual Diagnosis

Chapter Summary

In this chapter we will begin to:

- explore the definition and context of dual diagnosis;
- observe the prevalence and correlation of mental health & substance use;
- understand the social conditions under which substance use is created – normalisation.

Medicine, like all crusades, creates a new group of outsiders each time it makes a new diagnosis stick. Morality is as implicit in sickness as it is in crime or in sin.

(Ivan Illich 1976)

Dual diagnosis: a 'contested' term and a 'real' issue

In writing about dual diagnosis as a social phenomenon, we must first acknowledge that dual diagnosis as a term of reference is contested within the fields of health and social care, as highlighted by the opening quote by Ivan Illich. The concept of dual diagnosis has been applied to individuals that have been identified as having two existing physical or mental health issues; this process of identification usually falls under the professional discipline of medicine and its associated specialisms of physical health and mental health. The two predominant areas of dual diagnosis can be attributed to combined 'disorders' under the following categories: that of learning disability and mental health; and substance use and mental health (Rassool 2009).

> Within the professional disciplines of health and social care the terms 'dual diagnosis' and 'co-morbidity' are used interchangeably; the one interlinking commonality is a mental health problem that is compounded or made worse by either a learning disability or substance use–misuse. Within the text we are looking at dual diagnosis from the position of substance use combined with a mental health problem.

We are deliberately using the term 'substance use' rather than 'misuse', as the relationship between mental health and substance use often hides a complex interaction between self-medication and dependency – through the self-administration of chemical comforts (Gossop 2007). Despite the deliberate attempt to avoid a morally loaded term such as '*substance misuse*' within this text, it must be noted that within the context of health and social care practice, the term 'misuse' is often used in practice. Practitioners within the community often come into contact with individuals, who become service users or clients, who identify that they have a problem. Equally, the person who becomes dually diagnosed may be brought to the attention of local services through complaint or concern, perhaps via the police, local authority or a GP. Given this context it is important that we unpack and analyse what is meant by the term 'substance misuse'.

> Substance misuse is the use of substances that may be deemed legally or medically unacceptable. Substance misuse becomes defined as problematic when an individual encounters the following harmful consequences as a result of substance use–misuse:
>
> * Legal (criminal justice);
> * Social (relationship/familial);
> * Economic (employment/finances);
> * Health (physical/mental).

The medical–psychiatric-based approach to the identification of substance misuse and mental health has seen the development of two systems that support classification and diagnosis: these systems are the World Health Organisation's *International Classification of*

Diseases (ICD) and the American Psychiatric Association's *Diagnostic and Statistical Manual* (DSM-5) (APA 2013). The ICD is currently in version 10, but work is beginning on ICD-11. Both systems offer a codified health- and medicine-led approach to classification and diagnosis and cover legal, illicit and prescribed medications offering a range of medically led responses to substance misuse; both systems allow for an assessment to establish how harmful the substance use is and allow clinicians to diagnose a substance use disorder. In the context of dual diagnosis within this text we are using the DSM-5 criteria of:

1. an individual who has an identified substance use disorder with a coexisting psychiatric disorder that may be a secondary substance-induced mental health disorder;
2. or a primary mental health disorder that was present before the use of substances.

Within this book we are not trying to establish what came first. We are taking a social model standpoint position, that we will work with a solution to the presenting issues rather than attempting to separate them at point of assessment or service contact. This position is supported by the *Dual Diagnosis Good Practice Guide*, issued by the Department of Health (2002); this guide for service provision and practice has been in operation for some time supporting the contemporary DSM-5 classification (in 2002 the previous version of DSM in use was DSM-IV-TR).

The Department of Health (2002) guide describes four possible interlinked relationships:

1. A primary psychiatric illness precipitating or leading to substance misuse;
2. Substance use worsening or altering the course of a psychiatric illness;
3. Intoxication and/or substance dependence leading to psychological symptoms;
4. Substance misuse and/or withdrawal leading to psychiatric symptoms or illness.

The Department of Health (2002) guidance itself recognizes the contested nature of the link between mental health and substance use, with no clear pathway or pathology. The only clear issue is that taking a psychoactive substance or withdrawing from one changes and alters mood, with either positive or negative consequences for existing or emerging symptoms of mental distress.

Taking a psychosocial perspective involves moving away from the medicalization of complex social problems such as those seen in dual diagnosis. In fact, critics of medicalization have argued that there is a persistent process of medicalization of complex social issues. Fitzpatrick (2001) argues that it has become commonplace for governments and medical professionals to intrusively monitor the health of citizens by 'nudging' or 'managing' them for their own economic good, often encouraging the population to accept complex mental health or physical problems as an individual responsibility brought about by personal deficit, rather than as a result of the complex interactions between bodies and the environment. Ivan Illich (1976) takes this further in his critical text *Medical Nemesis* through highlighting that by focusing on individual responsibility for health and mental health, we lose sight of the bigger picture of the social situation in which complex mental health issues arise and are constructed. Thus, the impact of poverty and economic inequality on mental health is disguised by a complex layer of assessment, treatment and diagnosis by medical and allied health professionals, locating the problem as an individual responsibility. In disguising the complexity of causation it can be argued that the individualized-medicalized system protects those aspects of society that support the economic conditions and that contribute to the social reproduction of mental and physical health problems.

Given such arguments, and the contested professional disciplinary nature of psychiatry and the disease model of biological approaches to mental health (we return to such arguments in the first half of this book), we can begin to take a pragmatic social perspective. Despite using a codified manual and having clearly demarked guidance from the Department of Health (2002), it is important to recognize that there is no single uniform dual diagnosis presentation; it can be argued that there are many different patterns of consumption and multiple and complex presentations of mental distress. It is important from a critical standpoint perspective to recognize that psychiatry places itself within medical science; however, it can be argued that it does not have the same medical pathology of reproducible diagnosis and observation/recording of a standard form of pathology for 'mental illness', as disease does within standard physical-health-based medicine. We are not advocating working outside the medical model in a practical sense. Practitioners encountering acute mental health and substance misuse presentations are required to work in the best interests of the service users, and this currently is found within the medical- and health-based models of service delivery. Given this context it may be viewed as improper and unhelpful to explain to an acutely 'unwell' individual the sociological foundations of their distress; however, in reflecting on the context of the presenting distress and understanding a wider framework of the presentation beyond a medical individualized model, we hope that future work with dually diagnosed individuals may be planned in a more psychological and socially informed manner. At this point it is also worth acknowledging that there are established user and survivor movements and groups that will take these strident critical positions and locate distress and disturbance socially and politically, and furthermore they would not necessarily accept that distress is something to be treated and hidden. Similarly, when in the second half of the book we look at interventions, the notion of formulation is helpful, and indeed there are social formulations that contextualize distress. For instance, Harper and Spellman (2006) discuss 'social constructionist formulation', of which a tenet is the 'radical doubt in the taken-for-granted world' (p. 99). There remains, therefore, a dilemma for current practitioners about the extent to which they feel able, and are supported by professional bodies and employers, to align with mental health activists and other activism, and in deciding where that leaves them in supporting people within a service context.

Adopting a psychosocial perspective involves making a break with the thinking that is integral to an individualized model of mental health and substance use. To do this effectively we must understand the limitations of the current psychiatric–medical model, as Paul Moloney (2013) highlights within his seminal text, *The Therapy Industry – The Irresistible Rise of the Talking Cure, and Why It Doesn't Work*:

> There are no physical signs, such as tumours, by means of which your mental disorder might be identified. This fact alone distinguishes psychiatric categories from almost every other kind of illness that doctors treat. In contrast to the diseases of physical medicine, anchored in the material world, the constructs of psychiatric illness have a free floating nature. They are no more or less than someone else's judgement about meaning of what the sufferer is saying and doing, of the extent to which it is normal or abnormal. (2013:34)

In fact, it is often difficult for two psychiatrists to reach the same diagnosis with an individual service user (Bentall 2010). The foundation for this inconsistency is that we are dealing with a range of external biological factors; individuals are responding to the lived experience of varying social forces that shape mood and behaviour. We all experience life differently and we all consume psychoactive substances differently, in multiple social contexts. Despite the contested terminology, inconsistent identification and fluid definition, people who use psychoactive substances and experience mental distress are a consistent feature of late modern society that is here to stay.

Research conducted from 1993 to 1998 in the form of a survey of NHS primary care services reported that coexisting substance dependency and psychiatric conditions had increased by up to 62%, with rates of substance use, psychoses, schizophrenia and paranoia increasing by 147% (Frisher et al. 2004, 2005). This increase in primary care reporting was also supported by research within mental health services and substance use service provision: Weaver et al. (2003) reported that up to 75% of drug service users and 85% of alcohol service users reported a coexisting mental health problem, mostly affective and anxiety disorders; it is also noteworthy that further research highlighted that up to one third of drug users and half of all alcohol users had multiple co-morbidity, meaning that they reported multiple psychiatric conditions alongside their alcohol or drug use. The social context for this increase in presenting dual diagnosis service users will be explored later in this book.

Why do substances and mental health go together?

Dual diagnosis is at once a simple and thoroughly confusing concept; within a complex world that places extreme pressure on our lived experience, we often experience conflicting mental states of varying degrees. At all times we can administer psychoactive substances both legal and illicit as a chemical comfort to alter or enhance mood and mental state, allowing us to function better or relax when we need to. Abdulrahim (2001) has developed some broad links for understanding the correlation between mental health and alcohol use; however, in this book we are treating alcohol and substances as similar, as they are both psychoactive substances that are only separated by prohibition. Prohibition refers to both historical and contemporary limits placed on the use and legal status of some psychoactive substances. The rationale for psychoactive substance use follows a similar pattern of behaviour, as they act as chemical comforts and salves, in some way, to individuals in contemporary society.

- Psychoactive substances can be used to medicate psychological and social distress symptoms (self-medication).
- Psychoactive substances can contribute or cause psychological or social distress symptoms (side effect).
- Psychoactive substances can be used with no casual or preventative mechanism for psychological or social distress symptoms (social–recreational use).
- Underlying traumatic life events result in use of psychoactive substance use and associated mood and mental health disorders.

Reflective point: *When does a substance use issue and mental health problem become a dual diagnosis issue?*

Reflective Exercise

Reflecting on what you have read in Chapter 1 up to this point, imagine you are a mental health practitioner within a community mental health team. Please read the case studies below.

❏ Case study 1.1

Case study A

Paul is a 35-year-old male expressing suicidal thoughts. He tells you that he is tired of everything, tired of drugs, tired of his family and tired of life. The drug worker has made a call for a mental health assessment after Paul reported that he had a plan to end his life by taking an overdose. Paul reports that he has ordered over a £100 of heroin to 'finish himself off'. Clinical case history at the drug service reports that Paul is maintained on 30ml of methadone; he is on a structured detox programme and is having a planned detox this month. His treatment history records multiple failed detoxifications and one residential detox. He has two children under 5 and he lives with his partner Sue, who is unaware of the current situation. Paul had one previous mental health inpatient admission five years ago after making an attempt on his life after failing the residential detox.

Case study B

Alice is found walking through the university grounds at 4am by security; she has been dancing in the water fountains outside a central university building. Alice's pupils are dilated and her speech is confused; she keeps making reference 'to the power of the Internet' and intermittently laughs about 'magic parcels in the post'. In her more lucid moments she tells you that she is fine and wants to go home. You observe her responding and laughing to unobservable stimuli. Her student ID tells you that she is 19 and studying philosophy at the university; she is staying in a residence hall, and her nearest family are in Hampshire.

Case study C

The police have picked up John, who is a 25-year-old businessman; he was found in a public place dressed inappropriately (boxer shorts only), trying to buy a large bottle of whiskey. When the staff refused to sell to him, he became agitated, made a grab for the whiskey and the police were called. In the cells John maintains that he was a 'victim of circumstance' and that he was 'denied his rights as a consumer'. He wants you as a social worker to contact the consumer complaints service and advocate for him about the appalling service at the local shop where he was found. John has fully dilated pupils, and he presents as restless and agitated; he is perspiring heavily and his speech is pressurized. The police have no previous record of contact with criminal justice services. John tells you that he needs to get out of this cell because he needs to prepare his presentation for marketing services tomorrow; this is why he needed the whiskey as he was up late working hard. He denies any drug use and tells you that with a 'mind as quick thinking as his, he requires no adulterants'.

Issues to consider include:

- Substance use (frequency/dependency);
- Mental health presentation (prior to or after taking substances);
- Risk (individual and community);
- Outcomes (what interventions would you like to put in place);
- Does having a dual diagnosis assessment label change the outcomes of your initial assessment?

Understanding complexity

In each of these case studies you are presented with social complexity. What should be important to you as a practitioner is the realisation that the assessment of dual diagnosis is both complex and requires careful consideration. As mental health practitioners it is important that we support the person, not a label. An effective response to situations such as these requires a pragmatic and balanced social perspective: to meet complex individual needs – rather than organizational categorization and formal diagnosis.

What comes first, mental health symptom or substance use effect?

It is important to note that the broad range of psychoactive substances described below are often taken to produce a desired effect on mood or behaviour, often as a response to the management of social distress (as mentioned above), or to produce pleasant emotional states to escape the social constraints of work, family and other commitments that we have to manage on a daily basis. The positive effects of psychoactive substances are often observed as having a complementary social relationship masking and managing mental and social distress; however, long-term use of psychoactive substances as a panacea for social situations and mental distress often produces consequences, as the positive impact of the substance use becomes negative and part of a longer, more complex mental health presentation.

This complex relationship between the positive and negative impact of psychoactive substances on mental health is drawn from the work of Hamid Ghodse (2009) and can be observed below:

Stimulants

- This group includes cocaine, crack cocaine, meth amphetamine and amphetamine.

Positive factors (short term):

- These drugs speed up the central nervous system and produce feelings of confidence and energy.
- People often feel the best they have ever felt (euphoria) and experience increased social functioning including talkativeness, confidence, increased humour and empathy.
- Stimulants also reduce appetite and tiredness.

Negative factors (long term):

- Stimulants can lead to cardiovascular issues and result in fatal heart problems and strokes.
- Users can experience hyperactive social presentation, self-reinforcing behaviour (tapping, rocking) and anxiety.
- Withdrawal from stimulants can leave users restless, irritable, sleepless and paranoid, anxious and with suicidal thoughts.

Depressants

- This group includes opioids, alcohol and benzodiazepines.

Positive factors (short term):

- These drugs can slow the central nervous system down and produce feelings of relaxation, euphoria and general well-being.
- They can make the user feel warm, protected and worry free and relieve anxiety and tension.

Negative factors (long term):

- Users can experience social detachment and anxiety during withdrawal or detoxification.
- Risk issues with polysubstance misuse (alcohol, opiates, benzodiazepines), overdose and death may occur.
- Depressants often slow down reactions; hazards and accidents are more likely to occur in social contents.
- A physical dependency (recognized by medicine) that has an acute withdrawal when these drugs are taken over extended periods in large amounts can have an impact on social functioning and presentation within society.

Hallucinogens

- This group includes LSD, magic mushrooms and cannabis.

Positive factors (short term):

- Hallucinogens give a heightened appreciation of the sensory experience and perceptual distortion; essentially, hallucinogens are taken to induce a psychotic state.

Negative factors (long term):

- Negative experiences can occur on hallucinogens; the experience is directly related to the user's mental and emotional state.

These three categories are neither comprehensive nor ideal from a medical or pharmacological perspective. What they do offer is a social-model-informed perspective for substances such as depressants, stimulants and hallucinogens. For the practitioner in health and social care, the categories offer a broad understanding of how a psychoactive substance interacts with someone's physical and mental health and highlight the somewhat grey area between an effect of a substance and the presentation of a mental health symptom.

> **Reflective point:** *Consider the psychoactive substances prescribed in psychiatry such as major tranquilizers, antidepressants and anxiolytics. If you judged the drug by its effect could such prescribed drugs fit into the categories above? Could, and do, prescribed medications lead to issues of dual diagnosis based on notions of harm?*

Dual diagnosis: understanding patterns of consumption and the experience of mental distress

Given the critical perspectives taken here, and the limits we are suggesting, why is 'dual diagnosis' as a term important to us as practitioners within health and social care?

> Substance use and mental health are at the same time both old and new; since prehistoric times and the dawn of human civilization people have sought out and cultivated mind-altering substances (Gossop 2007, Shiner 2009).

Within Western Europe and the UK, mind-altering substances have played an important part in social and cultural practices; we often use psychoactive substances in religious rituals and cultural events. Psychoactive substances, be they legal or illicit, often form an important part of social celebration and the management of uncomfortable social and emotional situations. Within certain communities birth is often celebrated by a 'baby head wetting' ceremony, in which friends and family use alcohol to celebrate the birth of a child. Death can be marked with a wake in which family and friends often gather with the comfort of alcohol to mark the passing of a family member or friend. Within certain sections of the UK community, alcohol is both the alpha and omega and marks the beginning and end of a person's life. It is also important to recognize the in-between bits; alcohol often marks the end of the working week and acts as a catalyst for celebration of success or the management of failure, and within many UK communities alcohol can be seen as the social lubricant or glue that holds employment and recreational relationships together (Edwards 2000). Within the UK, the use of substances plays a complex cultural role, and even those communities and faith-based groups that abstain from all substances partly define themselves from a strict prohibitionist stance. The use and consumption of all psychoactive substances can be considered to form part of a diverse and complex pattern of social, cultural and religious networks.

Given this context within the UK, we often give priority to the cultivation of legal psychoactive substances. The best arable farmland is not used to grow food crops or sustain animals; instead we use the most fertile land for the ingredients required to produce alcohol. Priority is given to hops over crops, and hops are an essential component of the brewing process in creating beer. The underground world of illicit consumption operates parallel to legal society, with vast formal and informal criminal networks facilitating the production, transportation and supply of illicit psychoactive substances. Illicit substances form a part of escapism, relaxation and detachment from the everyday pressures of work, family and daily life. A significant section of the UK population acquires and consumes illicit substances on a recreational basis, despite a legal framework that places them at risk of criminal justice measures. Vast amounts of political and criminal justice resources are spent to reduce the production of illicit substances; within the UK we have been waging a 'war on drugs' for decades with no significant outcome in favour of prohibition, and despite the deployment of extensive criminal justice resources, consumption within the UK remains high (Keene 2010).

Supporting this social context of legal and illicit consumption of psychoactive substances is the experience of mental distress. There is something conducive to the experience of mental distress with late modern society in the UK. People are accessing mental health support as a preventative or as a means to manage presenting symptoms; counselling is one of the most popular forms of support. As Doward (2010) highlights, nearly one in five people in Britain has consulted a counsellor, and more than half the population admitted to knowing someone who had done so. Supporting this private or voluntary access to counselling is the public provision of mental health support within NHS general practice services. At the time of writing, up to 50% of GP services employed one or more practitioners who dealt primarily with mental health support (NHS 2014). On top of this open-access GP support via the NHS, there has been a growth in nationally funded and well-resourced services such as the *Improving Access to Psychological Therapies* (IAPT) at a community and hospital (outpatient) level; this service is to be free and on demand to those who would like to access it. Proponents advocate that this highlights a shift in thinking about the experience of mental distress and is a positive and psychosocial turn by medicine towards a less biological–medical way of working. It can also be viewed as a remedy or salve for contemporary living. As Moloney highlights, IAPT can be viewed as 'a shock absorber for social change, for the loneliness and loss of meaning that has gone with the decline of traditional religion and the shift to urban living' (2013:21). It is difficult to put an exact figure on the experience or prevalence of mental distress. Mental health is both stigmatizing and an unspoken taboo, and while many are coming forward and articulating their distress, many others remain hidden. We can see barriers are beginning to break down, with improved services access, but it is still taboo to talk about mental distress in social situations; within a social situation individuals must follow strict social etiquette, as we find with substance use, to maintain a positive presentation of self.

Organizations such as the Mental Health Foundation (MHF) highlight and propose that on average one in four people in the UK will experience some kind of mental health problem or distress in the course of a year; affective mood disorders such as anxiety and depression are the most prevalent form of reported mental distress. The MHF also highlights that we have some of the highest levels of deliberate self-harm within Europe (MHF 2014).

It is important to recognize that poor mental health is a common experience within contemporary society, and there appears to be improved access to talking therapies and support as a response to this. This voluntary intervention represents an informal level of recognition and support; however, it is also essential that we recognize that many individuals within society do not access mental health services informally and are subject to formal intervention under the Mental Health Act (MHA) 1983 (Amended, 2007, the Act) within England and Wales, and the Mental Health (Care and Treatment) (Scotland) Act 2003, which replaced the Mental Health (Scotland) Act 1984. The complexity of mental health legislation in the UK in turn complicates the arrangement for support and care. However, formal mental health legislation always carries aspects of formal detention to manage risk. Individuals across the UK can become subject to assessment and formal detention under mental health legislation. In such a situation they have been deemed to be at a significant risk to themselves or others due to their mental state and thinking at the time of assessment and intervention. In effect, the formal mental health legislation within the UK gives clinicians the power to, under certain circumstances, remove the liberty of individuals and treat them without their consent, which remains a legal but often controversial form of intervention. The example below offers a snapshot of information relating to the formal detention of those considered to require a formal mental health intervention within England and Wales.

> The Health & Social Care Information Centre (HSCIC 2013) highlights a total of 50,408 detentions in NHS and independent hospitals during 2012/13. This number was 4% (1,777) greater than during the 2010/11 reporting period. Supporting this increase in hospitalization was the application of community treatment orders (CTOs): there were 4,647 CTOs made during 2012/13, an increase of 427 (10%) since last year (HSCIC 2013).

The HSCIC highlights that year on year we are observing an incremental rise in the number of formal, involuntary admissions to hospital or community-based treatment; given this context it is also important to recognize the concurrent rise in recreational and problematic consumption of substances. Something about contemporary living and the breakdown of the traditional post-war structures of secure work, social housing and collective mechanisms of addressing inequality is having an impact on people that creates mental distress to such a level that it needs to be managed with formal–informal support or through the administration of medically prescribed chemical comforts under a statutory legislative framework.

Measuring the exact prevalence of drug use globally and across Europe and the UK is not an exact science. Like mental health, substance use is taboo within 'polite society'. Substance use as an activity both legal and illicit is considered a 'deviant behaviour', and even socially acceptable substance consumption such as using alcohol and nicotine follows a carefully prescribed etiquette that must be observed for an individual to be considered normal and within the safe range of consumption patterns. So, one of the effects of substance use being situated is that it is hard to quantify.

> People use substances for a variety of reasons: to escape from reality, to relax, to experience pleasure and to disassociate from the reality of everyday life.

Despite the difficulties in finding exact measurement, it must be noted that the UK has some of the highest levels of substance use, both illegal and legal, within Europe and the world (EMCDDA 2014).

England & Wales:

- Around 1 in 12 (8.2%) adults had taken an illicit drug in the last year in the UK – this equates to around 2.7 million people.
- 2.6% of adults in the UK aged 16–59 had taken a Class A drug in the last year – equivalent to almost 850,000 people (CSEW 2013).

Scotland:

- Just under 1 in 4 (23.7%) adults reported taking one or more illicit drugs at some point in their lives (ever), even if it was a long time ago.
- 1 in 15 (6.6%) adults reported using one or more illicit drugs in the last year, i.e. the 12 months prior to the survey interview.
- 1 in 28 (3.5%) adults reported using one or more illicit drugs in the last month, i.e. the month prior to the survey interview (SCJS 2011).

Northern Ireland:

- More than two-fifths – 41% – of adults reported lifetime illicit drug use.
- Up to 11% of adults in Northern Ireland had used illicit drugs within the last year.
- 6% of adults in Northern Ireland reported using illicit drugs within the last month (HSCT 2011).

Within the UK we have seen the illicit substance use level stabilize, albeit at historically high levels. Supporting the national crime survey data, Public Health England estimates that we have up to 298,752 problematic heroin and crack cocaine users in England (2013), while Hays and Gannon (2009) acknowledge up to 55,328 in Scotland, and there are somewhere between 1,000 and 2,000 in Northern Ireland (McElrath 2002). Supporting this level of illicit substance use, we have one of the highest levels of alcohol consumption within Europe: the Institute of Alcohol Studies reported total alcohol consumption in the UK at 10 litres per head for those aged 15 years and older and 8.3 litres per head on average throughout the entire population in 2011 (IAS 2013:4). The number of adults seeking help for alcohol related treatment in England and Wales alone stands at 109,683 presenting with alcohol as the primary issue, and another 33,814 reporting alcohol as problematic on top of another primary 'substance misuse' issue (PHE 2013).

The global is the local: economic liberalization and the normalization of substance consumption

Globalization and the opening up of the UK economy under a liberalized system of free trade has fostered and facilitated an economic system where goods and services move rapidly between continents, countries and free trade zones (Shiner 2009). With an increase in legal free trade there has been an increase in the narcotics-based global 'shadow economy'. This is a direct consequence of the development of a globalized free trade system; heroin, cocaine, ecstasy and ketamine move alongside the transportation of legal commodities in a fluid and undetectable manner, given the volume of shipping. The process of globalization and the opening up of global markets has also seen the development of mass instantaneous electronic communication through the Internet. The development of advanced technical communications has facilitated the marketization of illicit and 'legal' substance use on an unprecedented scale; the chaotic and ungovernable online market has created a thriving environment for the creation and consumption of illegal pharmaceutical drugs and traditional illicit substances alongside new psychoactive substances (NPS) or the mislabelled 'legal highs'. The modern substance consumer expects the market to respond and be available at the click of a button. The underground market has responded with the creation of online substance supply, in what can be considered a classic example of economic models of supply and demand. NPS such as methodrone, methoxetaminea and synthetic cannabis are prime examples of this fluid and evolving market: 'The number of identified NPS in the European Union rose from 14 in 2005 to 236 by the end of 2012' (UNODC 2013:xii).

The highest level of consumption of NPS within the European Union is located in the UK. The UK substance-use market takes the largest amount of NPS: on average, within the UK we consume an estimated 23% of all the European Union's NPS (UNODC 2013). This measurement of consumption and creation of NPS is also recognized by the UN *World Drug Report 2013* as the tip of the iceberg; the dynamic and fluid forces that drive the legalized free-market economy are also present as an inverse shadow economy of substance use. The use of NPS is considered by the *World Drug Report 2013* to be a 'hydra' like problem; when NPS are discovered and legislated against within nation states, manufacturers and retailers adapt and change the compound, creating even more diverse substances (UNODC 2013).

Global economic liberalization, it can be argued, has had a significant impact on the supply of illicit psychoactive substances; the opening up of global free trade has acted as a catalyst in the supply of chemical comforts to an eager and curious population. Supply is only one side, the other is demand, and it can be observed that demand and, what seems to be a common human need to collectively experience a range of new and diverse substances, has increased. The historic process of economic liberalization has been supported by a process of social liberalization; the emergence of radical social movements in the 1960s opened up a discourse that challenged traditional power structures and questioned gender, sexuality, social class, disability and race (Kohn 1992, Shiner 2009). Within this challenge to the established order was a need to explore and experiment, and during this process new subcultures emerged centred on substance use. The use of illicit substances was seen as aspirational and anarchic, challenging the dominant norm of prohibition and the virtue of upstanding sobriety within society. Initially this counterculture was contained within the urban-based liberal metropolitan elite; however, over time this change in attitudes towards a permissive and relaxed perspective on substance use began to diffuse out into wider society, and substance use was no longer the domain of the urban bohemians and cultural elite.

During the last quarter of the twenty-first century, a diverse range of national surveys began to highlight that somewhere between a quarter and half of young adults had used illicit substances at some point (ISDD, 1994). This process was named *normalization* and was identified by authors such as Howard Parker and Fiona Measham on the basis of the North West Cohort Study (Measham et al. 1994). The introduction of *normalization theory* has challenged the traditional model of criminological deviancy and psychology-based risk paradigms. Substance use could no longer be considered high risk if it was a 'normal' experience of a significant section of people within society. The normalization position does not advocate that all young people will take or experience drugs, as the sociologists Howard Parker, Judith Aldridge and Fiona Measham argue:

> Normalisation in the context of recreational drug use cannot be reduced to the intuitive phrase 'it's normal for young people to take drugs'; that is both to over simplify and overstate the case. We are concerned only with the spread of deviant activity and associated attitudes from the margins towards the centre of youth culture where it joins many other accommodated 'deviant' activities such as excessive drinking, casual sexual encounters and daily cigarette smoking. Although tobacco use is clearly normalised and most young people have tried a cigarette only a minority are regular smokers and even their behaviour is only acceptable to their peers in certain settings. So normalisation need not be concerned with absolutes; we are not even considering the possibility that most young Britons will become illicit drug users. It is quite extraordinary enough that we have so quickly reached a situation where the majority will have tried an illicit drug by the end of their teens and that in many parts of the UK up to a quarter may be regular recreational drug users. (Parker et al. 1998:22)

Despite a significant section of the population using illicit substances, people are doing so in what society considers normal parameters, and so it can be argued that illicit substance use has become more socially acceptable within strict parameters. Like nicotine and alcohol, illicit substances have developed an etiquette; central to this is recreational use – young people and adults are allowed to use in safe spaces. For young people, safe spaces include using substances as a rite of passage at the weekend or within the confines of self-exploration in further and higher education. For adults, substances may be used like alcohol to relax at the weekend, and all illicit substance use must be resolved and out of the system mentally and physically for the adult to return to work on Monday. To allow substances to impinge on work or family in a legal, physical or mental health form is to transgress what is considered recreational or safe.

Key messages:

- 'Dual Diagnosis' can be considered a contested term within society.
- Substance use and mental health in late modern society are common experiences within the general population.
- The contemporary economic conditions within late modern society, it can be argued, contribute to the production and consumption of psychoactive substances.

REFERENCES

Abdulrahim, D. (2001). *Substance Misuse and Mental Health Co-morbidity (Dual Diagnosis)*. London: The Health Advisory Service.

American Psychiatric Association (2013). *Diagnostic and Statistical Manual of Mental Disorders* (5th Ed.). Arlington, VA: American Psychiatric Publishing.

Bentall, R.P. (2010). *Doctoring the Mind: Why Psychiatric Treatments Fail.* London: Penguin.

Department of Health (2002). *Mental Health Policy and Implementation Guide – Dual Diagnosis Good Practice Guide.* London: DoH.

Doward, J. (2010). One in five Britons has consulted a counsellor or a psychotherapist. *The Observer.* 1 August. <http://www.theguardian.com/society/2010/aug/01/counselling-psychotherapy-survey> [Accessed May 2014].

Edwards, G. (2000). *Alcohol: The Ambiguous Molecule.* London: Penguin Books.

European Monitoring Centre for Drugs & Drug Addiction (2014). *European Drug Report 2014.* Lisbon: EMCDDA.

Fitzpatrick, M. (2001). *The Tyranny of Health: Doctors and the Regulation of Lifestyle.* London: Routledge.

Frisher, M., Collins, J., Millson, D., Crome, I., & Croft, P. (2004). Prevalence of comorbid psychiatric illness and substance misuse in primary care in England and Wales. *Journal of Epidemiology and Community Health,* 58, 1034–1041.

Frisher, M., Crome I., Macleod, J., Millson, D., & Croft, P. (2005). Substance abuse and psychiatric illness: Prospective observational study using the General Practice Research Database. *Journal of Epidemiology and Community Health,* 59, 847–850.

Ghodse, H. (2009). *Drugs and Addictive Behaviour: A Guide to Treatment* (3rd Ed.). Cambridge: Cambridge University Press.

Gossop, M. (2002). *Treating Drug Misuse Problem: Evidence of Effectiveness.* London: National Treatment Agency.

Harper, D., & Spellman, D. (2006). Social constructionist formulation: Telling a different story. In Johnstone, L., & Dallos, R. (Eds) *Formulation in Psychology and Psychotherapy: Making Sense of People's Problems.* Hove: Routledge.

Hay, G., Gannon, M., Casey, J., & McKeganey, N. (2009). *Estimating the National and Local Prevalence of Problem Drug Misuse in Scotland.* University of Glasgow: Information & Statistics Division Scottish Government.

Health & Social Care Information Centre (2013). *Inpatients Formally Detained in Hospitals under the Mental Health Act 1983, and Patients Subject to Supervised Community Treatment: Annual Report, England, 2013.* Leeds: HSCIC.

Illich, I. (1976). *Limits to Medicine – Medical Nemesis: The Expropriation of Health.* London: Marion Boyars Publishers.

Institute for the Study of Drug Dependency (ISDD) (1994). *Drug Misuse in Britain – 1994.* London: ISDD.

Institute of Alcohol Studies (2013). *Alcohol Consumption Factsheet.* London: IAS.

Keene, J. (2010). *Understanding Drug Misuse Models of Care and Control.* Basingstoke: Palgrave Macmillan.

Kohn, M. (1992). *Dope Girls: The Birth of the British Drug Underground.* London: Granta Books.

McElrath, K. (2002). *Prevalence of Problem Heroin Use in Northern Ireland.* Belfast: Queens University.

Measham, F., Newcombe, R., & Parker, H. (1994). The normalisation of recreational drug use amongst young people in North West England. *British Journal of Sociology,* 45(2), 287–312.

Mental Health Act 1983. London: HMSO.

Moloney, P. (2013). *The Therapy Industry: The Irresistible Rise of the Talking Cure, and Why It Doesn't Work.* London: Pluto.

National Health Service Choices (2014). *Can I get Free Therapy or Counselling?* <http://www.nhs.uk/Conditions/stress-anxiety-depression/Pages/free-therapy-or-counselling.aspx> [Accessed May 2014].

Parker, H., Aldridge, J., & Measham, F. (1998). *Illegal Leisure: The Normalisation of Adolescent Recreational Drug Use.* London: Routledge.

Public Health England (2013). *Facts & Figures.* <http://www.nta.nhs.uk/statistics.aspx> [Accessed March 2014].

Rasool, G.H. (2009). *Alcohol and Drug Misuse: A Handbook for Students and Health Professionals.* London: Routledge.

Shiner, M. (2009). *Drug Use and Social Change: The Distortion of History.* Basingstoke: Palgrave Macmillan.

United Nations Office on Drugs and Crime (2013). *World Drug Report 2013.* New York: UNODC.

Weaver, T., et al. (2003). Comorbidity of substance misuse and mental illness in community mental health and substance misuse services. *The British Journal of Psychiatry,* 183(4), 304–313.

2 | The Socio-Politics of Dual Diagnosis: Psychiatry, Law and Economics

Chapter Summary

In this chapter we will begin to:

- explore the historical development of mental health and substance use as social phenomenon;
- develop an understanding of the political and economic forces that have shaped both the understanding of mental health and substance use.

The social and political construction of dual diagnosis: understanding the context of mental health and substance use policy

In this text we are also undertaking a line of enquiry that has a standpoint perspective; based in the social, political and economic context of society, we suggest that substance use and poor mental health does not occur, and cannot be sustained, in a vacuum. Following this, we are making the case that the structure of society and its associated social forces, as well as individual choices and personal responsibility, play an important role in the development of the discourse surrounding dual diagnosis. Dual diagnosis and its construction as a term of reference, it can be argued, can be closely linked to the development of society under liberal capitalism and its associated moral, political and economic models of governance. In this section we will explore the social policy perspective and locate it within the historical narrative and discourse of the time; this will allow us to observe and understand the interlinking commonalities of contemporary mental health and substance-use legal and policy context.

The one common theme that underpins all the supporting technical and professional discourses is that of punishment and removal from normal society. Under prohibition, the substance user runs the risk of detention within the criminal justice system for the production, supply or consumption of illicit substances; even the consumption of legal substances is conducted within specially constructed public social spaces that are regulated. The breaking of these constraints puts the user at risk of civil penalties and exclusion from social zones. The individual experiencing mental distress faces confinement and exclusion from normal society under formal mental health legislation or informal professional support and guidance; at best, the individual must seek counselling and support away from friends and family. This low-level form of support places a barrier to resolving distress wherever it is constructed, be that at home, work or in the community, and asks us to place the individual's distress in the hands of a professional in isolation. At worst, the individual experiencing distress is deemed too high a risk to themselves in the community and is confined in the hospital or home and medicated until they are 'recovered' or compliant with 'treatment'. It can be argued that to transgress and deviate from normal parameters of society places you are at risk of removal from polite society: until you are educated, treated or corrected by a variety of professional disciplines within multiple institutions. Within the context of policy provision we are exploring substance use and mental health and the construction of the historical dual diagnosis discourse under the following thematic areas:

- Moral–medical;
- Medical–criminal justice;
- Psychiatric–criminal justice;
- Economic–criminal justice.

These discourses, or areas of historical development, are not definitive; they represent significant policy and social responses to the social and political construction of mental health and substance use, and as such it must be recognized that one shift in discourse does not represent a break with the previous era of provision. What we must recognize is that each change in direction of emphasis leaves a significant marker on the next period; what we are left with is a complex and interlinked narrative. What we are positioning within this discussion is that all the discourses represent institutional models of practice, and that the roles of all of these disciplines, such as health, education, welfare and criminal justice services, have been to support a disciplinary society. This has been done through their institutional roles by the inculcation and diffusion of a work ethic: as such all social policy and its associated technical professions in either medicine, health, social care and criminal justice operate to individualize complex social problems and reshape individuals back to societal norms of work and self-sufficiency. Psychiatry and addiction services have had a unique and special role within this process; as Nona Glazer notes, work and the acceptance of it is a 'central goal of schooling, a criterion of successful medical and psychiatric treatment, and an ostensible goal of most welfare policies and unemployment compensation programmes' (1993:33). Helping individuals to be work-ready and return to work are the central goals of social work and all allied health professionals. The term 'recovery', especially in mental health and dependency areas, is intertwined with the idea of self-support through employment and independent living in an economically productive role within society. If the dominant norm within society is to be sober, conscientious and committed to work, the combined issue of substance misuse and dual diagnosis presents a significant barrier to inclusion in the dominant form of society.

Reflective questions

- *Why do you think mental health and substance use as a social presentation within society requires a legal and social policy response?*
- *What purpose and whose interests does it serve to have legislation that manages issues such as mental health and substance use?*

Moral–medical

Key Legislation:

- The Poor Law Amendment Act 1834;
- The Lunacy Act 1890;
- The Public Health Act 1848.

In taking a psychosocial perspective on dual diagnosis it is important to understand the historical conditions that seem to have led to both the growth of the human sciences that derive and measure populations and define abnormality, and the socio-economic conditions (including the physical changes in work and domestic landscapes) by which we arrive at 'mental illness' and 'addiction'.

The process of industrialization and urbanization during the late eighteenth and early nineteenth century had a necessary, associated movement of populations from rural living to the growing urban environments. It is with this urbanization that society encountered problems in living, often drawn from the unequal social conditions. As populations moved from the rural to the urban there began a concentration of power and wealth in the hands of a new urban industrial elite – this new social class of elite were named the *bourgeois*, and they demarked a shift in power relationships from the historical rural aristocracy and agricultural labour system to the industrializing city. The bourgeois elite amassed great historical wealth through the employment of urbanized labour within the service economy and manufacturing sector. With this vast wealth came great inequality: the populations that had moved to urban settings were often engaged in unregulated labour that paid minimal wages. The work was dangerous, difficult and was undertaken with minimal regard for the safety or well-being of employees. Outside work, individuals often lived in difficult social conditions, in tightly packed urban environments, housing was multiple occupancy, and health, education and welfare services were neither universal nor supportive. This industrial urban revolution saw not only the abundance of production through manufacturing, but also an abundance of mental distress and unregulated substance consumption:

> The age of coal and iron had come in earnest. A new order of life was begin-
> ning, and the circumstances under which it began led to a new kind of unrest.
> Immigrants to the industrial and mining districts were leaving an old rural world
> essentially conservative in its social structure and moral atmosphere, and were
> dumped down in neglected heaps that soon fermented as neglected heaps will do,
> becoming highly combustible matter. (Trevelyan 1944:475)

Legislation of this industrial revolution period had initially followed a classical liberal system of free market economics; this economic system advocated a laissez-faire social system that was based in the physiocratic philosophy of private property and individual liberty. However, as we can discern by the legislative response to urban living, individual liberty was confined to those further up the social hierarchy who held economic and political power. The mentally distressed and intoxicated urban poor required coercion and adjustment to maintain the economic and social order. Urban living had created great opportunity for the bourgeois elite, but they also recognized the potential for social upheaval if the social and political system was not managed. The 1848 revolutions on the European mainland sent shock waves through the social, political and economic elite of the rest of Europe; alternative political, economic and social systems based on communism and collective redistribution were developed in response to the individualism and inequality of the classical liberalism of the day (Marx & Engels 2011).

The distress and disturbance of the industrial revolution saw the development of a moralistic punitive system of state welfare and mental health provision. It must be recognized that the Poor Law Amendment Act 1834 (PLAA) was one of the first pieces of legislation that attempted to address mental distress and moral backsliding through the consumption of substances. The PLAA core requirements produced a set of structured premises for the provision of welfare and social support. Welfare was composed of 'outdoor' relief to be supplied at home to the most deserving cases (deserving people were orphans, widows and the disabled) and 'indoor' relief at the work-house for able-bodied working-age adults who could work but choose not to (these individuals were often known as 'sturdy rogues', and these rogues were composed of the mentally distressed and addicted). The PLAA supported the development of 573 Poor Law Unions, each with an associated workhouse. We must have no false understanding of what historical welfare was and some may argue still is today; the workhouse system was a deterrent and punishment, and the conditions were so harsh that individuals would be deterred from seeking help if they could instead find work (Trevor 1987). It is estimated that up to 6.5% of the population during the mid-nineteenth century were housed in workhouses for support (Derek 2009).

The segment of the population in workhouses operated as both a societal safety valve for social distress and a means of inculcating and diffusing classical bourgeois liberal values from the upper class to the larger working-class population. Firstly, this system allowed the most vulnerable and potentially dangerous sections of society to be sectioned off in large industrial warehouses providing a safety net for both the urban poor and industrial elite. Secondly, the workhouse system enshrined the ideology of individual responsibility for complex social and economic problems, and the cyclical nature of capital and irregular employment made workhouses essential. Thirdly, the workhouse system introduced the premises of deserving and undeserving to the lexicon of health, welfare and social policy; this theme is an essential component of tested contemporary health, welfare and social policy and holds particular resonance for debates within contemporary society. Finally, it must also be recognized that the workhouse system was one of the structural government interventions that finalized the industrial revolution through transfer of populations from rural to urban. Vast numbers of poor people in outlying rural parishes were moved towards the urban centres where they could find employment. What we can also begin to discern is the development of the disciplinary technical professions that deal with social and mental distress within welfare provision. The PLAA enshrined the role of the legal professional within both the Poor Law Commission and the multiple local Poor Law Unions, and supporting this was the development of early social work and residential care professionals. Additionally, the workhouses provided a disciplinary system of employment both at the site and through the Charity Organisation Society (COS) within the community, and the COS can be seen as prototype community social workers, managing the community-based charitable resources and administering the workhouse assessment for those considered underserving.

The development of a comprehensive welfare system and workhouses facilitated the development of a new system of mental health provision through the Lunacy Act 1845 and the County Asylums Act 1845. Previous legislation had dealt with mental health from the beginning of the eighteenth century, however, the nationwide development of Poor Law Unions had created a system where vast numbers of people were warehoused in punitive conditions as a deterrent to idleness.

It was recognized that many of the people in the workhouses, including children along with adults, were suffering and developing mental health issues as a consequence. The development of country-wide asylums to deal with this population was promoted as a significant social development by social reformers of the time; the asylum was to be, in practice, a more humane way of warehousing people than the punitive system of hard work and discipline embodied within the workhouse. The system of mental health provision was fully developed in the 1890 Lunacy Act, which further developed the system of confinement, giving it a robust, legally defined mandate via specialized mental health magistrates for up to one year; this detention could be further extended by application to the Lunacy Commission (Rogers & Pilgrim 2001). The development of legislation and comprehensive social policy for mental health also enshrined two distinct professional disciplines in the delivery of mental health services: that of the legal professional in the form of the specialist magistrate, who can be considered an early mental health social worker or Approved Mental Health Professional, and the clear demarcation of medicine as the primary profession in managing distress as we see individuals moved from workhouses to asylums. The social reformers behind this legislation offered a medically led cure to the issue of mental distress that differed from the custodialism of workhouses. In reality, asylums became little more than medical workhouses, with a regimented regime that promoted confinement and docility. The medical pioneers and social reformers became the managers and superintendents; the staff working within were often ill-trained and poorly paid to deal with such complex issues (Tomes 1988; Porter 1989).

Supporting this enclosure of madness and idleness, the nineteenth century also saw the first attempt to develop a coherent public health system and some regulation of the sale of psychoactive substances, in the form of the Public Health Act 1848 and the Pharmacy Act 1868. Both these statutory instruments represent a formal shift in the management of individual health and substance use. Inadequate health care provision in a chaotic urban environment that promoted disease and poor health outcomes had resulted in high consumption of opiates and stimulants as cheap alternatives to expensive private medicine. The establishment of health legislation established the dominance of medicine and allied health (involving professionals such as pharmacists) professional disciplines for the management of moral as well as physical health. The introduction of the Public Health Act 1848 created a local board of health within local government, improved hospital provision, introduced vaccinations, and promoted better water and sanitation for urban populations. The introduction of the Pharmacy Act 1868 saw the registration and examination of pharmacists; previously a range of unregulated 'chemists' and entrepreneurs had supplied poisons and drugs to an eager population looking for remedies, relief and panacea to the pressure of everyday living. The legislation created a two-part schedule for poisons and controlled substances, building on the 1851 Pharmacy Act that had fallen short as an effective intervention due to industry pressure. The schedule had some limited impact, and the introduction of controlled sales of opium resulted in a decrease of opium-related deaths from 6.5 million people to 4.5 million people in 1869 (Berridge & Edwards 1981). Despite regulation, the sale of opium was still freely available and over the counter in mixtures of less than 1% opium; all the pharmacists had to do was formally record the sale of the controlled substance. There was no form of structured drug treatment at the time unless you had the private means to resource it. However, the supply of illicit substances beyond the pharmacy was widely available, with opium, cocaine and marijuana products remaining popular, facilitated by a global movement of trade with the UK as the hub of the British Empire. What we can discern from the Public Health Act 1848 and the Pharmacy Act 1868 is a considerable move towards an established medical and health system, with medicine having a prime role in the management of health and social conditions within the urban environment; we also observe a move beyond the dominance of medicine to the establishment of allied supporting health professionals such as pharmacists. The complexity of urban living required a complex web of legislative interventions to maintain social order and promote some stability within urban society.

Within the late eighteenth and early nineteenth centuries we can see two dominating discourses arise alongside the social conditions that assisted the development of mental health and substance use: that of the moral and that of the medical standpoint. As society began to manage the distress caused by industrialization, concurrently key social reformers of the time recognized the negative impact that alcohol and open access to illicit substances were having on the health and well-being of the population. The proponents of social reform were drawn from the ranks of the social, cultural and polite elite; therefore, much attention was focused on the moral backsliding of the population who chose vice over sobriety and addiction over hard work and clear thinking. As Harrison (2000) highlights through the historical discussion between two social reformers and pioneers of early social work, Ella Pycroft and Beatrice Webb, who at the time were members of the COS, a powerful organization that administered workhouse assessments and community-based social support:

> Do you remember telling me when I first met you how you had helped bringing about the death of an opium eater in Soho? I couldn't understand then how you could have done such a thing but now I have come to think you were right, and right in a most large-minded, far-seeing way. I am coming to see more and more that it is useless to help the helpless, that the truly kind thing is to let the weak go to the wall, and get out of the strong people's way as fast as possible. (2000:108)

What we begin to observe over this period of urbanization and industrialization is the establishment of a disciplinary and technical model based upon the moral virtues of liberalism as proposed by the bourgeois elite: one of hard work, independence and self-sufficiency underpinned by sobriety. Despite the promises of medicine delivering a cure for social distress in the form of lunacy, medicine instead followed the same pattern of custodialism and confinement of the workhouse system by the end of the nineteenth century:

> The realities of the pauper asylum bore little relation to the aspirations of the social reformers. Although some asylums tried to copy the moral treatment regime, this was quickly abandoned, as were all other therapeutic regimes. Like the workhouses, asylums became large regimented institutions of the last resort which, if anything, were stigmatising. Although they were run by medical men, they failed to deliver the cures that a medical approach to insanity had promised. (Rogers & Pilgrim 2001:49)

Following this thread, and with this history in mind, it becomes evident that the entire welfare and mental health system is underpinned by individual responsibility and the notions of deserving and undeserving recipients; these principles have resonance for all subsequent social welfare provision and remain firmly embedded within contemporary society. The dominant model of this period, that supports this thematic account of a moral–medical approach between the workhouse and the asylum, was the bio-deterministic knowledge base of welfare, health and psychiatry. The recipients of welfare and mental health were considered mad or wanting, due to faulty brains and or a flawed gene pool. This philosophy was in line with the values of the economic classical illiberalism of individual responsibility and self-support; it was not society but your deficits that placed you within a problematic social context: mental health and substance use were symptoms of your individual inadequacies.

The moral–medical phase established the following:

- a legislative welfare framework for welfare provision;
- a system of institutional health and mental health provision;
- the control of psychoactive substances to professional regulation;
- the establishment of legal, social and medical professional disciplines in the administration of welfare, health and mental health service provision.

Key messages:

- Individuals encountering social problems, mental distress and substance use during this period were to be assessed and treated according to both a moral and economic framework (deserving and undeserving).
- Mental health and substance use were considered the result of poor moral character and biological hereditary factors (individualization of complex social problems).
- Welfare and social support during this time were constructed as deterrents to seeking help (work is the primary model of social reproduction).

Reflective exercise (moral–medical)

Can you think of any examples of the concept of 'deserving poor' and 'undeserving poor' (enshrined in the PLAA) within contemporary social policy and legislation?

What terms do contemporary practitioners use to describe 'deserving' and 'undeserving' within contemporary mental health and substance use services?

Do any of these terms have a resonance for you:

- eligible/ineligible for service provision;
- complex needs/high threshold;
- non-compliant with treatment/difficult to engage with.

How far have we really moved on from the moral–medical phase?

Medical–criminal justice

The key legislative and policy anchors of the period are as follows:

- The Defence of the Realm Act 1914 (esp. reg. 40B);
- The Dangerous Drugs Act 1920;
- The Departmental Commission on Morphine and Heroin Addiction 1924–6;
- The Royal Commission on Lunacy and Mental Disorder 1924–6.

With the process of industrialization and urbanization becoming more settled during the early-twentieth century, the mechanism for managing substance misuse and mental health became more focused and developed by the technical professions operating them. The early-twentieth century saw a shift in discourse to a medical-led criminal justice response to substance use, with tighter controls by the Home Office and restrictions placed on supply and consumption controlled by the medical profession. There was a shift in discourse within the context of mental health from an individualized model of biological degeneracy (bio-deterministic model) to a more psychotherapeutic model of causation and management of symptoms; during this period we also see the move towards viewing mental health as having a similar basis to physical health. The period represents the dominance of medicine and justice as the prime mechanisms for dealing with substance use and mental health. During this period the social representation and portrayal of psychoactive substances had moved into the popular imagination, as Terry Parssinen highlights:

> In the period between 1910 and 1930, it would have been virtually impossible for a literate Briton to have avoided the subject of narcotic drugs. In newspapers, fiction, and films, the public was deluged with a mass of fact and opinion (often the latter masquerading as the former) about drugs. The perception of danger, expressed in a clear but controlled way in the previous four decades, gave way to near hysteria. Narcotic drugs, it seemed, were no longer confined to a handful of grimy opium dens in Limehouse, serving Asian seamen and a few offbeat Englishmen: their corrupting influence reached out into London's West End and beyond. (1983:115)

The legal and disciplinary 'capture' of substances from an 'over the counter' panacea for social distress and physical problems to control by both medicine and criminal justice disciplines clearly demarks the end of the period of the inert comfort-giving substance, and redefines substances and those that supply and take them as agents of corruption. This process establishes medicine as the dominant mediator between 'good' and 'bad' behaviour, and as the gatekeeper to treatment and recovery from not only poor physical health but poor social behaviour. In essence we are beginning to see the social construction of the deviant and internal other, the discourse of the social enemy within as a drug user; this can be seen as the prototype for contemporary understanding of the dual diagnosis discourse, with the methods of intervention being prohibition and exclusion from society through criminal justice measures, or treatment and recovery through medical adjustment and intervention.

Regulation 40B of the Defence of the Realm Act 1914 (DORA) came into effect in December 1915, in wartime Britain, after a scandal involving the sale of intoxicants, namely stimulants, to troops by sex workers; the legislation passed undebated in the Houses of Parliament and was a major moral panic of the period. The case involved the use of cocaine, which at the time was viewed as a German narcotic, thus fuelling wartime xenophobia, and opium was seen as an oriental form of moral degeneracy (Parssinen 1983). Such medico-legal conditions establish a dominant criminal justice role within substance regulation, a national external threat to the nation as a collective, supported by sensationalist vice and moral corruption, and within such publicity something had to be done. What we can observe within this period is the conflation of a criminal justice deviance discourse around substance use. Substances are portrayed as a threat to the war effort, in the form of reducing efficacy of service personnel, and on top of this external threat we are introduced to the internal threat of substance use as illegal underground activity that is morally dubious; the contemporary media and literature of the day portrayed drug use as vice connected to both sex work and foreign threats. The legislation made the supply of stimulants, opiates and hallucinogens initially illegal to members of the armed services; this was extended in 1916 to all members of society. DORA represents a significant break in the sale and consumption of substances, because from then on prohibited psychoactive substances would only be provided through a prescription from a registered medical practitioner, clearly establishing medicine as the dominant profession within substance misuse management.

The development of the criminal justice discourse can be traced back to the International Opium Convention at The Hague in 1912, signed by 12 nations including Great Britain. The convention recommended that opium be restricted to the medical profession for administration and that possession should become a criminal offence (Spear & Mott 2002). Prior to the Hague Convention, Great Britain was a reluctant partner in the prohibition of substances. However, the United States (US), as a protestant world power, with its ethical roots in abstinence-based values and also a subtext of challenging British dominance of the opium trade in the far east, was one of the first global powers to push for international regulation, as Parssinen highlights:

> The British position was ambivalent. Throughout the nineteenth century, British India had been the largest supplier of opium to China, and the resultant revenues had been one of stable financial supports of the Indian government. By the early twentieth century, however, those revenues had fallen considerably, and a vocal anti-opium lobby in Britain had maintained strong pressure on Britain to pull out of the trade altogether. (1983:129)

The criminal justice discourse as a model of governance becomes firmly entrenched once the national and business interests of the British Empire become reconciled to the diminishing profit returns, often due to smuggling rather than the righteousness of the anti-narcotic lobby (Taylor 1969). As with contemporary criminal justice discourses, the prohibition of substances on a national and international level serves dual purposes. Firstly, it regulates the behaviour of individuals at a national level, inculcating values of hard work and sobriety within the population, and it also allows the state to interfere with the private lives of its citizens by regulating the individual at a micro level. Secondly, prohibition at an international level extends the spheres of influence of a nation, allowing world powers to regulate and intervene with developing nations or competitors; such is the power of the narcotic trade, as it can cause internal markets to fluctuate under external pressure. The control of substances at local and national levels allows narratives to be constructed about the enemy within (the moral degenerate) and the enemy beyond (the Orientalized other); this narrative, it can be argued, provides a mechanism for both social control by the state and social reward for the normal abstinence-based population. This forms an important set of governance practices for helping citizens to identify with the system of government within society.

The rise of the medical-based practitioner reached its logical conclusion in the Dangerous Drugs Act 1920 (the Act); the Act enshrined and formalized the expert status of medicine in the treatment of substance use and misuse. Only medical practitioners were given the right to prescribe controlled substances and treat drug addiction; however, all was not without controversy throughout the 1920s. The criminal justice discourse began to challenge the treatment of substance misuse under the Act through the mechanism of the Home Office; this was done through a challenge to the dominance of medicine's role in treating substance misuse under the Act and alluded that it may not have constituted proper medical treatment. In response to this, the Departmental Commission on Morphine and Heroin Addiction 1924–6 was launched, headed up by Sir Humphrey Rolleston; its report became known as the *Rolleston Report* (1926). The scope of the committee was to consider and advise what circumstances are appropriate, if any, for the treatment of substance misuse through morphine and heroin or preparations. The report concluded that the treatment of addiction by a medical practitioner was a legitimate form of medical intervention. The *Rolleston Report* began a system of drug treatment known as the 'British System' and affirmed the disease model of addiction, with medicine as the primary gatekeeper for treatment. Supporting this embedment of the medical discourse within drug addiction and drug treatment was the move in mental health towards a more medical and psychiatric approach to detention and treatment. The Royal Commission on Lunacy and Mental Disorder 1924–6 (HMSO 1926) recommended that mental health be placed on the same level as physical health, in that it was to be viewed as a medical condition and not a form of degenerate deviancy. What we can begin to discern during the medical–criminal justice period is the establishment and dominance of a codified medical–legal framework for the management of society. We still have excess of the previous discourse behind the moralism of prohibition and the inculcation of sobriety as central to promoting the good society, focused on the constant economic need for work under economic liberalism, but what we can see is a break with the classically liberal physiocratic laissez-faire philosophy of minimum state intervention. The rapid expansion of society has seen the need for structured institutions and professionals to deal with the contemporary issues of urban living. We also begin to see the breakdown of the previous moral order's instruments of management; the Poor Laws and their workhouses begin to be gradually dismantled as the moral guardians of society as they are replaced by medical guardians. This process began with the creation of the Royal Commission on the Poor Laws and Relief of Distress 1905–09; the commission produced two conflicting reports, the majority and the minority report. These reports demarked the political differences of government of the day; these differences included key social reformers and trade unions, and despite the differences, both reports recommended that the Poor Law provisions had to be reformed. One significant outcome was that some workhouses were allowed to be absorbed by municipal health and converted into mental health asylums and institutions for those considered disabled or infirm; from this we can observe that the discourse was shifting to a medical approach to the management of complex social issues such as substance use and mental health.

The early-twentieth century shifted the understanding and discourse of mental health and substance use from the individualized concept of biological degeneracy and moral backsliding of the bio-deterministic model to a medically led disease pathology, with medicine establishing a prominent role within legislation and social policy as the technical officers of health, disease and social distress. One significant event on the understanding of mental health was the outbreak and end of World War I (1914–18). The conditions of modern industrial war had seen combat and death on an unprecedented industrialized scale, and the young men who were sent out to fight at the front lines in western and eastern Europe returned not only with broken bodies but also broken minds. The experience of combat and trauma led to a new, medicalized way of thinking around the management of mental distress. Supporting front-line combat and the recognition of shell shock was the development of a new concept, that of industrial fatigue. Women and men who were left in the factory producing the materials for the war effort were often working in appalling conditions for extensive periods of time, with some workers working in excess of 90 hours a week by 1916. As a result, women often miscarried and workers collapsed physically and mentally through exhaustion. Such were the crises that in 1915, Lloyd George set up the prototype Health of Munition Workers Committee, which was later to become the Industrial Fatigue Board (Rodgers & Pilgrim 2001). What is important is the clear demarcation from the bio-deterministic model of mental health to a more enlightened understanding of the environmental impact of social conditions on the human experience. Industrial fatigue combined with shell shock changed the mental health landscape, as Stone (1985) summarizes:

> The monolithic theory of hereditary degeneration upon which Victorian psychiatry had based its social and scientific vision was significantly dented as young men of respectable and proven character were reduced to mental wrecks within a few months in the trenches ... Not only had shell shock effectively blurred the distinction between the 'neuroses' and 'insanity', but many chronically 'war strained' ex-servicemen were, by the early 1920s, being transferred to asylums as inpatients.

World War I forced medicine to evaluate and explore Freudian-based psychotherapeutic methods of recovery for the shell-shocked men and fatigued workers; the development of these models of talking, listening and recovery saw the development of what we would call modern psychiatry (Stone 1985). We begin to see a move from insanity to a more nuanced understanding of mental distress, in the form of neurosis and not just psychosis. This understanding allowed for complexity, allowing an environmental and social discourse to develop around mental health. If hard-working and responsible soldiers and workers could be broken by trauma and fatigue, there must be something beyond the hereditary model of poor character and genetic background.

This development of thinking formed into a cohesive body of social policy with the Royal Commission on Lunacy and Mental Disorder. The development of the psychiatric discourse located in a Freudian psychotherapeutic model was a primary driving factor behind the commission. The Tavistock Clinic was founded in 1920 with senior support from the British elite; both Admiral Beatty and Field Marshall Haig were vociferous supporters. The government responded by establishing a series of outpatient centres for shell shock cases returning from the war. This statutory funding established a medical-led psychiatric base that would develop a community of therapeutic practice within psychiatry beyond the asylum walls. It is important to note that the shift in discourse and attitudes to mental illness facilitated by World War I caused a period of social reflexivity in government to the pre-war treatment of the mentally distressed within the asylums. This reflexivity had the result that no asylum doctors were invited to the Royal Commission on Lunacy and Mental Disorder. It was the case that 'people with severe mental distress were visible from all class backgrounds in the wake of the war. Their treatment in the community in outpatient settings made this visibility greater' (Rogers & Pilgrim 2001:54).

The visibility and the social class dimension of mental distress allowed society to conceptualize mental health as something that was experienced by all rather than just those lower down the social hierarchy. It is interesting that when those further up the social hierarchy experience trauma and mental distress, it becomes something worthy of support and acceptance in the community, and the softening of attitudes had a clear link to the experience of the political and business elite on the Western Front during World War I. With the Royal Commission on Lunacy and Mental Disorder, we begin to see an early discourse around dual diagnosis develop as physical health is linked to mental health. The Report of the Royal Commission (HMSO 1926) highlighted the four following key areas in mental health policy development:

- The interaction of mental health and physical illness was formally recognized; physical and mental health were to be viewed as overlapping and not distinct with common features;
- Voluntary treatment was encouraged; the key treatment in the past was detention, whereas contemporary intervention should be prevention and treatment;
- Class distinctions were to be abolished; with the removal of difference between pauper and private patients to separate mental health from Poor Law provisions.
- Community care was recommended; the commission recognized the principle of community care by recommending the establishment of national aftercare to support mental health recovery in the community (Jones 1972: 108–111).

It is in legislative changes that we can begin to discern what within this historical discourse is the foundation of medicine, and the birth of psychiatry as a theoretical model beyond the confines of the asylum. We can begin to observe the separation of welfare and medicine, as mental health distances itself from the punitive custodial methods of the Poor Laws. With these developments in medicine and psychiatry, and the subsequent establishment of therapeutic treatment, we also begin to see a new age of drug treatment and recovery.

The latter part of the nineteenth century and the early-twentieth century saw the development of a medicalized system of drug treatment enshrined by statutory legislation. Supporting this method of opioid and stimulant substitution was the development of therapeutic treatments, some of which would be considered dangerous and unsafe by modern standards (Parssinen 1983). One of the first established forms of treatment was the abrupt method for opiate dependence; under this method people were rapidly withdrawn over two days. This intervention was later developed into a semi-rapid and gradual withdrawal technique, and so popular at the time was this system of enforced abstinence that it became known as the 'English treatment' (Berridge & Edwards 1981). Addiction was also viewed as a form of poisoning, and some methods used were similar to the treatment of a drug overdose; less severe forms of poisoning through addiction were dealt with by administering sodium bromide, potassium, codeine, marijuana or cocaine. Medical practitioners also began to recognize that poor physical health impacted on substance consumption, as Berridge & Edwards (1981:163) highlight, 'physical antidotes' such as removing decayed teeth and recommending wearing warmer clothes to reduce opiate consumption. Supporting the early detoxification process and physical antidotes was a system of moral enlightenment that can be compared to contemporary complimentary therapy and self-help intervention; individuals seeking help were offered therapeutic hypnotherapy to inculcate self-control and restore values more in line with conventional society, and physical health changes were also promoted, including exercise and steam baths. During the early-twentieth century medical practitioners preferred a combined treatment approach, much like contemporary drug treatment, recommending substitute prescribing and therapeutic techniques to promote abstinence and recovery.

The medical–criminal justice phase established the following:

- a clear commitment to prohibition through formal legislation, via the restriction of the production, supply and consumption of psychoactive substances;
- the establishment of medicine as the dominant profession in the treatment of drug dependency and mental health through the 'British System' of treatment;
- the development of medical–psychiatric models of therapeutic practice for substance misuse and mental health in the form of voluntary treatment and community care;
- the recognition by medicine of the correlation between mental health and physical health.

Key messages:

- The treatment of substance misuse and mental health is to be viewed as having psychological foundations and contributing environmental factors.
- Medicine–psychiatry moves from a bio-deterministic model to a psychotherapeutic model of practice.
- Substance misuse is established under the medical–psychiatric model of treatment with a framework for substitute prescribing and therapeutic intervention.

Reflective questions (medical–criminal justice)
- *Which social group, or groups, of people benefits from the move from a 'moral–medical' framework to a 'medical–criminal justice' framework of intervention and treatment?*
- *Which professional disciplines and what institutions benefit from the shift in policy discourse?*
- *How significant is the issue of social class in the development of a 'medical–criminal justice' framework?*

Psychiatric–criminal justice

The key legislative and policy anchors of the period are as follows:

- The Report of the Inter-Departmental Committee on Social Insurance and Allied Services (1942);
- Mental Health Act 1959;
- The Interdepartmental Committee on Drug Addiction (1961, 1964);
- Dangerous Drugs Act 1967.

The British System of treating substance use and mental health remained broadly consistent up until the end of World War II. Drawing parallels with World War I, this period of significant global conflict reshaped social relationships, creating a new political and economic discourse within liberal capitalism: that of embedded liberalism or social democracy. This move from individual to collective responsibility on the behalf of business and political elites can be found within the outcomes of the wartime experience. Firstly, the mass mobilization of men and women across social classes had created a spirit of equality and solidarity; people were not willing to go back to the pre-war system of classic liberalism, and the token concessions as delivered after World War I were not appropriate. Secondly, Communism had established itself in the USSR and the People's Republic of China, representing dominant world powers and offering an alternative political and economic system to liberal capitalism. This discourse fundamentally challenged the principles of classic liberalism and individualization, moving collective responsibility and the provision of universal services for all to the centre of the political and economic discourse. The key policy document that anchored this discourse was the *Report of the Inter-Departmental Committee on Social Insurance and Allied Services* (1942), known commonly as the Beveridge Report. The Beveridge Report was a key piece of social policy that laid a framework for legislation that promoted nationalization and the opening up of universal public service provision. Beveridge recognized the need for liberal capitalism to adapt to the revolutionary conditions of the post-war world; his report identified five 'giant evils' in the world: squalor, ignorance, want, idleness, and disease. The 'giant evils' were addressed through systematic legislation covering universal health, education, housing and social security provision. The important development for mental health and substance use service provision was that the fractured regional health service provision for both mental health and substance use treatment and support was to now come under one overarching framework that was accessible to all.

Within this universal framework, psychiatry established dominance over both mental health and substance use as a professional discipline. The provision of universal services also created a vast array of allied health professionals in a coherent, nationally regulated framework: medicine, social work, nursing, occupational therapy, physiotherapy and psychology all benefited in the nationalization of universal health care, taking prominent roles in hospital and community care provision. Universal social services were also developed in post-war society, culminating in the development of universal social services at a local government level through the recommendations of the *Seebohm Report* (1968) that developed into a formalized body of legislation under the Local Authority and Personal Social Services Act 1970. The clear message for substance use and mental health was comprehensive treatment available within the community, free on demand, at point of entry, for both health and social care services. This liberalization and opening up of service provision was also a theme within mental health provision. The Percy Commission (1954–57), through the *Report of the Royal Commission on the Law Relating to Mental Illness and Mental Deficiency* (1957), recommended that voluntary treatment as an inpatient or in the community should be explored as a meaningful intervention rather than formal detention; these recommendations were translated into legislation through the Mental Health Act 1959, which while universally applauded as a piece of liberal social reform did also receive criticism because detention and control were still key features of its legal framework.

The shift in the discourse opened up by the Mental Health Act 1959 expanded during the late 1960s, as medicine and psychiatry became viable targets of social movements critiquing the structure and context of society. Medicine and psychiatry had historically positioned themselves as professions that acted as the guardians of the addicted and mentally distressed throughout history. In the late-eighteenth and nineteenth century, medicine and the specialism of psychiatry had a leading hand in supporting and nurturing the idea that all antisocial behaviour or moral deviancy in the form of vice, addiction, sin or crime was actually mental disorder (Porter 1989). When this social intervention, moral correction and therapy failed, psychiatry responded by institutionalizing individuals as chronic and degenerate (Porter 2002:89–123). This enclosure of madness under health (medicine–psychiatry) had come under criticism from social reformers; after all, medicine and psychiatry had promised to cure the insanity they had enclosed behind the walls of the asylum. Given the failure of medicine and psychiatry to deliver, cracks began to appear in the medicalization and internment of vice (addiction) and insanity (mental distress). This reform in services and shift in attitudes was brought about by the experience of conflict and new models of understanding of mental and physical health and its treatment. Post-war society was opening up service provision and changing attitudes to the established discourse and structures of pre-war society:

> Across a 20 year period starting from 1960, it became acceptable to blame society for every type of difficulty, including mental illness ... When combined with the critiques of the civil liberties lobby and the opponents of institutional care, a new window was created through which madness could be viewed, not as a permanent and bizarre affliction, but as an understandable response to a disordered world. (Moloney 2013:16)

This social change and change in thinking supported a challenge to the expert status of medicine and psychiatry, and even elements of psychiatry and psychology were questioning the efficacy of established modes of treatment. The theories of R.D. Laing (1961; Laing & Esterson 1964; Laing & Cooper 1964) were in harmony with this widespread critique of society and anti-establishment discourse; their critique, alongside others, helped to give birth to the 'anti-psychiatry' discourse. This anti-psychiatry discourse was supported by academia with the work of Erving Goffman (1961) and Jock Young (1971), opening up the hidden world of the mental patient and illicit drug users, questioning the social construction and social reproduction of both mental health and drug use. It is from this context that we begin to see dual diagnosis as a contemporary issue emerging during the move from institutional mental health care to community care during the twentieth century; at first it was a small flow of numbers leaving asylums, which during the last quarter of the century became a steady stream (Moloney 2013; Gossop 2007). The move away from centrally planned mental health services, in the form of large institutional hospitals during the latter half of the twentieth century, had a significant impact on the visibility of mental health and substance use service users in the community; previously those deemed as unfit to work or cope with the pressures of contemporary living would be placed within these institutions and effectively warehoused for indefinite periods of time. As the power of psychiatry was beginning to be challenged in the asylum system, we can see a shift in its responsibility and focus to the community-based care of individuals encountering substance misuse, as highlighted in the two reports issued by the Interdepartmental Committee on Drug Addiction (1961, 1965).

The significance of substance use as a social phenomenon began to be acknowledged within this changing social landscape: the Home Office set up the Interdepartmental Committee on Drug Addiction, also known as the Brain Committee, after its chair, Sir Russell Brain. This committee worked across health, social welfare and criminal justice to develop a response to problematic substance misuse, and the committee published two reports, in 1961 and 1965. The first report of the Interdepartmental Committee on Drug Addiction in 1961 made recommendations similar to the *Rolleston Report*, including the principle of treatment by a community-based doctor and that the prevalence of substance use was small. One interesting point was that substance misuse was to be viewed as a mental disorder rather than a criminal justice issue. This initial report was followed up by the second report of the Interdepartmental Committee on Drug Addiction in 1965: the second *Brain Report* (Interdepartmental Committee on Drug Addiction 1965) disclosed that the total number of addicts known to the Home Office had risen from 454 to 753, and this included a rise in heroin addicts from 68 to 342 and cocaine addicts from 30 to 211. The small increase in substance misusers may seem insignificant when compared to the historic growth in substance use; however, it heralded a significant shift in societal and social policy discourse surrounding substance misuse and mental health. The messages delivered along with this increase in presenting substance misusers followed a pattern of moral panic and the creation of an enemy within discourse; we see once again the use of a moral panic to facilitate or shift policy and societal thinking in relation to substance misuse.

The previous system of drug treatment first developed by the the Departmental Commission on Morphine and Heroin Addiction following its report, also known as the *Rolleston Report* (1926) after its author, was portrayed as corrupt and incompetent. Localized health services and general practice were at best unable to respond to the complexity of, or the demand for, treatment, and at worst were facilitating this problem of addiction by poor prescribing practice in the community. The second *Brain Report* developed a different discourse for drug treatment and mental health provision: firstly, this report highlighted a shift in responsibility from general medicine and general practice to a specialized system of psychiatric intervention. Secondly, the report recommended that addicts be treated at specialist psychiatric treatment centres removed from the community. Thirdly, the report recognized the limitations of medical treatment and built in requirements for long-term recovery and rehabilitation; this system recognized the importance of social services and local health services in supporting long-term recovery. Finally, the report instituted a system of notification of problematic substance misusers within the Home Office, building a clear relationship between mental health and criminal justice in managing problematic substance misuse. This shift in the treatment for substance misuses from general medicine to a psychiatric system supported by criminal justice lays the foundation for the development and funding of modern substance use service provision.

With the publication of the second report by the Interdepartmental Committee on Drug Addiction (1965) and the subsequent moral panic with the rise in drug dependency, we can see a shift within the criminal justice discourse concerning drug treatment. As we have mentioned previously, the 1960s and 1970s saw a rise in social-justice-based libertarian ideology that challenged the traditional structures and authority of society; these social liberation movements were drawn from across the political spectrum and represented a range of diverse perspectives. The late 1960s saw a direct challenge to capitalism and its associated professional and technical disciplines; mental health and substance use was one part of the emerging social movements. During this period we see a vocal mental health service user movement emerge with the eventual establishment of the Mental Patients Union as a social movement in the late 1960s early 1970s (Crossley 1999). This challenge to the social order of mental health and substance use was further supported by political and economic social movements that broadly challenged the established wisdom of the political, economic and social elite across the spectrum of society.

Given the context of social change, an increase in substance consumption led to a further, deeper involvement of the criminal justice model, with the further codification of substance use under a criminal justice framework. The passing of the Dangerous Drugs Act 1967, combined with the second *Brain Report* (Interdepartmental Committee on Drug Addiction 1965), ended the British system of drug treatment under general medicine and clearly established criminal justice and psychiatry as the dominant managers of problematic substance misuse. The Dangerous Drugs Act also established the police in an influential role managing those suspected of substance use: the introduction of stop and search powers under the Dangerous Drugs Act remains a controversial subject. Within this context of social change the criminal justice model was positioning itself as a key partner in the substance misuse landscape.

The psychiatric–criminal justice phase established the following:

- the development of universal service provision across health, education, welfare and mental health, free to all and accessible within the community through local social and health service contact points;
- addiction or substance misuse should be viewed as a mental health condition rather than a purely criminal justice matter, establishing a role for psychiatry in managing social deviance within the community;
- the development of a system of treatment for mental health that places emphasis on community care rather than treatment in the confinement of the asylum;
- the establishment of separate drug treatment provision under a psychiatric (drug dependency units) rather than physical health framework;
- the introduction of a criminal justice framework giving wide ranging powers to the police to manage substance misuse within the community.

Key messages:

- Patterns of substance use are changing – an increase in individuals presenting with substance misuse issues is observed.
- The treatment of substance use and mental health is to be viewed as a deviant behaviour that requires adjustment under the supervision of psychiatry.
- If not treated through the psychiatric model, substance misuse will be dealt with through a custodial model of criminal justice provision.

> Reflective questions (psychiatric–criminal justice)
> * How significant is the use of a 'moral panic' as a reaction to the increase in substance use to establish psychiatry as the dominant model of substance use treatment?
> * Should substance use be treated in isolated, specialized addiction units under the control of psychiatry?

Economic–criminal justice

> The key legislative and policy anchors of the period are as follows:
>
> * The Misuse of Drugs Act (1971);
> * UK Drug Strategies (1985, 1998, 2010);
> * Mental Health Act 1983;
> * The NHS and Community Care Act 1990.

For discussing the latter half of the twentieth century and early-twenty-first century, the dominant theme of substance misuse and mental health will be explored through the criminal justice and economic framework. However, it is important to acknowledge that these two themes are underpinned by both health and psychiatric discourses in shaping the policy, legislation and public attitudes towards mental health and substance use. The overarching political and economic framework of government during this period is characterized by a shift from post-war social democracy or embedded liberalism to that of neo-liberalism. This shift marks a move in policy and legislation that sees universal public service provision remodelled on a privatized business model; the impact on mental health, welfare and substance use policy can be considered significant and will be further explored within this section. Before we explore the social and political aspects of social policy under the context of neo-liberalism, it is necessary to define the ideological framework of the system we live within. David Harvey (2005) describes neo-liberalism as a set of government practices that promotes individual property rights and enterprise through the application of unrestricted free markets. The primary role of government within a neo-liberal context is to provide the rule of law, through the protection of individual and private property rights; the secondary role of government is to roll back its institutions and functions, creating private enterprise and profit within the previously public non-profit sector (Friedman 2002). Neo-liberalism, however, does not operate on a purely technical apparatus but has aligned itself within a philosophical framework through its academic proponents such as Milton Friedman (2002) and Francis Fukuyama (1992). The academic advocates of neo-liberalism directly conflate individual freedom, justice and human dignity with the freedom to pursue private profit within a free market context. This combination of economics with broad-ranging social values is a seductive and compelling foundation for contemporary capitalism (Harvey 2010).

The period from 1970 to the present day has seen a historical and unprecedented rise in illicit substance use; this rise cannot be fully explained by individual or bio-deterministic factors, and to fully understand it we must analyse the wider social forces that contribute to individual decision-making in relation to substance use. The structure of society and its political and economic foundation, it can be argued, have helped facilitate and support this rapid transition. The breakdown of the post-war settlement, and the lack of contemporary political and economic commitment to a collectivist redistributionist economic policy within government, has led to a situation where we have seen economic inequality rise over the last 40 years to levels not seen in the UK since the nineteenth century (Wilkinson & Pickett 2009). The free market principles of the neo-liberal model share common purpose with the entrepreneurial spirit of nineteenth-century classic liberalism. It can be argued this growth in inequality and the structural change within society, brought about by neo-liberalism, like its predecessor classic liberalism, has assisted the creation of social distress and social anxiety. The contemporary economic climate of permanent austerity brought about by the global economic crash of 2008 has nurtured social conditions where the average person faces more employment and financial insecurity and inequality than previous generations; given this context, the historic level of problematic and recreational substance use–misuse seems a rational response to a chaotic and unpredictable world, as Wilkinson & Pickett highlight:

> Low position in the social status hierarchy is painful to most people, so it comes as no surprise to find out that the use of illegal drugs, such as cocaine, marijuana and heroin, is more common in more unequal societies. (2010:70)

This inequality as advanced by neo-liberal economic practice, it can be proposed, has assisted in the creation of the necessary space for substance use and dependency; often the areas hit hardest by the economic restructuring of neo-liberalism are the hardest hit in relation to problematic substance misuse and mental distress. Parker (2005) highlights that the former mining, manufacturing and fishing areas have some of the highest concentrations of substance misuse and mental health issues within the UK. This is supported further by Bushell et al., who highlight that while it is becoming a more normal experience to use and experience substances within society, there is 'now strong evidence for indices of deprivation and social exclusion co-occurring with both psychiatric disorders and substance misuse as a triad of interlocking experiences' (2002:355). Given this context it is important to explore the correlation in problematic substance misuse with the shift in broad economic ideology and its associated policy.

Glatt et al. (1967) highlight that Home Office notifications for drug treatment during the social democratic Keynesian period show a slow, gradual increase, as can be seen below:

Year	Number of Home Office notifications
1959	454
1960	437
1961	470
1962	532
1963	635
1964	753

Table 2.1 Home Office Notifications for Drug Treatment 1959–1964

This low level of incremental increase in addiction is contradicted directly by the increase in individuals requiring structured treatment for substance use within the period of capitalism defined by neo-liberal ideology and economic practice. It can be argued that the move from a collectivist political and economic system to a monetarist-individualized neo-liberal ideology, with the associated break-up of the social system of nationalized public services, resources and utilities, has helped create a system of structural inequality that has seen the gap between the rich and the poor rise steadily since the 1970s (Wilkinson & Pickett 2009; Hills et al. 2009). Official figures on substance dependency highlight that England had 5,000 registered heroin users in 1975 (Reuteur & Stevens 2007), while contemporary figures reveal that 193,575 people accessed structured community drug treatment services within England during 2012–13 (Public Health England 2013).

One of the key periods of change in relation to substance use was during the late 1970s and early 1980s. This period saw a shift in the criminal justice focus of substance misuse management through the application of legislation to classify substances and regulate harm. The Misuse of Drugs Act 1971, which continues to inform and provide the foundation for all subsequent drugs law within the UK, made an attempt to classify the harm of substances within a legislative framework, as Shiner highlights:

> In an effort to ensure that the severity of punishment reflected the potential for harm, three classes were established (A, B and C) and drugs were allocated to them on the basis of the following criteria: whether they were being misused; whether they were likely to be misused; and whether the misuse in either case was having or could have harmful effects sufficient to constitute a problem. (2006:61)

The philosophy of British drug law is provided for by the principle of harmfulness; however, the principle of harmfulness is not clearly established and is a hybrid of medical, social and criminal models of practice; debates continue to this day around the social, medical and legal classification of harm as a concept and how harm is measured and established. Ruggiero (1999) has argued that regulation by harm is a paternalistic notion derived from a moral standpoint relating to the inherent wrongness of drug use. In 1985 a further amendment to the Misuse of Drugs Act 1971, by the passage of the Controlled Drugs (Penalties) Act, clearly entrenched the criminal justice framework, making the maximum penalty for importing, producing, and supplying – or possessing with intent to supply – Class A drugs from 14 years to life imprisonment. Despite the controversy over classification and its scientific evidence base for harm (or not), the fact remains that the system of classification is, and had become, entrenched as a foundation and cornerstone of the criminal justice response to managing substance misuse.

During the 1980s there was a shift in the discourse of substance *use–misuse* and the notion of the development of the 'problem drug taker' and the significant rise in uptake of illicit substances. The Advisory Council for the Misuse of Drugs (ACMD) formed a working group on treatment and rehabilitation. Its report (ACMD 1982) provided a framework for the construction and development of comprehensive treatment services, and central to this service provision was the principle of the problem drug taker:

> Thus a problem drug taker would be any person who experiences social, psycho-logical, physical or legal problems related to intoxication and or regular excessive consumption and/or dependence as a consequence of his own use of drugs or other chemical substances (excluding alcohol and tobacco). (ACMD 1982:13)

The problem drug user as a concept coincided with a new heroin epidemic that was emerging throughout the UK, as Lart highlights:

> In the early 1980s a new 'heroin epidemic' emerged, with very different features from that of the 1960s. Between 1980 and 1985, the average yearly increase in notifications was 30 per cent, with a single increase of 50 per cent in new notifications recorded for 1983. (2006:97)

By 1985 the total number of people on the index of drug use at the Home Office was 14,688 (Mott 1994). The increase in drug use has complex social and economic foundations: the 1980s saw a radical transformation of society with traditional industry and its supporting employment being allowed to 'go to the wall' in a planned dismantling of nationalized and heavily subsidized industrial organizations, as economic policy moved from embedded liberalism to a its new neo-liberal position (Harvey 2005). The UK government of this period, under the leadership of Prime Minister Margaret Thatcher, created the necessary space for the global free market and the transfer of public services and utilities to private business interests. This economic revolution created financial success for a small economic and business elite and assisted the immiseration of many communities within former industrial and manufacturing areas of the UK (Parker 2005). The rise in heroin use, it can be argued, can be viewed as a rational response to a disordered and rapidly changing world; as unemployment grew in the once industrialized areas, so did substance misuse and its associated health and mental health problems.

This period highlighted that substance misuse could no longer be contained by the psychiatric institutions in the form of the drug dependency and addiction units (DDUs). The DDUs and local addiction units were constructed under the post-war settlement and were created to deal with small numbers of users that they then managed through a comprehensive pharmacological and therapeutic model of practice. The new problem drug taker as identified by the ACMD (1982) and the rise in heroin use required a more multidisciplinary response. The ACMD (1982) had shifted discourse from the addict and addiction to a range of legitimate social and psychological concerns that required a multidisciplinary response, and what we can observe here is the birth of the psychosocial discourse within the management of problematic substance misuse. Many of the DDUs and local addiction units responded and became central players in the new multidisciplinary landscape, after all, they held the codified knowledge and established evidence base for the problematic treatment of substance use and acted as key repositories of research, education and specialist knowledge, shaping the practice of future criminal justice-based drug treatment services. Going against the national trend of privatization and free market principles, the government agreed to fund this nationalized drug treatment system; however, this was done in a context of rising numbers of drug users and the recognition by government of the research coming out of Edinburgh that injecting drug users were part of a complex problem relating to the emerging HIV epidemic (Robertson et al. 1986). This rational and pragmatic response to drug treatment and intervention saw services develop under the now historic Department of Health and Social Security (DHSS) that led to a 'flexible locally based network of services able to respond to the wide range of drug related problems' (Black 1988:84). These services had a two-tier system of direct providers and advisory committees at a regional and district level, and this provision was mapped to the general organization of the NHS during this period. At a regional and district level, the Drug Advisory Committees were set up and composed of social services, police, probation services, local education and local voluntary groups. The formation of these groups was the prototype organization of the subsequent Drug Action Teams (DAT) and contemporary local safety boards that manage substance use provision within metropolitan areas (DHSS 1984, 1985). Despite national funding, what we can observe is the embedded principles of the business model, because local advisory committees were also set up to audit and commission services; this principle of locally based commissioning and auditing of service efficacy is echoed within the contemporary 2010 UK Drug Strategy.

Despite, or possibly because of, the radical economic change and the rise in problematic substance misuse, we see a rise in the spending and service provision for the treatment of problematic substance misuse. However, this ten-year period of pragmatic health response and the consolidation of a multidisciplinary psychosocial response took a significant turn during the mid- to late-1990s, under the conservative government of Prime Minister John Major. In 1995, the Conservative administration published a three-year drugs strategy within its White Paper, *Tackling Drugs Together* (Home Office 1995); this White Paper continued the application of a pragmatic public health response to drug misuse and identified the following key thematic areas:

• Increase the safety of communities from drug-related harm;
• Reduce social acceptability and availability of drugs for young people;
• Reduce the health-related risks and other consequences of drug misuse.

With the election of a Labour government under Tony Blair in 1997, the health agenda took a back seat to the criminal justice agenda. The New Labour government published its own White Paper in 1998, *Tackling Drugs Together to Build a Better Britain* (Home Office 1998). As Lart highlights:

> When first published, the strategy contained four aims:
>
> • To help young people resist drug misuse in order to achieve their full potential in society;
> • To protect our communities from drug-related anti-social and criminal behaviour;
> • To enable people with drug problems to overcome them and live healthy crime free lives;
> • To stifle the availability of illegal drugs on our streets. (2006:103)

This White Paper, with its assertive criminal justice edge, was developed into a ten-year drug strategy. Critics at the time highlighted that the contemporary drug strategy was an 'unhealthy' one, having abandoned its public health value base (Stimson 2000). The 1998 Drug Strategy opening statements confirm to the reader that 'drugs are a threat to health, a threat on the streets and a serious threat to communities because of drug-related crime' (Home Office 1998:4), and this is supported by the subsequent statements from the 2008 Drug Strategy:

> Drug misuse wastes lives, destroys families and damages communities. It costs taxpayers millions to deal with the health problems caused by drugs and to tackle crimes such as burglary, car theft, mugging and robbery which are committed by some users to fund their habit. The drug trade is linked to serious and organised crime, including prostitution and the trafficking of people and firearms. Drugs remain a serious and complex problem that we – along with all modern societies – must face. (Home Office 2008:4)

The New Labour government was implementing the election mantra of becoming 'tough on crime and the causes of crime'; this conflation of crime with substance use can be observed as part of the wider neo-liberal approach to government of placing complex social issues within a set of individual choices and actions. The New Labour approach of attempting to reconcile neo-liberal business practices with social justice drivers, known as third way politics (Giddens 1998), led to the development of social exclusion as the complex problem that underpinned and nurtured problematic substance use. In reality, it can be argued that the term 'social exclusion' was a 'fig leaf' used to cover the embarrassment of rapidly growing poverty and inequality.

The 2008 Drug Strategy led to the creation of a drug treatment programme that was nationally coordinated, well financed and worked towards a harm reduction framework. The overall aims of the harm reduction initiative were to reduce crime through access and retention within treatment and reduce the financial and societal costs of drug-related harm. This framework for treatment of substance use through harm reduction involved increasing and retaining significant numbers in drug treatment, peaking at 206,889 in 2009, and retaining them on opiate substitutes (PHE 2013). The key assumption of the New Labour period was that 'treatment works'; the political mantra of the time was that for every £1 spent on treatment at least £9.50 would be saved in health costs (Godfrey et al. 2004). To support the comprehensive and well-funded treatment system the Labour administration built upon the 1985 Drug Advisory Committees and the 1995 Drug Action Teams. The newly developed (DAT) would become embedded within a local authority and eventually merge into Local Community Safety Partnership Boards that were set up through the Crime and Disorder Act in 1998. This embedment at a local level can be considered important as it located provision alongside reshaped NHS services; this provision followed a primary (community) and secondary (hospital) care model. Once again, provision within substance use services mirrored health sector organization; with the removal of regional health authorities in 2002, the responsibility for commissioning drug services was moved into the local NHS Primary Care Trust (PCT), and the PCT and DAT formed a joint commissioning group. The Health Act 1999 made possible the creation of shared budgets; this system embedded neo-liberal business values at a local level, establishing the essential components of competition-based commissioning, based on a system of what worked underpinned by cost efficiency. From this period what we can observe is the beginning of outsourced relationships, with public, private and voluntary sector service provision competing for local drug treatment service provision.

The National Treatment Agency (NTA) provided a comprehensive, evidence-based approach to substance misuse. One of the key features of the NTA was its codification of evidence-based practice into a publicly accessible format with its significant online presence. Historically, the localized drug service provision had failed to develop a robust and coherent evidence base, and a review of the evidence base for drug treatment highlighted a lack of evidence underpinning the treatment given to drug users (Task Force to Review Services for Drug Misusers 1996). This principle of evidence-based practice was central to both the New Labour administration and the historical criticism levelled by Cochrane (1972) that most treatments available on the NHS had not been evaluated in a systematic or rigorous manner. Within drug services, comprehensive auditing was developed with the creation of the National Treatment Outcomes Research Study (NTORS), later to become the

Treatment Outcome Project and the National Drug Treatment Monitoring Service, which firmly embedded a system of monitoring and evaluation that supported a treatment works discourse, allowing services to articulate what was successful on a national level. The combination of monitoring and nationally funded research through the NTA created an environment where service provision for the first time could become coherent and standardized. Alongside the creation of the NTA, the Audit Commission (2002) was tasked to review drug services on a national level, and the review found inconsistency in service provision with multiple service philosophies and practices that lacked evidence-based approaches and were delivered by undertrained staff. The result was a historic reshaping under the *Models of Care* (NTA 2002, 2006) that identified four tiers of standardized service provision:

- Tier 1 – non-substance misuse specific services requiring interface with drug and alcohol treatment, e.g. housing, social services.
- Tier 2 – open access drug misuse services, e.g. advice and information, needle exchange, outreach, low threshold prescribing, assessment.
- Tier 3 – structured community-based specialist drug misuse services, e.g. prescribing, structured counselling, care planned treatment.
- Tier 4a – residential substance misuse services, e.g. inpatient detoxification services, residential rehabilitation services.
- Tier 4b – highly specialized non-substance misuse services, e.g. HIV specialist units, liver disease units.

The *Models of Care* initiative represented a well-funded, nationally planned and evidence-based approach to treatment that aimed to raise the standard of delivery and experience of service users. Within its structure we can observe the influence of the 'trans-theoretical model' of practice (Prochaska & DiClemente 1983). The tiers of provision reflect the various stages of pre-contemplation and contemplation supported by Tiers 1 and 2, and preparation, action and maintenance being supported by Tiers 2, 3 and 4. This system was heavily supported by manualized therapy that was derived from the Project Match Research Group (1997) findings. These manualized therapies were built around the trans-theoretical model of practice; the three standard interventions aimed to develop motivation for change through the use of motivational enhancement therapy, the promotion of awareness around relapse prevention through the delivery of cognitive behavioural skills, and the development of long-term recovery through the introduction of 12-step facilitation that promoted awareness of both Narcotics Anonymous and Alcoholics Anonymous. The *Models of Care* structure and supporting evidence-based practice derived from Project Match (1997) and disseminated through the NTA in a comprehensive manual, *Treating Drug Misuse Problems: Evidence of Effectiveness* (Gossop 2002), are ongoing themes that influence the delivery of service provision and treatment within contemporary service provision: motivation, self-management and individual responsibility are core concepts of the contemporary recovery agenda. It is important to note that despite the significant change within drug treatment provision and service delivery, one consistent theme is the maintenance of the *Models of Care* system supported by the trans-theoretical model of practice. We may have moved from a harm reduction concept to a recovery-abstinence approach, but the structure and clinical delivery remains similar despite a change in the overarching discourse.

Previous strategies had established the reduction of harm to the individual drug user as a policy driver; during the late 1990s, harm reduction had moved towards a model of reducing the harm created by the drug user to society or, as New Labour highlighted, families and communities (Hunt & Stevens 2004). New Labour was significantly influenced by the evidence from the US that punitive enforced treatment had as much success as voluntary treatment (MacGregor et al. 1991). The New Labour project of nationally funded, research-minded and comprehensive drug treatment came with an increased criminal justice message; this message came in the form of Drug Treatment and Testing Orders (DTTO) and the later introduction of the Drug Rehabilitation Requirement (DRR). The introduction of these two orders further reinforced the link between substance use and crime, because both the DTTO and DRR used the 'threat' of imprisonment and confinement as a means to coerce the individual substance user to be maintained in community drug treatment services. Traditionally, the British system of drug treatment was built upon a medical, then mental, health premise of voluntary participation, and this shift to managing those who present in the criminal justice system, or the 'criminally needy' (Stimson 2000), presented an issue for drug treatment. Since the 1920s, medicine, public health and psychiatry had been the dominant disciplines within the treatment of substance use, and the inability for medicalized models of practice to cure or stop substance use may have contributed to the seeming necessity for a more punitive methodology for treatment. That is, one of coercion and enforcement, with the aim to reduce the cost to society of problematic substance use. Reduction in cost is a dominant theme within the contemporary 2010 UK Drug Strategy and the associated break-up of the harm reduction criminal justice model under the NTA. In the NHS White Paper (July 2010) (later to become the Health and Social Care Act 2012), the government announced that as part of the new law, the NTA would be abolished as a separate organization and its critical functions would be transferred to a new national service, Public Health England (PHE). It is important to note that the move to public health as a model for management has not seen a return to broad-based public health initiatives within structured drug treatment services. The restructuring of the NTA was part of a wider initiative to discredit the harm reduction approach to drug treatment, moving the discourse clearly from a medical–criminal justice model of harm to the individual and society, to a criminal justice economic model where the cost to society and the government is clearly a key feature of the social policy arrangement. Within this shift in discourse around substance misuse, the NTA was presented within the public media discourse as a failing agency. Mark Easton, a BBC Home Editor, reported that:

> The National Treatment Agency (NTA) yesterday published its annual figures showing yet another big increase in the numbers of people who were on the drug treatment programme last year – 202,000 altogether. (Trebles all round – government target achieved in style.) Not mentioned in the press notice, discretely lodged in a table near the bottom of the data release, was the number of people who left the treatment programme drug-free last year – 7,324. (Easton 2008)

The economic crisis of 2008 and ongoing austerity programme of central government created a visible shift in the political discourse surrounding drug treatment. It must be noted that the subsequent restructuring of the public sector on a deeper ingrained business model can be considered farcical in the light of the facts behind the austerity programme. The financial crisis of 2008–09 was one with deep roots in economic and financial mismanagement by a business elite within the financial sector. The ensuing crisis was revered from one of private financial capital within the banking sector to an austerity programme where public service provision needed to be restructured to reorder a balance of debts system to fund a financial sector bailout (Zizek 2009).

One of the first visible economic restructuring efforts was observed within drug treatment services. Drug users, with their historical marginalization and deeply entrenched perception of being undeserving and needing to do more to help themselves, are a primary group to begin a cost-saving exercise with. The premise of the attack was that drug treatment was not working. The coalition government, it can be argued, had moved the goalposts from reducing the cost of substance use to wider society – through harm reduction treatment services that aimed to reduce the cost to government and society – to looking at the cost of drug treatment through its output, which it focused on as abstinence from all drugs. Almost overnight a 40-year harm reduction evidence base that was backed up by empirical and robust evidence was almost wiped out. The local drug treatment service structure, now deeply entrenched in a business model of competitive tendering and commissioning, moved to secure its role in this abstinence-based future; this shift was supported by multiple voices in higher education and research, all sensitive to the shifting sands of research funding and government grants, joining the great debate critiquing service provision. A central myth was created, that of the drug user parked on methadone (Drug Scope 2009), and this myth was supported by an apologetic hierarchy within the NTA, desperate to secure a future for the technical workforce and hoping to maintain a dominant position within the newly emerged PHE workforce (Dawson 2012). Quite simply, drug treatment services were built under a harm reduction philosophy of reducing drug-related deaths and providing open access treatment to all who required it, and abstinence was a core requirement of drug treatment. However, exiting individuals from drug treatment services is not as simple as removing a drug from the system of a human being. Effective drug treatment requires a complex interlinked system of housing, education, welfare, employment and health service provision.

The economic context had created a society where service provision across the entire social welfare sector was being rolled back and retrenched on economic lines, and supporting this service roll back was an a increasingly difficult employment market. Historically, we have seen a 40-year stagnation in wages for employees and a system where inequality has grown at unprecedented rates not seen since the nineteenth century (Harvey 2005). Supporting this, there is a system of precarious underemployment, wherein those 'locked out' of the labour market have to compete in a dwindling job resource pool that comes from a poorly paid service sector. It is from this economic context that we begin to discern the true face of neo-liberal government policy; that of individualism and self-help. Under neo-liberal practices the government and its policy must be one of minimum intervention that seeks to regulate and inculcate values of independence, completion and self-support; abstinence and employment are central factors of this as can be observed clearly within the 2010 Drug Strategy.

The practices of neo-liberalism can be observed as having become firmly embedded within drug policy discourse by the time the 2010 Drug Strategy came into existence. The acceptance of partnership service provision, in the form of competitive tendering, had firmly become entrenched as the model of service design and delivery supported by the 2010 NHS White Paper and the later publication of the Health and Social Care Act 2012. The principles of New Labour, its culture of managerialism and audit, through the introduction of the Treatment Outcome Project and the National Drug Treatment Monitoring Service, have helped create a culture that must provide evidence and record information accurately. This level of audit diligence has primed the practice context for measuring successful outcomes as directed by government policy. Within this context we can see the beginnings of monitoring and evaluation that can be developed directly to a payment by results system. The conflation of treatment working and economic savings developed a harm reduction discourse that was centred on reducing the cost to society of substance use. When reduction of harm is confused with economic cost it is no major leap of faith to move the discussion into the domain of individualized treatment and recovery capital.

The contemporary drug strategy can be considered an excellent example of a highly individualized economic-model-based recovery process. The failure of the New Labour project to move the discourse surrounding drug treatment from the 'individual' as a dependent user, to addressing the underlying factors within society that cause substance dependency, has assisted the creation of the necessary conditions for a further neo-liberal approach to community drug treatment. It must be noted the New Labour model did recognize contributing external factors; however, it developed a working model of social exclusion. Social exclusion as a concept avoided the real politic of economic and social inequality by hiding mental health and addiction in a complex social model where no central causation can be located. The core prohibition stance and criminal justice framework behind the strategy remains the same as its predecessors, with emphasis placed upon enforcement with the aim of reducing demand and supply. One core change from the previous strategies can be found in the replacement of social justice drivers with the provision of harm reduction measures, as Theresa May, Home Secretary, describes in her opening statement:

> A fundamental difference between this strategy and those that have gone before is that instead of focusing on the harms caused by drug misuse, our approach will be to go much further and offer every support for people to choose recovery as an achievable way out of dependency ... The causes and drivers of drug and alcohol dependency are complex and personal. (Home Office 2010)

It can be read that the coalition government was ideologically opposed to collective responsibility for the factors that contribute to substance use and dependency. The government acknowledges that the root causes of use and dependency are 'complex' but 'personal'. This individualization of complex social problems strikes to the very core of the neo-liberal ideology. The main statements support a picture of 'recovery that is an individual, person-centred journey', but this individual journey is underpinned by independence from drug treatment, support structures, abstinence and an ability to be financially independent. The policy fails to acknowledge what wider factors have contributed to the journey of individual substance dependency; a clear message emerges from the government that you are on your own, and the 'big society' is creating your 'own society'.

The government highlights that although it will not be supporting harm reduction as an approach ideologically, harm reduction does have positive outcomes:

> Substitute prescribing continues to have a role to play in the treatment of heroin
> dependence, both in stabilising drug use and supporting detoxification. ... There
> are many thousands of people in receipt of such prescriptions in our communi-
> ties today who have jobs, positive family lives and are no longer taking drugs or
> committing crime. (Home Office 2010:18)

The success or failure of drug treatment is to be clearly measured in 'work' or economic
independence. The ability of drug treatment services to produce people who are independent
and economically contributing to society through meaningful prescribed production is an
essential message.

The conflation of substance use with worklessness, poverty and economic stagnation can
be considered a natural development of discourse for a system that relates the harm caused
by prohibition of substances with the use of a substance. The contemporary drug strategy
develops the idea of displacement further by stating that 'drug and alcohol dependence is
a key cause of intergenerational poverty and worklessness.' For example, in England, 80%
of heroin or crack cocaine users are on benefits, often for many years and their drug use
presents a significant barrier to their employment' (Home Office 2010:23). Unsurprisingly,
the contemporary UK drug strategy does not acknowledge that capitalism or its neo-
liberal framework has supported the creation of the necessary social conditions from which
substance use is created or promoted. The neo-liberal economic context is further built into
the recovery process with the introduction of 'recovery capital'. Recovery capital is central
to promoting independence from dependency and is made up of the following components:
social capital, physical capital, human capital and cultural support (Home Office 2010).

All of these 'capital' based components are highly individualized and involve the dependent
individual interacting structurally with society building upon their own family, finances,
relationships, skills, values and beliefs to create the conditions to reduce their abstinence
and reintegration. Within the contemporary drug strategy the government is implementing a
complex system of medical, judicial and economic coercion and repression. The drug strategy
fails to acknowledge that individuals presenting at crisis within drug treatment services have
often failed to manage their 'recovery capital', and substance use and dependency is part of
a complex social and environmental response to the functioning within wider society, both
on an individual and collective level.

The central premise of the 2010 strategy that promotes the occupation of neo-liberal
values and business culture can be found in the introduction of a payment by results system
(PBR). PBR, if introduced fully, will create a dedicated system of drug treatment that works
within the 'recovery capital' framework; to use the government's catch phrase, 'money
will follow success' (Home Office 2010). The system of PBR began in 2011 with a series
of regional test sites, and a full scale evaluation will be available in 2013. PBR will create
a system of drug treatment that is dedicated to providing abstinence within the framework of 'recovery capital'. We have moved beyond New Labour's evidence-based approach,
measuring what works best, to delivering a system of drug treatment that provides best
economic value for government and best economic opportunity for the private sector.
The withholding of funding until outcomes can be measured within a timescale will have
considerable implications for service delivery. PBR requires drug services to have significant capital and financial resources to be able to provide long-term delivery. The localism

and big society approach feels very hollow within this context; careful reading highlights that localism is primarily concerned with local-based commissioning rather than ownership by central government. This devolution is far more concerned with the transfer of responsibility to local authorities rather than the provision of directly owned and managed local sustainable services. PBR could be construed as a platform for the introduction of multinational corporations. Local, regional and national third-sector organizations lack the economic and financial capacity to manage financial risk on this scale; large organizations such as Serco and G4S will be the only providers big enough to manage the financial risk posed by the PBR system.

As we have explored previously, it can be argued that the latter half of the twentieth century has seen the necessary social conditions for drug use to flourish and become structurally embedded as a significant social phenomenon in late modern UK society. Within this period we have seen a shift in policy provision to a criminal justice and economic thematic arrangement. These themes of correction and business ideology are both present and intertwined with contemporary mental health legislation, policy and community care arrangements. The discourse surrounding mental health during the late-twentieth century moved from one of internment within large scale institutions to confinement within the community. Central to this was the introduction of the Mental Health Act 1983 and its subsequent amendments under the amended Mental Health Act 2007; the shift in mental health legislation has moved from institutional care to community care approaches and compulsory community based treatment. This process of deinstitutionalization within mental health had been happening slowly since the 1950s, but it became structurally embedded with the introduction of the NHS and Community Care Act 1990. In the 1950s within the UK there were approximately 150,000 people detained within large-scale mental institutions – this number had decreased significantly by the 1980s to around 30,000 (Porter 1987) – and according to our current figure we have 16,989 detained in a hospital setting, with a further 5,218 people subject to confinement at home under a community treatment order (Health & Social Care Information Centre 2013). This process of community care highlighted a classic combination of social change married with a sharp application of economic neo-liberal business practice. The NHS and Community Care Act 1990 shifted economic responsibility from large-scale institutions to regional NHS and local government, introducing a system that placed a cap on care provision and reduced costs through a criteria-based local assessment of eligibility of care. The process of community care also saw the introduction of a mixed economy of care opening up the health and social care sector for future business practices further embedded by the Health and Social Care Act 2012, allegedly liberating the NHS from state control through providing freedom via the business model of operating for-profit service provision within a once restricted nationalized health and welfare sector.

It is the opening up of the institutions and location within the community that begins to show the emergence of the dual diagnosis discourse as a visible social phenomenon. Previously, those who suffered from long-term mental health problems and substance misuse issues were often hidden within vast institutions for significant periods of time (see Ferguson 2014, for a moving account of the US context of long-term incarceration), unable to cope with the demands of work, family and society: the institution operated as both a salve and a mask to hide those who fell through the safety nets provided by capitalism within the UK. The appearance of large numbers of people in the community often unresponsive or difficult to manage within existing frameworks of intervention required a new policy and service provision to match the task at hand.

The first evidence of a dual diagnosis discourse began to emerge as a solid term of reference during the 1980s, with formal recognition being signalled within the professional domain of psychiatry in the third edition of the *Diagnostic and Statistical Manual of Mental Disorders* (DSM-III), published in 1980. As we have explored earlier, the 1980s in the UK also established the presence of the problem drug taker as a social construction. The problem drug taker was an important part of the component of understanding the management of complex individuals within the community through multiple service provision. It can be argued that the development of a dual diagnosis label is an attempt to articulate the difficulty in dealing with complex individuals that can neither be cured nor coerced back to the dominant norms of acceptable society. Within a contemporary mental health and substance misuse treatment system based upon the business model, we require a label to give people that do not easily meet treatment outcomes. In a competitive environment where success and continuity of service provision requires positive outcomes, we require a narrative that places the individual at fault rather than society or the treatment provision. It can be argued that the term 'dual diagnosis' is a collective fig leaf from which government, health and social care professionals can hide their collective embarrassment for failing to address the complex social problems that can contribute to mental distress and problematic substance misuse.

The criminal justice–economic phase established the following:

- a national drug treatment service that is well funded and resourced;
- a comprehensive system of community mental health provision;
- the introduction of coercion in drug treatment through criminal justice measures;
- the introduction of a business model of practice within mental health and substance misuse.

Key messages:

- Substance use is viewed as a complex yet individual problem.
- The treatment of substance use is to be based upon a model of abstinence.
- 'Dual diagnosis' is a relatively new term that can be traced through a number of discourses: social, clinical, political.

Reflective question (criminal justice–economic)

The 2010 UK Drug Strategy (Home Office) reports that 'the causes and drivers of drug and alcohol dependence are complex and personal.'
- *Do you think this is an accurate description of the causation of substance dependency?*

REFERENCES

Advisory Council on the Misuse of Drugs (1982). *Treatment and Rehabilitation*. London: HMSO.

Berridge, V., & Edwards, G. (1981). *Opium and the People: Opiate Use in Nineteenth-century England*. London: Allen Lane.

Black, D. (1988). Drug misuse: Policy and service development. *Journal of the Royal Society of Health*, 3, 83–89.

Bushell, H.D., Crome, I., & Williams, R. (2002). How can risk be related to interventions for young people who misuse substances? *Current Opinion in Psychiatry*, 15(4), 355–360.

Cochrane, A. (1972). *Effectiveness and Efficiency: Random Reflections on Health Services*. Oxford: Nuffield Provisional Health Trust.

Crossley, N. (1999). Fish, field, habitus and madness: On the first wave mental health users movement in Britain. *British Journal of Sociology*, 50(4), 647–670.

The Dangerous Drugs Act 1920. London: HMSO.

The Dangerous Drugs Act 1967. London: HMSO.

Dawson, P. (2012). Why the methadone doesn't work. *The Guardian*. 10 January. <http://www.theguardian.com/society/2012/jan/10/why-methadone-drugs-dont-work> [Accessed May 2014].

Department of Health and Social Security (1984). *Health Service Development: Services for Drug Misusers*. HC(84)14. London: DHSS.

Department of Health and Social Security (1985). *Drug Misuse: Prevalence and Service Provision: A report on Surveys and Plans in English National Health Service Regions*. London: DHSS.

Derek, F. (2009). *The Evolution of the British Welfare State* (4th Ed.). Basingstoke: Palgrave Macmillan.

Drug Scope (2009). *Drug Treatment at the Crossroads: What It's for, Where It's at and How to Make It Even Better*. London: Drug Scope.

Easton, M. (2008). Drug treatment: Success or failure? *BBC*. 3 October. <http://www.bbc.co.uk/blogs/legacy/thereporters/markeaston/2008/10/drug_treatment_officials_were.html> [Accessed May 2014].

Ferguson, P.M. (2014). Creating the back ward: The triumph of custodialism and the uses of therapeutic failure in nineteenth-century idiot asylums. In Ben-Moshe, L., Chapman, C., & Carey, A.C. (Eds) *Disability Incarcerated: Imprisonment and Disability in the United States and Canada*. New York: Palgrave Macmillan.

Friedman, M. (2002). *Capitalism & Freedom*. Chicago: Chicago University Press.

Fukuyama, F. (1992). *The End of History and the Last Man*. New York: Free Press.

Galanter, M. (2000). Self-help treatment for combined addiction and mental illness. *Psychiatric Service*, 51, 977–979.

Giddens, A. (1998). *The Third Way: The Renewal of Social Democracy*. London: Wiley.

Glatt, M.M., Pittman, D.J., Gillespie, D.G., & Hills, R. (1967). *The Drug Scene in Great Britain*. London: Edward Arnold.

Glazer, N. (1993). *Women's Paid & Unpaid Labour*. Philadelphia: Temple University Press.

Godfrey, C., Stewart, D., & Gossop, M. (2004). Economic analysis of costs and consequences of drug misuse: 2-year outcome data from the National Treatment Outcome Research Study (NTORS). *Addiction*, 99(6), 697–707.

Goffman, E. (1961) *Asylums*. London: Penguin.

Gossop, M. (2002). *Treating Drug Misuse Problems: Evidence of Effectiveness*. London: National Treatment Agency.

Gossop, M. (2007). *Living with Drugs*. Aldershot: Ashgate.

Harrison, R. (2000). *The Life and Times of Sydney & Beatrice Webb 1858–1905: The Formative Years*. Basingstoke: Palgrave Macmillan.

Harvey, D. (2005). *A Brief History of Neoliberalism*. Oxford: Oxford University Press.

Harvey, D. (2010). *The Enigma of Capital: And the Crises of Capitalism*. Oxford: Oxford University Press.

Health & Social Care Information Centre (2013). *Inpatients Formally Detained in Hospitals Under the Mental Health Act 1983, and Patients Subject to Supervised Community Treatment, Annual Report, England, 2013*. <http://www.hscic.gov.uk/catalogue/PUB12503> [Accessed April 2014].

Health and Social Care Act 2012. London: HMSO

Hills, J., Sefton, T., & Stewart, K. (2009). *Poverty Inequality & Policy Since 1997*. York: Joseph Rowntree Foundation.

Home Office (1995). *Tackling Drugs Together*. London: TSO.

Home Office (1998). *The 1998 Drug Strategy: Tackling Drugs Together for A Better Britain*. London: TSO.

Home Office (2008). *Drugs: Protecting Families and Communities: The 2008 Drug Strategy*. London: TSO.

Home Office (2010). *The Drug Strategy 2010 Reducing Demand, Restricting Supply, Building Recovery: Supporting People to Live A Drug Free Life*. London: TSO.

Hunt, N., & Stevens, A. (2004). Whose harm? Harm reduction and the shift to coercion in UK drug policy. *Social Policy and Society*, 3, 333–342.

Jones, K. (1972). *A History of the Mental Health Services*. London: Routledge.

Laing, R.D., & Cooper, D.G. (1964). *Reason and Violence: A Decade of Sartre's Philosophy* (2nd Ed.). London: Tavistock Publications Ltd.

Laing, R.D., & Esterson, A. (1964). *Sanity, Madness and the Family*. London: Penguin Books.

Laing, R.D. (1961). *The Self and Others*. London: Tavistock Publications.

Lart, R. (2006). Drugs and health policy. In Hughes, R., Lart, R., & Highgate, P. (Eds) *Drugs: Policy and Politics*. Maidenhead: Open University Press.

MacGregor, S., Ettorre, B., Coomber, R., Crosier, A., & Lodge, H. (1991). *Drugs Services in England and the Impact of the Central Funding Initiative, ISDD Research Monograph One*. London: Institute for the Study of Drug Dependence.

Marx, K., & Engels, F. (2011). *The Communist Manifesto*. London: Bookmarks.

Misuse of Drugs Act 1971. London: HMSO.

Moloney, P. (2013). *The Therapy Industry: The Irresistible Rise of the Talking Cure, and Why It Doesn't Work*. London: Pluto.

Mott, J. (1994). Notification and the home office. In Strang, J., & Gossop, M. (Eds) *Heroin Addiction and Drug Policy: The British System*. Oxford: Oxford University Press.

National Treatment Agency (NTA) (2002). *Models of Care for Treatment of Adult Drug Misusers*. London: NTA.

National Treatment Agency (NTA) (2006). *Models of Care for Treatment of Adult Drug Misusers*. London: NTA.

Parker, S. (2005). *Mentor UK Coastal and Ex-mining Areas Project: A Review of the Literature*. London: Mentor.

Parssinen, M.T. (1983). *Secret Passions, Secret Remedies: Narcotic Drugs in British Society 1820–1930*. Manchester: Manchester University Press.

Porter, R. (1989). *A Social History of Madness: Stories of the Insane*. London: Phoenix Giants.

Porter, R. (2002). *Madness: A Brief History*. Oxford: Oxford University Press.

Prochaska, J.O., & DiClemente, C.C. (1983). Stages and processes of self-change of smoking: Toward an integrative model of change. *Journal of Consultant Clinical Psychology*, 51(3), 390–395.

Project Match Research Group (1997). Matching alcoholism treatments to client heterogeneity: Project MATCH posttreatment drinking outcomes. *Journal of Studies on Alcohol*, 58(1), 7–29.

Public Health England (2013). *Facts & Figures*. <http://www.nta.nhs.uk/statistics.aspx> [Accessed March 2014].

Report of the Departmental Commission on Morphine and Heroin Addiction (1926). London: HMSO.

Report of the Inter-Departmental Committee on Social Insurance and Allied Services (1942). London: HMSO.

Report of the Interdepartmental Committee on Drug Addiction (1961). London: HMSO.

Report of the Royal Commission on Lunacy and Mental Disorder (1926). London: HMSO.

Reuteur, P., & Stevens, A. (2007). *An Analysis of UK Drug Policy: A Monograph Prepared for the UK Drug Policy Commission.* London : UK Drug Policy Commission.

Robertson, R., Bucknall, A.B.V., & Welsby, P.D. (1986). Epidemic of AIDS related virus (HTLV-111/LAV) infection amongst intravenous drug users. *British Medical Journal,* 292, 527–530.

Rogers, A., & Pilgrim, D. (2001). *Mental Health Policy in Britain.* Basingstoke: Palgrave Macmillan.

Ruggiero, V. (1999) Drugs as a password and the law as a drug: Discussing the legalisation of illicit substances. In South, N. (Ed.), *Drugs: Cultures, Controls and Everyday Life.* London: Sage

Second Report of the Interdepartmental Committee on Drug Addiction (1965). London: HMSO.

Shiner, M. (2006). Drugs, law and the regulation of harm. In Hughes, R., Lart, R., & Higate, P. (Eds) *Drugs: Policy and Politics.* Maidenhead: Open University Press.

Spear, H., & Mott, J. (2002). *Heroin Addiction, Care and Control*: The British System. London: DrugScope.

Stimson, G.V. (2000). Blair declares war: The unhealthy state of British drugs policy. *International Journal of Drug Policy,* 11, 259–264.

Stone, M. (1985). Shellshock and the psychologists. In Bynum, W.F., Porter, R., & Shepherd, M. (Eds) *The Anatomy of Madness* (Vol. 2). London: Tavistock.

Task Force to Review Services for Drug Misusers (1996). *Report of An Independent Review of Drug Treatment Services in England.* London: DoH.

Taylor, A. (1969). *American Diplomacy and the Narcotics Traffic, 1900–1939.* Durham, NC: Duke University Press.

Tomes, N. (1988). The great restraint controversy: A comparative perspective on Anglo-American Psychiatry in the nineteenth century. In Bynum, W., Porter, R., & Shepherd, M. (Eds) *The Anatomy of Madness: Essays in the History of Madness.* London: Routledge.

Trevelyan, G.M. (1944). *English Social History.* London: Longmans, Green & Co.

Trevor, M. (1987). *An Economic and Social History of Britain 1760–1970.* London: Longman Group.

Wilkinson, R., & Pickett, K. (2009). *The Spirit Level: Why Equality is Better for Everyone.* London: Penguin.

Young, J. (1971). *The Drugtakers: The Social Meaning of Drug Use.* London: Paladin.

Zizek, S. (2009). *First As Tragedy, Then As Farce.* London: Verso.

3

Key Models for Understanding Dual Diagnosis

Chapter Summary

This chapter will:

- outline the main areas of critique for learners, lecturers, the helping professions and their disciplines;

- outline the main models that are applied in the treatment of poor mental health and dual diagnosis;

- describe and discuss the social model, with roots in disability discourse that offers a practice orientation.

Introduction

Despite the historical separation in the way addiction and dependency, mental health and their combined dual diagnosis have been categorized, there is a striking resemblance in the kinds of models and perspectives that have been taken to understand, conceptualize, treat and delineate them. In fact, it is arguable that the very separation of these three areas reflects more of a disciplinary concern and separation, rather than a set of naturally occurring categories. And, were we to take a Foucauldian (a term that refers to the work and positions of the highly influential French thinker Michel Foucault) view, it could be suggested that the act of making these arbitrary separations might in fact be a disciplinary power effect and strategy to demonstrate the efficacy of the models being applied and of the disciplines doing the modelling. We might also argue that while there is a progression through perspectives and models of understanding that can be periodized, in practice, such perspectives have perhaps accumulated and become parallel. For instance, moral and religious perspectives sit alongside and interact with contemporary clinical scientific models. Furthermore, the main and dominant models and theories of explanation, which will be discussed further below, are applicable in a range of circumstances, and we might see that the applications, and the objections to their application, are thematically similar. While the tendency in many accounts of mental health, dependency and dual diagnosis begin in the main models as a means of orienting the reader, this section will begin at the critical edges, and this is to enable readers to gain the most in appraising the main models for their own learning and practice.

Critical accounts

Currently, there are two main dilemmas facing clinical models. Penson (2014) outlines these as being on the one hand the need to increase scientificity, and on the other, the workings of sociology of science and knowledge. Taking the first, this thrust is towards improving the science of 'madness', and so here an empirical and positivistic paradigm is favoured. This orientation raises objections to current models and practices on the basis that they have lost their scientificity in favour of commercial interests such as serving Big Pharma (the name given to the pharmaceutical industry in recognition of both its lucrative financial turnover and its lobbying power and influence), and are also slavishly dominated by the privileged guild interests of the helping professions (Moncrieff 2011). These concerns are not mutually exclusive in that some of the recent criticisms of the American Psychiatric Association (APA) on the publication of its *Diagnostic and Statistical Manual* (DSM-5) have been its close ties with Big Pharma and the APA's relatively opaque methods for arriving at the new manual. The objections raised by the British Psychological Society (BPS) (2013) and the US National Institute for Mental Health (Insel 2013) to the new DSM-5 were in part because the manual lacks validity, and in part because it renders everyday experiences as increasingly pathological. The recent DSM-5 now adopts the term 'addiction' rather than the earlier term 'dependency', and both decisions to use these terms were a matter of a vote between committee members tasked with revising the new manual; with only one vote cast in favour of the original use of 'dependency' (as was used in DSM-III), this was hardly a scientific method to arrive at clinical models (West & Brown 2013).

Boyle (1993) outlines at least part of the problem for mental health and psychiatry. She notes that medical science requires that to identify an illness or disease there should first be an observation of a pattern and a guess at what is happening (i.e., to infer non-observables) to form what is called a 'hypothetical construct'. If this best guess, or construct, is to be valid, then it must go on to satisfy two things. Firstly, it must be derived from the observable pattern which becomes the criteria for inferring the construct: this means the pattern can be identified when it is repeated. Secondly, the construct must lead to new observations – new findings, greater clarity of the construct, and better predictability. These are necessary conditions for construct validity, so if the construct is not derived from a pattern it cannot be valid. Validity is increased when certain events go together in a cluster, or are linked to independent and reliably measured signs (observables). Boyle argues throughout the rest of her text that psychiatry, in the case of schizophrenia, fails to demonstrate rigour in this process by medicine's own criteria.

West and Brown (2013) reiterate a similar process to that of Boyle and suggest that a theory ought to also account for four further criteria:

Is it contradicted by observations?
Does it fail to encompass important relevant observations?
Does it have more elements than are needed?
Is it misleading? (West & Brown 2013:23)

They proffer these questions within a critique of both research and theory development in addiction studies and with social and behavioural sciences more broadly. In light of their concerns that theories tend not to be rigorously evaluated against the 'natural world', there are often multiple examples of events and circumstances that cannot be accounted for within social science models. While critical of attempts towards scientificity when those attempts lack robustness, they do note the value of theory as a *sensitizer* 'that generate[s] ideas and concepts that help understanding' (West & Brown 2013:29). Broadly speaking, models represent the world or part of therein, and theories explain it (good theories do so in line with the data).

Feyerabend (1975: 2010) argues that disciplinary influence is a result of the pre-eminence of tradition in scholarly thought and research, which he terms the 'material effect', that is, the force of the authority of an established position or argument over the 'logical force', being the reasoning of the argument which includes viable alternatives. The obedience demanded by material effect is 'nothing but a political manoeuvre' (ibid.:9). Such practices as diagnosis become questionable as practices and perhaps reflect power relations, or 'empowered taxonomies' (Penson 2011), rather than natural categories. Larsson (2013) highlights this in two ways in relation to the growing evidence of the 'social determinants of mental health'. He notes that this is a conceptual gap that fails to account for this evidence, and this interacts with a rhetorical gap that is typified by dominant biomedical and psychological views that neglect to account for the growing evidence of social determinants in interventions and policy. In effect, while it is hoped that scientists are ethical and unbiased in their research, in reality, there are a range of biases, distortions, incompetence, hierarchies, conflicts and habits that raise crucial concerns over the veracity of models, theories and research publication (Marshall 2002; Goldacre 2012; West & Brown 2013).

Writers and researchers who are hopeful of increasing the scientificity of the human sciences as applied in our field include Bentall (2003; 2010) on psychosis and treatments; Moncrieff (2005) on understanding modes of psychotropic mediation drug action, depression and antidepressants (Moncrieff 2011); Lewis (2006) and Trueman (2013) on the activity and effects of professional guild interests; and Mosher et al. (2004) and Goldacre (2012) on Big Pharma.

The second thrust, which is the sociology of science and knowledge, still argues that there is something to be *known*, but it is more inclusive of a range of perspectives on the basis of factors like culture and geography. In effect this approach relativizes the human sciences and suggests there are multiple truths. This is by no means a more humanistic approach and may include a range of problematic ideas, if, for instance, a certain spiritual view is still stigmatizing and results in poor treatment. Again, these views are not entirely exclusive from the first dilemma above, in that often a relativizing critique can draw attention to commercial and supposed empirical concerns as with the emerging field of the postcolonial critique of psychiatry within the mental health field (Mills 2014; Penson 2014). A postcolonial critique notes that cultural and social objections to the Western human sciences are only part of the problem, and there is a long history of imperial, colonial and neo-colonial activity that aims to advance Western perspectives in the continuation of the civilizing colonial mission. Contributors to the relativizing camp include: Fernando (2008; 2011), who argues that psychiatry and the helping professions should customize their approaches to account for cultural difference; Appignanesi (2008), who provides a gendered account and critique of psychiatry as a male dominated discipline; and Clarke (2001), who philosophically questions understandings of psychosis from within a Western, realist paradigm.

Increasingly, there is a cross, or interdisciplinary, critique of the major models that traverses the boundaries of psychology, sociology, history, political science and ethics domains. Such critique(s) ask penetrating questions about what actually happens in psychiatry and the helping disciplines, not just what is thought about dual diagnosis and madness, or written about it. In this area there are powerful critiques that outline concerns about the conduct of the helping human sciences and professions and, maybe by doing so, reduce some of the models, policies and values to rhetorical device rather than actuality. Read (2004) suggests that whatever the history of madness may be, it has three recurring themes:

> One of the functions of 'treatment' for 'mad' people is to suppress thoughts, behaviours and feelings thought unacceptable to those with the power to determine and enforce social norms. The 'treatments' are frequently unhelpful and sometimes damaging and violent. Experts of the day often camouflage the sociopolitical function, and the damaging nature of the 'treatments' behind theories that the people concerned have personal defects that are reduced by the treatments. (Read 2004:9)

Read is not alone, and the activities of psychiatry have been linked, from the late 1800s to the mid-twentieth century, to the eugenics movement in the US and Europe (Whitaker 2002; O'Brien 2011) and the application of medical science in mass murder in hospitals and death camps in Nazi Germany and beyond (Read & Masson 2004), and, more broadly, the sterilization of the disabled and 'defective' (including the mad) in institutions (Snyder & Mitchell 2006). More recently there are concerns that contemporary treatment approaches raise serious human rights concerns (Spandler & Calton 2009), and it may even be the case that the United Nations views aspects of contemporary care, such as having forced treatment without a person's consent and seclusion, as meeting international criteria for torture (Mendez 2013). Current first line treatments may be more harmful than good but remain highly recommended due to the pressures of key commercial and professional interests (Whitaker 2002). There is a history of exploitive medical experimentation in former colonies (Schiebinger 2013) predicated on Euro models of racial superiority. Rembis (2014) points out that despite the discourse of de-institutionalization in the US, there is a very large 'mad' prison population, which raises all kinds of issues as to what constitutes good care and support and where that should be delivered. And so the histories across the caring professions and human sciences have remarkable similarities and often only become separate in accepting the systems of classification that have already been imposed. This remains a tension in such areas as 'mad' activism and the application of the social model of disability to the mental health field (Penson 2015).

In summary, before going on to describe and discuss the main(stream) models for understanding mental health and dual diagnosis, the objections and critiques have a number of overlapping objections. Psychiatry and the helping disciplines claim a scientific rigour that they do not demonstrate and represent Western epistemologies which come with a history of colonial and imperial practices at the expense of other social and cultural views. Therefore, these disciplines have arguably poorly served a range of groups who have been pathologized, incarcerated and mistreated, such as women, LGBT people, the disabled and people of colour; and psychiatry and the helping disciplines have little moral or ethical high ground (especially in the absence of a clear break with older practices) in practice but continue to be used through continued guild privileges ensconced in Western society and institutions. It is with these critiques in mind that we can now, and in a more informed way, engage with the main models as they are applied in contemporary service provision.

Key messages:

- While there are dominant models that health-based, clinical disciplines operate within; ones that aim to explain distress and dependency in clinical ways, there are substantial critiques of their assumptions and methods.
- Some of the concerns are *epistemological* (i.e., concerns about how we think we know what we say we know), and others are human-rights based and ethical.
- Critical perspectives offer novel angles that assist in appraising the realities of practice.

The main models

Table 3.1 outlines the main models and the assumptions of these.

All the models in Table 3.1 make assumptions about how mental ill health and substance use come about and in doing so also advance the means by which treatment and reparation can be made. Table 3.2 takes each model in turn and gives the main treatment or interventions for each model. In practice, however, this may well be very flexible in that some nurses prescribe medications, some doctors undertake talking therapies and some social care practitioners advocate medications.

Model	Assumptions & principles
Medical	There are mental illnesses, like physical illnesses, that cause distress and dysfunction. These arise out of the body, e.g. genetic expression, brain structure and function. Such disorders can be diagnosed and treated.
Social	Two main areas exist: (1) distress and disability is interpreted within social conventions and culture, so what we call mental illness is actually what we interpret it to be (social construction); and (2) the *Glasgow effect* – poverty, urbanicity, isolation and early adversity cause poor mental health.
Psychological	This refers to what and how we think: processes such as learning, socialization, memory, perception, attention, etc. can be different to those of general population norms, and that difference or impairment results in dysfunction and distress.
Legal/administrative	For example, the Mental Health Act, Mental Capacity Act and the Protection of Freedoms Act enshrine in law what it is to be 'mentally disordered' or 'to lack capacity', allowing for state intervention through the police, medics, nurses and approved mental health professionals, such as AMPHs, where there is concern.
Psychosocial	This involves a mix of psychological and social (and bio), and acknowledges the link between internal and external experiences.
Disability/activist	This ranges from the user involvement movement to the survivor movement and is rooted in the physical disability movement from the 1970s.

Table 3.1 The main models in contemporary mental health and substance user practice

Model	Area of intervention
Medical	Interventions act on the body – drugs, ECT, psychosurgery.
Social	Interventions act towards the environment – maximizing income, changing material conditions.
Psychological	Strategy is to change meaning and distress through behaviour change and discussion – talking therapies, behaviour modification.

Legal/administrative	Definitions and processes are placed in law and policy and regulate such things as mental capacity, mental disorder and risk, diminished responsibility and access to help/benefits. There are strong links to medical and psychological professions.
Psychosocial	Approach blends a bit of all the above; curiously the bio is often implied rather than clearly stated.
Disability/Activist	Methodology refuses to accept that something is simply 'wrong' with the person and demands the environment and attitudes are inclusive of a diverse population.

Table 3.2 The main models and their areas of intervention

> **Reflective point:** *Think about your current role and contact with service users and imagine a pie chart. Divide up the pie chart based on how much time you tend to spend drawing on practices within the different models. Having done that, think about the following:*
> - *How far does this reflect the needs of clients?*
> - *Does the pie chart need to be drawn with different segments? What would you want them to be?*
> - *How would colleagues fill in theirs? Does this suggest a team culture in practice?*

Clearly, while the models above can be separated out to an extent, as mentioned above, with the blurring of professional roles comes the sharing of who does what. Nurses deliver psychological interventions, for instance. There is a worthwhile final note on the issue of pharmacological interventions; Moncrieff (2005) suggests that psychiatric drugs (and others) could be better put to use through a 'drug-centred model' approach rather than the 'disease model' which is often a criticism of psychiatry. What this means is that professions need to forego dubious theorizing about underlying disease states and instead offer prescriptions based on the intended effect of the drug. So, for someone who is agitated, a sedative may be of worth, and a stimulant may be worthwhile for people struggling with their energy and motivation. It would bring other psychoactive substances into the clinical range, for instance an antihistamine with sedating effects may be far safer, with fewer unintended effects, than a major tranquilizer.

Psychosocial perspectives

Many practitioners would claim to practice a 'psychosocial perspective', but what this is exactly is hard to settle on. In one sense it may be that practitioners are staking their claim to be more well-rounded workers and supporters than by practising treatment offered by the medical model, despite medical model dominance in psychiatry, mental health and substance use. However, for clinical guidance and for many practitioners, medications remain the first line treatment, with talking therapies and social interventions coming afterwards. Psychosocial models look to the interaction between the clients internal worlds, their social relationships and material conditions to explain both the problems experienced and the solutions. Thylstrup and Johansen (2009) report that there is little robust evidence for psycho-social interventions in dual diagnosis, and it appears that the degree of *psychosociability* of interventions tends to reflect the service context and blend rather than a coherent set of strategies or delivery. As such, a psychosocial approach might be integrated at the level of delivery but not at the level of understanding the complexity of a set of problems. What this means in actuality is that stating something to be a 'psychosocial intervention' merely articulates the modalities that are attempted rather than an integrated explanatory model. 'Psychosocial' may be a case of what Hacking (2000) refers to as an 'elevator' word, which is a term, when used, that aggrandizes the point being made without qualifying the quality by which it can do this. In effect it sounds better than what it means.

Psychosocial models seem to be regularly based on personal vulnerability models that suggest a set of physical and psychological characteristics, acquired through physical and psychological development, which make a given person prone to certain experiences or pathologies when triggered by environmental pressures, stressors or events. Vulnerability is 'a process that increases the liability for mental disorder but of itself is insufficient to cause disorder' (Goldberg & Goodyer 2005:168). The most cited version is the stress vulnerability model for schizophrenia and psychosis (Zubin & Spring 1977; Clements & Turpin 1992), and there are also such models for personality disorder (Perris 1998), anxiety and depression (Goldberg & Goodyer 2005) and the similar 'kindling model' for bipolar disorder (Lam et al. 2000). Despite the regularity of such models and the speculation for their accuracy, the evidence remains relatively weak, relying on correlations, self-reporting and, as discussed above, questionable diagnostics. Williams (2002) sums this up in saying that

> the stress vulnerability model is at least a convenient if temporary starting point
> in ensuring that people with diagnoses of schizophrenia receive appropriate
> and helpful psychosocial interventions. In time such a unifying concept may
> prove inappropriate or even unhelpful in the understanding of the treatment of
> psychosis; at the current juncture it appears a helpful concept. (Williams 2002:15)

Certainly, over ten years on, it is arguably not leading to great advances in the care and support of people with psychosis when we know that despite rhetoric about recovery, and the application of such models, the life outcomes for people diagnosed with schizophrenia remain poor. The Schizophrenia Commission (2012) found that those with a schizophrenia diagnosis lose on average 15–20 years of life compared to a non-clinical population.

In 2005 the Canadian Psychiatric Association published guidance for psychosocial inter-vention for schizophrenia which included the following points:

- There is a need for medical and psychosocial approaches to complement rather than compete.
- However, despite that lack of competition, the psychosocial interventions seem to affiliate to medical norms through a view whereby 'effective psychosocial interventions may improve medication adherence, reduce risk of relapse and the need for readmis-sion to hospital, reduce distress resulting from symptoms, improve functioning' (Canadian Psychiatric Association 2005:29).
- The '[p]atients, their families, and caregivers should be educated about the course and treatment of the disorder, as well as about ways to reduce risk of relapse. It is also

important to provide a realistically hopeful attitude for the future. The physician is an extremely important contributor to this process' (ibid.).
- And, [s]taff providing psychosocial interventions should be appropriately trained' (ibid.).

So, while psychosocial models seem to be offering, an alternative to the medical model, it seems that there remains an implied hierarchy of intervention that also favours current professional hierarchies. Psychosocial approaches remain predicated on models of pathology and by extension treatment and reparation. However, Lewis (2006) offers a more hopeful view for the future and one that relies on psychiatry becoming a more *humble* discipline, about power sharing and more closely aligned to solving the problems of service users, and less about treating arguably demonstrable diseases. Critical perspectives hinge on the break with the medical model, and one of the few areas this is provided is through activist and survivor perspectives such as that articulated by the social model of disability. We would suggest then that a psychosocial perspective is not just one that identifies a range of treatment modalities which includes psychological treatment, but it would also consider political, wider social and contextual factors and physical well-being.

The social model of disability in dual diagnosis

There is a long history of disability activism, beginning in the 1970s, that resulted in a reformulation of what was believed to be the problem for disabled people. Medical models tend to locate the problem in the person, that is, the impairment is the same as the disability. However, the social model of disability disputes this and instead argues that disability arises out of attitudes and environments that are inflexible and operate on the basis of physical and sensory norms that in fact exclude those people outside of those norms. The social model of disability intervenes by demanding an adaptation and changing those attitudes and environmental inflexibilities to enable disabled people to participate fully in life. Given the roots of this model in activism, it comes closest to aligning with the wishes of service users and asks difficult questions about the nature of helping relationships.

Penson (2011) suggests three processes, or areas of belief, that underpin a disabling process or experience – a disability triangle. Firstly, there is the 'myth of normalcy' which suggests that there is a norm, constant and measureable, and it is one that is achievable, and so it is one which disabled people fall beyond but can aspire to. By extension this myth becomes the benchmark by which full participation is measured, and so the normative benchmarks of employment, civic participation, etc. become naturalized. Secondly, there is the 'negative ontology' that evokes the disabled person as tragic or undesirable, which may be expressed in terms of horror, disgust, pity, sympathy, stigma or hostility. Finally, there is a 'myth of autonomy' that is the notion that the normal population (operating the 'myth of normalcy' allows a normal population to be constituted) are wholly independent, and the disabled are not, but strive to be, and this autonomy is achieved through the reparative effects of the helping professions and state. This is a paradoxical task in that the definitions of a 'normal population' and 'autonomy' mean the disabled can only ever achieve a facsimile of their able counterparts. These are termed myths on the basis that each embodies unstable categories and designations that are applied to parts of the population, but to some more than others. By extension, such myths are arguably underpinning helping relationships.

Oliver (2013), one of the originators of the social model of disability, outlines that one of the current objections to the social model is the notion of impairment. This is no truer than in the mental health and dependency fields, given the lack of clear indications of impairment (Penson 2015). The lack of an evidenced account of disease and pathology in models of dependency does not prevent dominant models acting as though this is the case, but rarely are people with dependencies viewed as being applicable for the meagre benefits, in real terms, that a disabled identity confers. Curiously, one of the key practices of the social model, collectivism, appears in the mental health survivor movement and substance use population. Edward and Robins (2012) found that 'individuals make more visits to self-help groups for support with their substance use and mental illness than to all mental health professionals combined' (Edward & Robins 2012:555). At present, while the application of the social model of disability is growing in the mental health field with some protections in law, despite disease models in the field of dependency and addiction, the social model has a very low profile. However, perhaps there are two reasons for the lack of impact of survivor and user movements in mental health and dual diagnosis, as compared to (other) civil rights groups. Firstly, as covered in Chapter 2, there is the sociological function of the *other* and the scapegoat. Secondly, there is the extent of what Foucault (1975) calls dividing practices – these are the physical and psychological deployments of the 'mad, bad and disabled', both physically and psychically in highly individualizing disciplinary practices. In *Discipline and Punish*, Foucault (1975) refers to these dividing practices in terms of space (this would include the use of cells, dormitories and treatments that reduce social interaction), psychology (the panopticon that induces the sensation of an unceasing surveillance that is internalised and teaches self-limitation) and time (routines, jobs, tasks that order the day and how time is spent). And while some deinstitutionalization has occurred, some critics would argue that this did not result in a reduction of disciplinary power and dividing practice, but rather a proliferation and diffusion through community service, treatment and surveillance embodied in community care, mental health, and public protection policy and law (Penson 2011).

Key messages:

- There are a number of models used within the dual diagnosis arena – each with its own assumptions, limits and uses.
- There are viable alternatives to the dominant biomedical model, and even options such as drug-centred prescribing within the medical model.
- The critical perspectives, and those offered by service users and activists, are essential to working out what is the actual outcome of help and support.
- Psychosocial perspectives should also consider sociopolitical factors in dual diagnosis practice.

REFERENCES

Appignanesi, L. (2008). *Mad, Bad and Sad: A History of Women and the Mind Doctors From 1800 to the Present*. London: Virago.

Bentall, R.P. (2003). *Madness Explained: Psychosis and Human Nature*. London: Penguin.

Bentall, R.P. (2010). *Doctoring the Mind: Why Psychiatric Treatments Fail*. London: Penguin.

Boyle, M. (1993). *Schizophrenia: A Scientific Delusion*. London: Routledge.

British Psychological Society (2013). *DSM-5: The Future of Psychiatric Diagnosis (2012 – Final Consultation): British Psychological Society Response to the American Psychiatric Association*. Leicester: British Psychological Society.

Canadian Psychiatric Association (2005). Clinical practice guidelines: Treatment of schizophrenia. *Canadian Journal of Psychiatry*, 50 (Suppl. 1), 29S–36S.

Clarke, C. (2001). Construction and reality: Reflections on philosophy and spiritual/psychotic experience. In Clarke, I. (Ed.) *Psychosis and Spirituality: Exploring the New Frontier*. London: Whurr.

Clements, K., & Turpin, G. (1992). Vulnerability models and schizophrenia: The assessment and prediction of relapse. In Birchwood, M., & Tarrier, N. (Eds) *Innovations in the Psychological Management of Schizophrenia*. Chichester: Wiley.

Edward, K.L., & Robins, A. (2012). Dual Diagnosis, as described by those who experience the disorder: Using the Internet as a source of data. *International Journal of Mental Health Nursing*, 21, 550–559.

Fernando, S. (2008). Institutional racism and cultural diversity. In Tummey, R., & Turner, T. (Eds) *Critical Issues in Mental Health*. Basingstoke: Palgrave Macmillan.

Fernando, S. (2011). Cultural diversity and racism. In Rapley, M., Moncrieff, J., & Dillon, J. (Eds) *De-Medicalizing Misery: Psychiatry, Psychology and the Human Condition*. Basingstoke: Palgrave Macmillan.

Feyerabend, P. (1975; 2010). *Against Method* (4th Ed.). London: Verso.

Foucault, M. (1975; 1991). *Discipline and Punish: The Birth of the Prison*. London: Penguin.

Goldacre, B. (2012). *Bad Pharma*. London: Harper Collins.

Goldberg, D., & Goodyer, I. (2005). *The Origins and Course of Common Mental Disorders*. London: Routledge.

Hacking, I. (2000). *The Social Construction of What?* London: Harvard University Press.

Insel, T. (2013). Director's Blog: Transforming diagnosis (29 April). *National Institute for Mental Health*. <http://www.nimh.nih.gov/about/director/2013/transforming-diagnosis.shtml> [Accessed June 17 1600]

Lam, D., Jones, S.H., Hayward, P., & Bright, J.A. (2000). *Cognitive Therapy for Bipolar Disorder: A Therapist's Guide to Concepts, Methods and Practice*. Chichester: Wiley.

Larsson, P. (2013). The rhetoric-reality gap in social determinants of health. *Mental Health Review Journal*, 18, 4.

Marshall, M. (2002). Randomised controlled trials – Misunderstanding, fraud and spin. In Preibe, S., & Slade, M. (Eds) *Evidence in Mental Health Care*. Hove: Brunner-Routledge.

Méndez, J.E. (2013). *Report of the Special Rapporteur on torture and other cruel, inhuman or degrading treatment or punishment*. United Nations General Assembly/Human Rights Council.

Mills, C. (2014). *Decolonizing Global Mental Health: The Psychiatrization of the Majority World*. Hove: Routledge.

Moncrieff, J. (2005). Rethinking models of psychotropic drug action. *Psychotherapy and Psychosomatics*, 74, 145–153.

Moncrieff, J. (2011). The myth of the antidepressant. In Rapley, M., Moncrieff, J., & Dillon, J. (Eds) *De-Medicalizing Misery: Psychiatry, Psychology and the Human Condition*. Basingstoke: Palgrave Macmillan.

Mosher, L., Gosden, R., & Beder, S. (2004). Drug Companies and Schizophrenia: Unbridled capitalism meets madness. In Read, J., Mosher, L., & Bentall, R.P. (Eds) *Models of Madness: Psychological, Social and Biological Approaches to Schizophrenia*. Hove: Brunner Routledge.

O'Brien, G.V. (2011). Eugenics, genetics, and the minority group model of disabilities: Implications for social work advocacy. *Social Work*, 56(4), 347–354.

Oliver, M. (2013). The social model of disability: Thirty years on. *Disability & Society*, 28(7) 1024–1026.

Penson, W. (2014). Insanity. In Taylor, P., Corteen, K., & Morley, S. (Eds) *A Companion to Criminal Justice, Mental Health & Risk*. Bristol: Policy Press.

Penson, W.J. (2011). Reappraising the social model of disability: A Foucauldian reprise. In Moore, D., Gorra, A., Smith, H.M, & Reaney, J. (Eds) *Disabled Students in Education: Technology, Transition and Inclusivity*. Hershey: IGI Global.

Penson, W.J. (2015). Unsettling impairment: Mental health and the social model of disability. Spandler, H., Anderson, J., & Sapey, B. (Eds) *Distress or Disability? Mental Health and the Politics of Disablement.* Bristol: Policy Press.

Perris, C. (1998). Defining the concept of individual vulnerability as a base for psychotherapeutic interventions. In Perris, C., & McGorry, P.D. (Eds) *Cognitive Psychotherapy of Psychotic & Personality Disorders: A Handbook of Theory & Practice.* Chichester: Wiley.

Read, J. (2004). A history of madness. In Read, J., Mosher, L., & Bentall, R.P. (Eds) *Models of Madness: Psychological, Social and Biological Approaches to Schizophrenia.* Hove: Brunner Routledge.

Read, J., & Masson, J. (2004). Genetics, eugenics and mass murder. In Read, J., Mosher, L., & Bentall, R.P. (Eds) *Models of Madness: Psychological, Social and Biological Approaches to Schizophrenia.* Hove: Brunner Routledge.

Rembis, M. (2014). The new asylums: Madness and the mass incarceration in the neoliberal era. In Ben-Moshe, L., Chapman, C., & Carey, A.C. (Eds) *Disability Incarcerated: Imprisonment and Disability in the United States and Canada.* New York: Palgrave Macmillan.

Schiebinger, L. (2013). Medical experimentation and race in the eighteenth-century Atlantic world. *Social History of Medicine*, 26(3), 364–382.

The Schizophrenia Commission (2012). *The Abandoned Illness: A Report from the Schizophrenia Commission.* London: Rethink Mental Illness.

Snyder, S.L., & Mitchell, D.T. (2006). *Cultural Locations of Disability.* London: University of Chicago Press.

Spandler, H., & Calton, T. (2009). Psychosis and human rights: Conflicts in mental health policy and practice. *Social Policy & Practice,* 8(2), 245–256.

Thylstrup, B., & Johansen, K.S. (2009). Dual diagnosis and psychosocial interventions: Introduction and commentary. *Nordic Journal of Psychiatry*, 63(3), 202–208.

Trueman, J. (2013). The mirage of mental health reform. In Walker, S. (Ed.) *Modern Mental Health: Critical Perspectives on Psychiatric Practice.* St Albans: Critical Publishing.

West, R., & Brown, J. (2013). *Theory of Addiction* (2nd Ed.). Chichester: John Wiley.

Whitaker, R. (2002). *Mad in America: Bad Science, Bad Medicine, and the Enduring Mistreatment of the Mentally Ill.* Cambridge, MA: Basic Books.

Williams, S. (2002). The nature of schizophrenia. In Harris, N., Williams, S., & Bradshaw, T. (Eds) *Psychosocial Interventions for People with Schizophrenia.* Basingstoke: Palgrave Macmillan.

Zubin, J., & Spring, B. (1977). Vulnerability – A new view of schizophrenia. *Journal of Abnormal Psychology,* 86(2), 103–126.

4 | Working with Individuals: The Broader Picture and Getting Started

Chapter Summary

The aims of this chapter are to outline and explore:

- the varied and complex nature of the relationship between substance use and mental health problems when working with individuals;
- factors impacting on motivation to change;
- the importance and essential skills needed in risk assessment when working with individuals with dual diagnoses;
- problem formulation and conceptualization;
- the contemporary psychosocial interventions employed in working with dual diagnosis and their efficacy;
- the Care Programme Approach (CPA);
- relapse prevention and issues and complexities;
- strength-based approaches;
- the importance and centrality of the therapeutic relationship.

Introduction

> You will get further with a patient with a good therapeutic relationship and lousy techniques, than you will with good techniques and a lousy relationship.

> (Victor Meyer cited in Aubuchon & Malatesta (1998:141))

In this chapter we begin to focus on working with individuals who have dual diagnoses. We start to explore the different psychosocial interventions employed when working with this client group, but in this chapter we remain fairly generic. The quote above from Aubuchon and Malatesta (1998) gives a good indication of where our argument will go – although we will recommend both good technique and relationship! Chapter 6 then goes on to look at specific models. However, we do make reference here to specific therapeutic approaches such as formulation, which can be a great aid to adding focus and structure to your work with clients. In the first instance this chapter takes a broad outlook, including considering the role of the relationship, our values as workers and the organizing frameworks of the Care Programme Approach (CPA), the Mental Health (Wales) Measure 2010 and case management. It is worth noting here that up until 2012 in the UK the CPA was the main way of assessing and identifying the needs of individuals with mental health problems. Since June 2012, however, the CPA was superseded in Wales by Part 2 of the Mental Health (Wales) Measure 2010. The Mental Health Measure, from 2012, which constitutes Care and Treatment Planning in Part 2 of the Mental Health Measure in Wales highlights that people who receive secondary mental health services have two important new rights: the right to have a Care Coordinator appointed to work with them to coordinate their assessment, care and treatment, and the right to an individual and comprehensive on-going Care and Treatment Plan to assist their recovery.

Working with dual diagnoses is complex, and we begin to give a sense of that in this chapter, along with the necessity to 'feel your way' with the client along their path to recovery. Our practice suggestions are based on views of current best practice, which in turn draws on a research evidence base which enables us to explore how diverse psychosocial interventions are employed in different professional and socio-cultural contexts. Some case examples given in this chapter include the challenges that may be faced when conducting an assessment to inform which interventions are appropriate, the challenges in assessing risk and gaining an understanding of the client's subjective experience in order to support them. Challenges can also include choosing the appropriate intervention.

There has been much research and theoretical literature which has suggested that the therapeutic relationship is the key ingredient in achieving successful therapeutic outcomes (Lambert et al. 2004; Haugh & Paul 2008; Norcross & Lambert 2011; Charura & Paul 2014). The key issues and challenges often associated with the importance of the therapeutic relationship are in relation to the practitioner's competencies in formulating and maintaining a relationship in settings where clients may present with complex mental health problems as well as substance use problems. The very nature of this work often means that practitioners are faced with complex challenges which may manifest as clients continuing to use substances and relapsing, their mental health getting worse and them consequently self-destructing through use of different substances. In this chapter we therefore explore the importance of practitioners having the relevant skills and competencies in not only conducting assessments but also in using interventions such as motivational interviewing (MI), CBT, psychodynamic principles and so on.

Safran and Muran (2000) make the case that irrespective of the therapeutic model, the therapeutic alliance is essential and has three components. Firstly, the alliance needs a sound bond (that the two people can connect sufficiently to work together); secondly, that there is agreement on goals, and these should be the client's goals. Finally, there is agreement on the tasks and activities that lead the person closer to her or his goals. If the therapeutic alliance lacks part of this formula the effectiveness is reduced. This should be borne in mind in settings or relationships where the client is subject to some form of compulsion, which may have an impact on all three dimensions.

The varied and complex nature of the relationship between substance misuse and mental health problems

As outlined in Chapters 2 and 3 of this book, there is a varied and complex relationship between substance use and mental health problems/distress. Some key points we have noted from practice include, for example, that alcohol and most drugs are depressants; hence it is often difficult to know which problem to tackle first. On one hand, an individual client may be using substances to 'mask', or help them cope, with the mental health problem. On the other hand, they may be experiencing mental ill health due to their substance use. These challenges also impact on service delivery. For instance, in practice, clients have often been referred to services with multiple admissions and interventions, which could be an indication of the complexity of problems a dually diagnosed client may face. To be fully reflective though requires us to consider the service experience as one which may also fail to engage recovery, and also consider the broader social context for clients, which may work against their best efforts such as living in poverty and experiencing multiple stigmas. On reviewing the client's personal history, a common 'revolving door dynamic' of having a detox/rehabilitation then relapsing may often be identified. Usually, this is because the client could not cope with the psychological distress arising from circumstances or experiences when sober/drug free, and then got in contact again with services. It should be understood that while clients may be unhelpfully labelled as 'revolving door cases', they cannot become so without revolving door clinicians to admit them, and return visits to a service area can be reframed as a help-seeking behaviour that is encouraging. To expand on this with an example from practice, consider the following case study.

❑ Case study 4.1 Mental health and substance use: the 'revolving door'

Sue is a 28-year-old client who has been in contact with substance use and mental health services at least five times in the last three years. She states that she started drinking and taking drugs as a 16-year-old girl following an incident in which she was sexually assaulted after a night out. She also states that during that time she accessed some support from mental health services because she became anxious about going out, and consequently was depressed and started using unprescribed drugs. Through the support she received, she managed to control her substance use, became abstinent and got engaged. However, she describes the relationship to have been a violent one. Sue had two children in this relationship. Following the birth of her second son, she was diagnosed with post-natal depression. At that point she started drinking and smoking heroin. She also attempted to commit suicide by hanging. Consequently, her relationship ended and her children were taken into care.

Services were contacted again and she was admitted onto a psychiatric ward, and then after a month she was referred for residential rehabilitation. While in rehab, her mother, whom she was close to, became terminally ill and died. Following this, Sue had another episode of depression, dropped out of rehabilitation and her drinking and drug taking spiralled. Over the last three years, she has received support through an alcohol residential detox, two community detoxes and a six-month residential opiate rehabilitation. Social services had been involved initially when her two children were taken into care, and also recently to support her with supervised contact with her children during the times that she has been abstinent.

Case study 4.1 highlights the challenges, complexities and interlinks between mental health and substance use. Many clients we have worked with present with a wide range of reasons for why they use substances. It is also evident in most cases that multiple life traumas and experiences can perpetuate substance use as well as mental disease. It is therefore important for those in training, as well as practitioners, not only to be aware of this complex interlink, but also to explore ways in which clients can be supported to avoid where possible the continual revolving door dynamic of going in and out of services. An example of this can be considering long-term rehabilitation treatment options. Another important aspect of support is the involvement of the family and social network of the client in their treatment plan. We will go into more details of this later in this chapter, as well as in Chapter 5.

Values-based practice

We have highlighted the importance of the therapeutic relationship in the helping role, but it is essential to understand that relationships are formed out of the values (the beliefs) that both parties hold, and these are particularly of importance to the practitioner who is expected to show values that are conducive to enabling and helping. Much has been written about values for practice, and this is often enshrined in organizational statements, equality and diversity policies and professional body guidance and identity. With the latter, often professional bodies use value-based language to delimit their roles and particular contribution to the care of individuals and families they see. Such value-based practice is entirely dependent on practitioners being open and reflective, including being open to the possibility that they are wrong and make mistakes. Below are the Ten Essential Shared Capabilities for Mental Health Practice, originally introduced in 2004, and which despite being over ten years old, remain a sound checklist for value-based practice:

The Ten Essential Shared Capabilities for Mental Health Practice (National Institute for Mental Health England 2009)

Working in partnership. Developing and maintaining constructive working relationships with service users, carers, families, colleagues, lay people and wider community networks. Working positively with any tensions created by conflicts of interest or aspiration that may arise between the partners in care.

Respecting diversity. Working in partnership with service users, carers, families and colleagues to provide care and interventions that not only make a positive difference but also do so in ways that respect and value diversity including age, race, culture, disability, gender, spirituality and sexuality.

Practising ethically. Recognizing the rights and aspirations of service users and their families, acknowledging power differentials and minimizing them whenever possible. Providing treatment and care that is accountable to service users and carers within the boundaries prescribed by national (professional), legal and local codes of ethical practice.

Challenging inequality. Addressing the causes and consequences of stigma, discrimination, social inequality and exclusion on service users, carers and mental health services. Creating, developing or maintaining valued social roles for people in the communities they come from.

Promoting recovery. Working in partnership to provide care and treatment that enables service users and carers to tackle mental health problems with hope and optimism and to work towards a valued lifestyle within and beyond the limits of any mental health problem.

Identifying people's needs and strengths. Working in partnership to gather information to agree on health and social care needs in the context of the preferred lifestyle and aspirations of service users, their families, carers and friends.

Providing service user–centred care. Negotiating achievable and meaningful goals; primarily from the perspective of service users and their families. Influencing and seeking the means to achieve those goals and clarifying the responsibilities of the people who will provide any help that is needed, including systematically evaluating outcomes and achievements.

Making a difference. Facilitating access to and delivering the best quality, evidence-based, values-based health and social care interventions to meet the needs and aspirations of service users and their families and carers.

Promoting safety and positive risk taking. Empowering the person to decide the level of risk they are prepared to take with their health and safety. This includes working with the tension between promoting safety and positive risk taking, including assessing and dealing with possible risks for service users, carers, family members, and the wider public.

Personal development and learning. Keeping up-to-date with changes in practice and participating in lifelong learning, personal and professional development for one's self and colleagues through supervision, appraisal and reflective practice.

In simple terms, when a practitioner manages to show good values in their skills they are probably showing LUV (they **listen, understand** and **validate**). Below is the LUV triangle that orients our practice intentions:

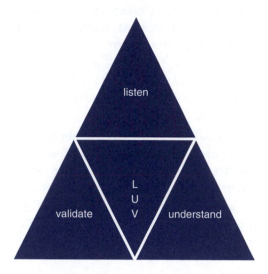

Figure 4.1 The LUV triangle (Echterling et al. 2005)

Importance of acknowledging issues of difference and diversity and their impact on treatment

It is important to recognize that now more than ever we live in a multicultural society. And when working with individuals or families, cultural factors impact on how clients access services. From our experience we have often questioned the lack of access or limited access by particular members of society. Paul and Charura (2015) highlighted in their work on working relationally the importance of considering the social context, which includes the way in which the client relates to other members of the community and the impact of the following:

- Cultural factors – these include collective ideas, values, beliefs, attitudes and behaviours which the client shares with a particular group.
- Political factors – these relate to laws, policies and other governing influential structures on the client's life in society.
- Economic factors – these relate to the client's experience of the impact of financial and other material resources in society.

In line with this they considered that it is important for practitioners in their work to have the awareness that difference is not just about skin colour or visible features but includes an awareness of all dimensions which influence the therapist and client. They used Moodley's (2005) synonymously inclusive definition, which extends difference and diversity to seven major categories. These are named as race, gender, class, sexual orientation, disability, religion and age (Moodley 2005). We believe that these areas are also central to any work practitioners do in the dual diagnosis field. Some examples may include asking questions like:

- How many clients from the major seven categories access your service?
- What may be the barriers and how can the service be made more accessible?

We believe that having such openness and awareness to working with issues of diversity adds to the practitioner's competencies.

The Care Programme Approach – case management

In addition to psychological models and medical treatment there are quasi-bureaucratic approaches, like case management, which in mental health services consists of the Care Programme Approach (CPA) and the more value-based strengths model. CPA is the main organizing principle for specialist care in the UK, and so it is important to contextualize work undertaken with clients within it. You will see that the tasks of case management reflect the tasks and processes of structured therapeutic work that starts with relationship building, then problem/goal identification, assessment, doing the work or treatment, relapse prevention and exit. This chapter follows this process broadly, although in the following chapter you will read more about the models and kinds of interventions involved in working with dual diagnosis. Taking case management first (a mainly problems-based approach), we discuss CPA and the strengths-based model below.

For a while in the late 1980s and through the 1990s, case management was seen as having an essential role in the delivery of successful services. Organized at the level of the service user, case management was the critical application of a range of community care policy thrusts. Historically, case management has been a term more affiliated to health-based or nursing care, with care management being the social care equivalent. Despite the disciplinary separation, both are organized around the key tasks of assessment, planning, intervention and evaluation (Challis 1994), which in turn echoes such activities as the nursing process.

In 1991, the CPA was introduced in the UK as a means to coordinate the care and support of mental health service users, irrespective of whether their mental health service career began in the health or the local authority setting. CPA designates a coordinator who is a clinician involved with the service user and who has the job of producing a care plan addressing health and social care needs. CPA began with tiers that sifted service users on the basis of presumed complexity, diagnosis and risk, and while this has changed to an extent, the drive is still to make sure those people assessed as having greater risks and more complex problems remain a priority.

Since its inception, CPA has been blighted by poor cooperation in its delivery, resulting in a series of position and review papers such as *Building Bridges* (DoH 1996), *Still Building Bridges* and *Refocusing the Care Programme Approach* (DoH 2008). Each in turn reiterate the centrality of CPA to effective service delivery and improved service user outcomes. Unfortunately, the evidence for effectiveness was lacking, and since the early 2000s research in the area has dropped off. A Cochrane Review (Marshall 2002) found that while a lot of research in the area could not be included due to issues of quality, standard case management failed to show improved social or clinical outcomes; it did not show financial value and even showed an increased frequency of hospital admissions and duration of hospital stay (there was a modest increase in medication compliance). While the review did not specify it was looking at CPA, the review was looking at the most relevant and closest evidence base. Ziguras and Stuart (2000), in their meta-analysis, found some modest positive gains, particularly for carers, from case management, but the best results were for assertive community treatment. Assertive community treatment, or assertive outreach, is another model of case management which offers intensive contacts to service users who are not engaging with routine mental health services, and this is done by a team with relatively smaller caseloads and who team-work individual service users with persistence. Setting aside the ethics of this at a time before Community Treatment Orders, the Mental Capacity Act or Deprivation of Liberty Safeguards, assertive case management was more effective than standard case management when it came to reducing hospital admission and duration of stay; the other measures where either unattainable due to poor research or equivalent (Marshall & Lockwood 2002). Curiously, Marshall (2002) speculates on why this might be so:

> [W]hen one looks back at policy documents justifying the introduction of case management into the UK, they generally refer to US trials of assertive community treatment, not to US trials of case management. Thus an ineffectual intervention was promoted as a result of a misunderstanding that arose from the confusing nature of 'case management' terminology – assertive community treatment was mistaken for ordinary case management. By the time the UK trials had confirmed that case management was ineffective it was too late; the care programme approach had arrived. (Marshall 2002:63)

This may account for why CPA has been so hard to implement over three decades – case management was never supposed to have great outcomes, but assertive outreach was. While CPA has been criticized for its bureaucratic outlook, other case management models have foregone the stages of 'assessment to delivery' in favour of setting out a value base first.

Strengths–based models in mental health

> A strengths approach is about connecting with service users, and with ourselves as practitioners, in ways that help to unearth mutual creative potentials and by doing so restoring all that is fun and exciting in our work. (Ryan & Morgan 2004:5)

The strengths-based model (Ryan & Morgan, 2004), as mentioned above, is one such case management approach developed initially in US forensic settings where the traditional problem-based approaches were not engaging service users. The strengths-based model works to the following tenets:

1. The focus of the helping process is upon the client's strengths, interests, abilities and competencies, not upon their deficits, weaknesses and problems.
2. All clients have the capacity to learn, grow and change.
3. The client is viewed as the director of the case management helping process.

4. The client–case manager relationship becomes a primary and essential partnership.
5. The case management helping process takes an outreach perspective.
6. The entire community is viewed as an oasis of potential resources rather than an obstacle. Natural community resources should be considered before segregated mental health services. (Morgan 1996:55–62)

Despite the strengths-based model having been around for a while, it remains a challenging approach for services to deliver, not least because services work on the premise of problem and need as an entry point. However, the strengths-based model can be used as the ethos that informs the broader case management tasks, as shown in Figure 4.2, which houses a range of interventions. The strengths-based approach also links to specific therapeutic work; for instance, Kuyken et al. (2009) suggest that within a cognitive behavioural frame 'once strengths are identified, clients often are able to transfer skills from areas of strength to manage areas of difficulty with greater ease' (2009:54–55).

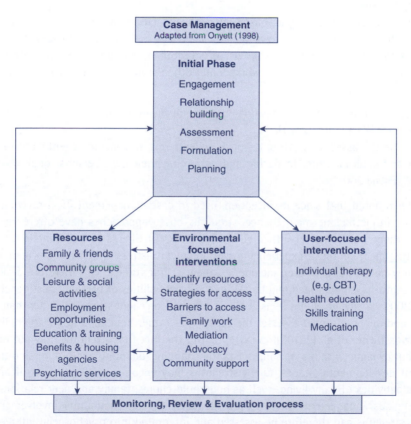

Figure 4.2 The case management model (Thanks to Neil Bottomley for this adapted version of Onyett's (1998) model)

Some links can be made here between the CPA, the Mental Health (Wales) Measure 2010 and a strengths-based approach. Both CPA and the Mental Health Measure are frameworks which are about connecting with clients, and with ourselves as practitioners, in ways that enable coordination in their assessment, care and treatment, and work to ensure the right to an individual and comprehensive plan, an ongoing Care and Treatment Plan to assist their recovery.

In addition to strengths-based models applied in individual case work, there has in recent years been interest in community development models such as ASSET-based approaches that work at a community level mobilizing local people around things they want to achieve with the assets they have to bring (Glasgow Centre for Population Health 2011; Improvement & Development Agency 2010).

Strengths-based models for substance use

Consideration needs to be given to problem solving and social skills training so clients can develop relationships with abstinent friends, to minimize social pressures to use substances (Bellack & DiClemente 1999). Strength-based approaches have become the grassroots recovery movement.

As the title suggests, strengths-based perspectives focus on the client's strengths at every phase of the helping process, as developed by Saleebey (1997, 2008; da Silveira Nunes Dinis 2012). There is much literature on the use of strength-based approaches in substance use and dual diagnosis work by social workers and other professions. Essential ingredients of strength-based approaches include:

• Focus on the importance of developing personal meaning and life purpose in recovery (Moxley & Washington 2001).
• Focus on the assets and attributes of the client. This may include client's utilization of own self-determination, to decide and determine their own personal goals (Saleebey 1997; Payne 2005).

It has been noted that since its inception, used in case management of intravenous drug users and in methadone maintenance, strengths-based approaches have offered a bridge for practitioners to better serve their clients (Karoll 2010). Clients participating in substance abuse treatment or those experiencing psychological distress which affects their motivation may not initially, or ever, include abstinence. Practitioners can therefore draw from this strength-based approach and be affirming of possibilities of personal abstinence goals (Wilke 2001; da Silveira Nunes Dinis 2012). The focus is on client strengths rather than weaknesses, and the practitioner assesses the capabilities rather than liabilities of their clients.

Biswas-Diener et al. (2010) drew attention to the fact that strengths may not be fixed traits, but dynamic within a person, constantly changing, adapting and progressing through different developmental stages. Client strengths may encompass all contexts of an individual's activities of daily living, such as household chores, family and peer relations, spiritual/religious engagement, interests, vocational skills, and community involvement. The client's strengths can therefore be assessed and integrated into psychosocial interventions to enhance clinical outcomes and further facilitate shifts to positive outcomes (Duckworth et al. 2005; da Silveira Nunes Dinis 2012).

> ## Benefits of strength–based approaches
>
> Harris et al. (2012) noted in their research some examples of clients' experiences of prac-
> titioners using a strength-based approach in their work with them.
>
> Participants frequently talked about the importance of the identification and use of
> one's strengths. For example, participants reported 'identifying my strengths was difficult
> at first, but it is important to do because if you know what you are good at you can make
> the effort to use them' and 'knowing what I am good at, like basketball and having a good
> sense of humour, has made me want to do these things'.
>
> Several participants discussed the importance of practising and further developing
> one's strengths. For example, 'we learned that continuing to practice and further develop
> our unique strengths is more important than medicating our weaknesses by using drugs'
> and 'we need to look for what we are good at so that we can practice these things and
> become better people'.
>
> This research shows the importance of incorporating strength-based approaches from
> the client's perspective. It outlines how such an approach can help in the utilization of
> clients' own self-determination, in deciding or determining their own personal goals and
> in shifting clients' own perceived limitations.

Risk

Another major challenge for practitioners is around the management of risk. The complex
nature of the impact of mental ill health and substance use on clients often means that there
are many issues of risk to be considered. These include:

- health risks associated with the use of the substance, or with withdrawing from the
  substance;
- risk to self-harming or harming others – risk to others should always be considered to
  include neglect of children, and in the UK this would invoke the use of local safeguarding
  of children procedures;
- risk of combining prescribed medication and substances/unprescribed medication.

Furthermore, there are many other issues to consider for which each service in which practitioners work will have protocols and guidance. These include:

- information governance;
- confidentiality;
- referral and treatment pathways;
- pathways of reporting issues pertaining to protection of vulnerable adults and children;
- discharge pathways;
- aftercare/post-discharge support packages.

There are, however, a number of tensions and problems in risk assessment and management.
Current models and approaches are still predicated on actuarial risk assessment thinking,
which tries to profile a population to arrive at a risk judgement. However:

In the drive for evidence-based practice, a more objective and reliable form of risk assessment was sought. This emerged with the development of actuarial risk assessment instruments (ARAIs), an approach utilized successfully by the insurance industry for many years ... Such instruments were constructed by statistically analyzing the correlates of violent behaviour across wide population groups. Individuals presenting with particular attributes and characteristics could be mapped on to a risk continuum to gauge the likelihood of them committing future violent acts ... It is a process that deliberately disengages practitioners in order to eliminate the problems of inter-rater reliability that had been associated with unstructured clinical judgment. (Turner & Colombo 2008:166)

While risk becomes a catch-all term for things that cause worry, in fact we should distinguish between different aspects of the matrix of issue that is actually being discussed. We can see this helpfully when we separate the areas of concern out:

- **Risk** is the probability that a given thing will happen in a certain time frame.
- A **hazard** is the situation arising in a certain circumstance that could lead to harm.
- **Danger** is the extent of the hazard or the degree of harm. (Prins 2005)

Assessment of risk usually covers risk to self, to others, to property, of deterioration in state and health but rarely considers what is known as iatrogenic risk, which is risk arising from treatment itself. The box below suggests some of the iatrogenic risks that practitioners should consider if they are to be fully rounded in their risk assessments. This is best seen in discussion of psychotropic treatments (Whitaker 2004), which should be minimal with conscientious prescribing, routine health checks and unintended (side) effect monitoring.

Common iatrogenic risks in accessing services and treatment (Tummey & Tummey 2008)

- **Neurological/anatomical/physiological** – brain damage, cardiac function, immunosuppression, uncontrollable movements, side effects, changed sexual and other function, weight gain, toxicity, poisoning;
- **Interpersonal/psychological** – demoralization, poor application of psychological approaches, pathologizing formulations, passive aggressive interactions, neglect and dismissal, subjugation and domination, denial of access to personal preferences and personal space, use of role/professional status to further one's opinion;
- **Social** – stigma, exclusion, change to familial relationships, reduced hope, humiliation and teasing, labelling, disclosure to others through association, assumption of 'science' and 'truth', undisclosed conflicts of interest, closing ranks;
- **Abuse/assault** – physical assault, unwelcome physical and psychological intimacy, surveillance, seclusion, restraint, tranquilizing, sexual assault in care settings.

So far we have introduced some of the challenges and complexities of the relationship between substance use and mental health. Case study 4.1 has already built on some of the challenges and the links between mental health, substance use and the issues to consider in access to services which we started to explore in earlier chapters. The case study (4.2) that now follows outlines some basic information which may be presented often at the onset of a client referral. Our aim is to outline and explore some of the issues, including those that may not be explicit. It is important for practitioners to be aware of how the complexities and the challenges that arise in assessment and in working with clients as part of their caseload. The reflective questions which follow case study 4.2 encourage you to reflect on some of the issues you will have to consider in your assessment and consideration of engaging with clients presenting within the service you work in.

❏ **Case study 4.2**

Sam is referred for treatment and support with your service. In the referral letter from the community mental health team is some basic information which includes the following:

Sam is a 36-year-old mother of two. Her children are aged 4 and 8. Sam also has a diagnosis of generalized anxiety and depression for which she has been previously prescribed medication. Sam has a history of self-harming by cutting her wrists, and she attempted suicide twice in the last year. She has also previously used heroin for five years and has been in and out of treatment services. Sam had a detox and rehabilitation in prison six months ago and is currently stabilized on 80ml methadone. She is willing to engage with the service, hence this referral.

Reflective question: perspectives and challenges in conducting assessments

What are some of the issues you will have to consider in your assessment and consideration of engaging with Sam?

Case study 4.2 highlights a case that presents many complex issues relating to dual diagnosis which many practitioners working in this field will often face. Conducting a thorough and comprehensive assessment is essential in order to be able to gather all the information needed. A comprehensive assessment ensures that not only is the key information about the client's substance use and their physical and mental health obtained, but also their social circumstances. This then helps the practitioner in working collaboratively with the client to formulate and explore the best treatment/therapeutic options.

Before we outline some of the complexities associated with assessment and working with clients with dual diagnoses, we draw to the reader's attention here an important model that is often used in practice to illicit the stage of change that a client will be on. This *transtheoretical model* (also known as the cycle of change model) was hypothesized by Prochaska and DiClemente (1983) and is reproduced in Figure 4.3 below:

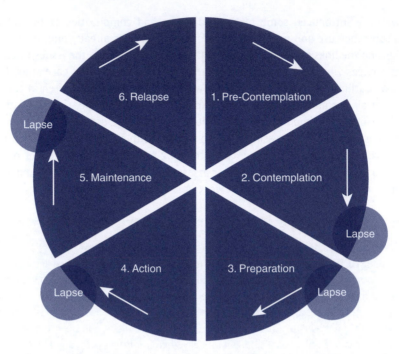

Figure 4.3 The transtheoretical model adapted from Prochaska and DiClemente (1983)

This widely used transtheoretical model, as hypothesized by Prochaska and DiClemente (1983), has six stages:

1. The pre-contemplation stage – this is the stage when the client denies, or does not recognize, that they have a problem.
2. The contemplation stage – this is when clients start to realize that they have a problem, but may still be ambivalent about change.
3. The preparation stage – this is when clients have decided to change and are actively making plans to do so.
4. The action stage – this is the stage in which individuals have made specific evident modifications in their lifestyles within the past six months. It is worth noting, however, that typically, not all modifications or changes of behaviour count as action in this model. The behavioural modifications would have to evidence change that moves the individual towards a desired outcome.
5. The maintenance stage – this is when clients have reached their goal and have made considerable progress. In this stage the client is ready to consider how to maintain change.
6. Lastly is the relapse stage, which is when clients return to their old patterns of substance using behaviours.

This model has proved to be effective because it emphasizes the need for individuals to develop functional attitudes and beliefs towards their substance abuse. When working with clients who have dual diagnoses, it is important to bear in mind that there are multiple factors that can affect their motivation. Practitioners and clients find this model helpful in a further way, in that it allows for progress to be gained without expectations of moving through the whole model before the client is able or willing to do so. For instance, a client may be able to engage with information on tobacco addiction, show understanding of it (pre-contemplative to contemplative), but want to think further about whether smoking cessation work is something they want to do at this point. The small but significant change from pre-contemplative to contemplative is a sign of progress even if it does not progress beyond this point at the present time.

Physical and mental health factors affecting motivation to change

As we have seen in Chapters 2 and 3, the combination of having poor mental health and being in distress, as well as depending on substances, can often result in a complex web of challenges around the individual's ability to make changes to her or his substance use. Some of these challenges are directly related to physical health deterioration, which can consequently influence motivation. It is therefore key that practitioners are aware of some of the possible physical health problems that can emerge as a result of substance use, as well as how they can impact on motivation.

❏ **Case study 4.3 Factors affecting motivation and impact of physical health**

Tim attends for assessment; he states that he has not engaged in service because he is too anxious to go out in public. He also states that he has been feeling very low in mood and lethargic. He was in hospital last year for three weeks following an accidental drug overdose. For about two weeks now he has been coughing up blood and states he also has an ulcer in his groin due to injecting drugs daily and it won't heal. He states it is painful but he has been managing it by taking codeine-phosphate tablets for pain which he gets from 'a friend'. He states that 'the gear and booze' are 'killing him slowly'. However, he states that he is motivated to stop drinking and using drugs. He also states he is very worried because he shared a needle twice 'a while ago' and later found out the person had hepatitis C.

Reflective questions

- *What may be some of the factors which may be affecting Tim's motivation?*
- *At what stage in the cycle of change is he?*
- *What would you need to consider in his assessment in order to best help him?*

Although the focus of this book has been on substance use and mental health, the impact of substance use on physical health is well documented (Schulte & Yih-Ing 2014). Intoxication, substance use (especially prolonged use over time) and the possibility of accidental overdoses can all be life-threatening factors which result in medical emergencies. Alcohol, marijuana, heroin and amphetamine/methamphetamines contribute to morbidity and mortality (Boffetta & Hashibe 2006). Opioid analgesic poisoning is also related to deaths, as is heroin or cocaine (Schulte & Yih-Ing 2014). Prescription medication used in excess of the prescription poses as much of a threat to health as traditional street drugs (Arria et al. 2011).

From our work in different health settings that support individuals who use substances, we have noted that the combination of multiple substances substantially increases the risk of health problems. For example, alcohol, tobacco, heroin, prescription stimulants and methamphetamine have been linked to increased risk of cardiovascular problems and heart disease (Schulte & Yih-Ing 2014). Increased risk of heart attacks and cardiac arrest seems an obvious problem (Kontos et al. 2003). Heavy drinking is purported to be the most common cause of secondary hypertension, with binge drinking being a significant risk factor for all subtypes of stroke (Schulte & Yih-Ing 2014).

Substance use can also increase the risk of transmitting infectious disease. Drug and needle-sharing practices can lead to infection of HIV, hepatitis C (HCV) and other blood-borne pathogens. It is noted that injection drug users (IDUs) are the highest risk group for acquiring HCV. Similarly, injection drug use is a significant contributor, both directly and indirectly, to the spread of HIV.

Dependence on substances can also indirectly lead to increased risky sexual behaviour and sex work (i.e. trading sex for crack, methadone, other drugs or money) (Azevedo et al. 2007). Regardless of sexual orientation, however, sexual risk practices such as reduced condom use, being 'high' during sex and having multiple sexual partners is prevalent among methamphetamine users (Schulte & Yih-Ing 2014). As noted so far there are many mental and physical health effects as well as behavioural challenges associated directly and indirectly with substance use. Schulte and Yih-Ing (2014) noted a summary of examples by life stage of mental and physical health conditions associated with substance use (Table 4.1 below).

Substance Use	Physical/Medical Conditions	Mental Health/ Psychiatric Disorders
Adolescence		
Alcohol	Accidental Injury	Suicidal Ideation/Behaviours
Marijuana/Cannabis	Ulcers from Injecting	Self-Harming Behaviours
Tobacco	Automobile Accidents	Depression
Inhalants	Physical/Sexual Violence	Anxiety
Psychotherapeutic	Poisoning/Overdose	Attention Deficit/
Drugs	Sexually Transmitted	Hyperactivity Disorder
Amphetamines	Infections	
Opioids/Pain Relievers	Respiratory Problems	
	Asthma	
	Pain-Related Diagnoses	

Adulthood		
Alcohol	Poisoning/Overdose	Suicidal Ideation/Behaviours
Marijuana	Ulcers from Injecting	Mood Disorders
Tobacco	Sexually Transmitted Diseases	Depression
Psychotherapeutic	Cancers (e.g. mouth, throat, lung, colon)	Bipolar I & II
Drugs	Heart Disease/Hypertension/Stroke	Anxiety Disorders
Opioids/Pain Relievers	Reproductive Morbidity/Fetal Damage	Panic Disorder
Tranquilizers/	Diabetes	Post-Traumatic Stress Disorder
Benzodiazepines	Respiratory Problems	Social & Specific Phobias
Cocaine/Crack	Asthma	Generalized Anxiety Disorder
Heroin	Infection	Eating Disorders
Methamphetamine	Liver Damage/Disease	Antisocial Personality Disorder
Older Adulthood		
Alcohol	Accidental Injury	Suicidal Ideation/Behaviours
Psychotherapeutic	Ulcers from Injecting	Depression
Drugs	Liver Cirrhosis	Anxiety Disorders
Opioids/Pain Relievers	Heart Attack/Stroke	Social & Specific Phobias
Sedatives/	Insomnia	Generalized Anxiety Disorder
Benzodiazepines	Cancers (e.g. mouth, throat, lung, colon)	Dementia/Wernicke-Korsakoff
Amphetamines	Diabetes	Syndrome
Marijuana		Insomnia
Tobacco		

It is important to note that this is not a comprehensive list of substances which individuals may use, and these physical/medical conditions are not inclusive of all conditions that may result from substance use. Furthermore, the list does not mean that a client will get all of these but rather are an example of some conditions.

Table 4.1 Substance use and related health impacts

Source: Adapted from Schulte and Yih-Ing (2014).

We urge some caution in reading these co-morbidities and consequences in a straightforward causal way. If the arguments of Part I are accepted, then these health and emotional problems are equally and often a result of poverty, social circumstances and distress rather than an underlying pathological state. Furthermore, we suggest caution where such correlations can lead to moralizing viewpoints such as arriving at the view that a certain condition results easily from choices a person makes. Often, people with dual diagnoses have hard, difficult personal histories, including trauma, exploitation and neglect. Similarly, service users and critics would find some of the pathologizing language of the area a barrier to understanding and getting help.

From practice we have noted that at times clients with a dual diagnosis go through a 'revolving door' of being informed that they have to seek support for their substance use first, then get support for their mental health (see case study 4.1). However, as we have shown throughout this chapter, having a dual diagnosis can present many challenges for the client and for practitioners. Whereas Department of Health (2002) guidance suggests that this should be resolvable in practice, the reality is clients are given a confusing picture of what needs to happen when. For example, a client who may be experiencing symptoms of depression, such as low mood and lethargy, or signs of anxiety may find it quite difficult to be motivated to change their behaviour. As would many clients who are prescribed a sedating medication. They may also struggle to engage in services, as leaving their home to attend for appointments may be a challenge due to poor mental health or to poor physical health. This link between mental/physical health and motivation is an important one for practitioners to be aware of.

Equally, it may be the case that a client is experiencing, or is informed, that their physical/mental health is deteriorating. This may be a catalytic factor to their motivation. From practice we have noted change at the point where individuals are informed that they are in the first stage of liver damage due to drinking, they survive a drug overdose or are informed their children may be taken into care. Such experiences can result in clients becoming more motivated to do something about their substance use. We are not advocating draconian and dramatic measures, or schedules of potential punishment, we are merely outlining that there are a range of motivators and barriers which we can map to the transtheoretical model and which may help us understand what will act as a motivator for one client and not another.

As we have noted so far, and particularly in case study 4.3 where the client, Tim, shows how dual diagnosis can manifest a complex web of challenges which include an impact on mental and physical health. Through a comprehensive assessment which takes into consideration the different stages of change and factors that may be influencing the clients motivation, the practitioner can be better equipped to help a client and choose appropriate interventions. It is therefore clear that there are many health complexities that arise from substance misuse, and the practitioner's competence in identifying how these may be impacting or influencing the client's motivation is paramount.

Key factors in assessment when working with dual diagnosis

The brief details in case studies 4.1 and 4.2 can serve as a platform from which the practitioner can have some information to start to work with the client. Each service/profession will have different forms and approaches to assessment. Our aim here is to present a working model that can be adapted to suit different settings. Furthermore, we highlight different aspects which enable blind spots to be identified that practitioners often miss in working with dual diagnosis. The National Institute for Clinical Excellence (NICE), in its (2007) guidelines, offers a list of important factors to consider in assessment. When making an assessment and developing and agreeing a care plan, staff should consider the client's:

- medical, psychological, social and occupational needs;
- history of drug use;

- experience of previous treatment, if any;
- goals in relation to her or his drug use;
- treatment preferences.

Staff who are responsible for the delivery and monitoring of the agreed care plan should:

- establish and sustain a respectful and supportive relationship with the client;
- help the client to identify situations or states when he or she is vulnerable to drug misuse and to explore alternative coping strategies;
- ensure that all clients have full access to a wide range of services;
- ensure that maintaining the client's engagement with services remains a major focus of the care plan;
- maintain effective collaboration with other care providers.

Furthermore, NICE guidelines note that healthcare professionals should use biological testing (e.g. of urine or oral fluid samples) as part of a comprehensive assessment of drug use, but they should not rely on it as the sole method of diagnosis and assessment.

We believe that these NICE guidelines are important for staff to incorporate into their assessments. There are, however, other specific services that may also add extra components, for example issues of risk management. In the following section, we present an example of an assessment template. We encourage the reader to consider the issues identified in the case studies presented so far in this chapter and to use this information to consider:

1. What information do you already have about the client from referral?
2. What other information is important to get when conducting an assessment in dual diagnosis that is different from standard assessments for those without a dual diagnosis?
3. Which of this information will you get from the client, and which from other sources (e.g. other professionals, family where possible/appropriate)?
4. What are the context, nature of assessment and intended service provision and limitations of your service/profession in conducting this assessment?
5. What challenges may emerge for the practitioner as well as for the client in conducting the assessment?
6. What stage of change is the client at, and what may influence her or his motivation or be getting in the way of them being motivated?

At the point of accessing services, clients may already have been in touch with mental health services and may therefore already have been labelled with a diagnosis. Sometimes, however, contact with you may be the first professional contact that the client has, and there may therefore be a need to identify other pathways that may be triggered in order to best support the client or protect vulnerable others impacted by their substance use or mental ill health. It is therefore important for the practitioner to be open about this from the outset and to explicitly state the boundaries of confidentiality, and the possible involvement of other teams/professions where possible. It is also important to state the possible benefits of involving the client's healthy social network/family in supporting the client.

Boundary rules	Your own examples and reflections as a practitioner
What are examples of boundary rules that are explicitly communicated to the client in the service you work in (e.g. you talk about it or have it in service information)?	
What are examples of boundary rules that are implicit and therefore assumed (e.g. social norms and expectations)?	
What boundary rules are non-negotiable and rarely change in your work with clients?	
What are the boundary rules that can be negotiated and changed with consent and agreement?	

Table 4.2 Working out what boundaries are needed and when they apply

It is beyond the scope of this book to outline in full professional demands and standards, but it can be useful, in the context of the therapeutic relationship, to reconsider the kinds of boundaries you might need to negotiate. Boundaries also refer to job role and the service context.

Table 4.2 above gives you the option of writing the common boundaries of your working relationships in one column of the table. Where a boundary rule does not easily fit, you may want to think about the circumstances under which it moves.

The figure below (Figure 4.4) notes the zone of helpfulness, which gives some latitude to personal style in practice while still being clear about where you need to locate your personal and professional boundaries (it refers to nurses, but in reality this could be any practitioner). While it is often the case that practitioners who become over-involved and self-disclose become the centre of professional actions or more necessary supervisory guidance, this figure also suggests that those practitioners that are aloof and withholding are equally problematic.

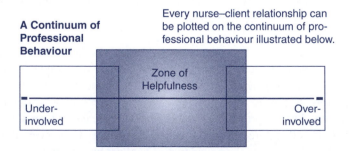

Figure 4.4 The zone of helpfulness in professional boundaries

Source: Oregon State Board of Nursing (2010).

Assessment form template	
Client and referrer details	In this section will be the client's name, date of birth, gender, telephone number and other relevant contact details. Also included will be the referrer's contact details. This makes it possible to easily contact the referrer when any information is needed and also to give feedback on progress or discharge following treatment completion.
Presenting circumstances	This section will include some of the information from the referral letter/other professionals. It may also be information given by the client's family if referred by family members. It will also include information gathered from interviewing and having dialogue in the face-to-face assessment with the client.
Substance use summary	What substances does the client use? Route: how do they take it (e.g. inject, smoke, drink?) How much does the client use per day/week? How long has the client used/been dependent on this substance for?
Substance withdrawal summary	Often the severity of withdrawal symptoms is one of the factors which perpetuate the use of substances. It is important for the practitioner to elicit the symptoms and experience that the client has when withdrawing from the substance. In working with dual diagnosis it is also important to be mindful of the link between the withdrawal and the impact on mental health.
Physical health summary	The clients are asked about their health and any impact the substance they use has had on them, including any periods of accessing health services. For those being assessed for residential detox or rehabilitation services, consent is also often gained to get a medication and health summary form their General Practitioner (GP).
Mental health	Any mental ill health/disorder diagnoses or any experiences of psychological distress are noted and assessed in this section. When working with known dual diagnoses, it is important to gather as much information as possible here.
Current medication	Any medication the client is prescribed/taking is also elicited. It is important to also ask if the client is taking any unprescribed medication because from our experience, clients can often be buying or taking medication without it being via prescription, including pain killers, methadone, sulbutex or any other drugs. Any allergies to any medication?
Social circumstances	Questions asked here relate to the client's living and wider social circumstances, for example: Where does the client live and who do they live with? Does the client have children? (If so, how old are the children, who looks after the children, and who is with them as the assessment is being conducted?) What social support/structure or network does the client have? Is the client employed, or when did they last work? Is the client on social security benefits? How does the client fund her or his substance use?

Table 4.3 Assessment template for dual diagnosis

Table 4.3 (Continued)

Assessment form template	
Issues of risk	Assessing risk includes asking the client about any risk behaviours, e.g. self-harming, overdosing, any suicidal attempts or ideation, and risk of self-neglect/exploitation by others. Furthermore, it also includes an assessment of risk to others including violence and risk to children.
	There may also be risks associated with the individual's health, and possibilities of infecting others, including blood-borne viruses, e.g. hepatitis B, hepatitis C, HIV.
	It is particularly important in dual diagnosis to also consider risks in mental ill health relapse and what some of the triggers may be.
	Depending on the organization, there are different tools that are used in assessing risk. Practitioners should familiarize themselves with the risk assessment tools used within their service.
Initial treatment plan	In exploring the treatment plan the following questions may be a guide:
	What psychosocial interventions are going to be employed in working with this client?
	What has worked for the client in the past?
	What the client would like and how this matches with what the practitioner recommends?
Any other information	In this section will be any other service-specific information that the practitioner can draw from the assessment.
Motivation	It is important to establish how motivated the client is to change. This can be established through their behaviour and dialogue in session. Important information includes drink/substance use diaries, periods of abstinence in the past, what the client wants from the service or what support they need. You may use skills of motivational interviewing in this part of the assessment.

Assessing clients and formulation

In working with dual diagnoses and considering psychosocial interventions, part of the role of assessment is to identify the 'suitability criteria' of the client. Suitability criteria refers to two things:

1. Whether the service area doing the assessment can work with the client, and this may be due to limits set in the service design.
2. Criteria recommended in clinical guidance which suggests what will work for which clients at what point.

Many services are not in the position of refusing help even where guidance suggests that the client may not be ready to engage in healthy change. But, optimism, coupled with goal oriented conversation, seems to be a supportive quality in mobilizing recovery (Law et al. 2012).

Often assessment leads to a care or support plan, but as we will see shortly, there is a possible stage between assessment and planning called *formulation* (more is written about this later in this chapter). A number of therapeutic models use formulations, and at its simplest a formulation is a shared model for understanding how a client's problems are being maintained, how they arose and what the direction of work together might be. Assessment supplies a substantial amount of the information that underpins this shared working model, and the assumptions about the problems and the work might viably shape the care plan. As can be seen from Table 4.2, assessment elicits what the client's problem is. It also asks 'What keeps the problem going?' And it elicits any risk behaviours that the client has. It also serves to enable the practitioner to find out a brief history of how the problem developed, eliciting the client's substance use and mental health history as well as finding out any general health issues, and lastly finding out about the expectations of treatment/support and identifying the main goals for treatment/support.

From practice, we are aware that the assessment can also give the practitioner any details about the client's frequency of using drugs/alcohol, the amount he or she uses, and the nature of withdrawal symptoms, as these may manifest in the room as the practitioner conducts the assessment.

The *problem list* – a tool for getting started

We come later to looking at strengths and ASSET-based approaches, but for the time being we will assume that clients discuss their problems. For clients with dual diagnoses we have acknowledged the complexity of problems in terms of intensity, range and longevity. For some clients, and practitioners, who are overwhelmed by their problems, a useful starting point can be generating a problem list. The box below explains how this can be used.

Using problem lists

Rationale: clients may need your help getting a 'helicopter' view of their situation and the range of problems they may be facing. You need to know how best to help through prioritizing and adding focus.

Task: You and the client list all the problems they are experiencing at present. You then prioritize from the whole list using 4 questions:

1. Is there a problem on the list that if solved would solve the others?
2. Is there a problem on the list that if not tackled will lead to crisis or higher risk?
3. Is there something that connects all/some of the problems?
4. Is there somewhere on the list the client would prefer to start?

Tips: Remember these are the client's problems not yours. Maintain an open, enquiring style. Asking the questions above, and doing the problem list, allows you to do LUV (see Echterling et al. 2005). You can negotiate the problem list as something to be carried on through homework tasks.

Use: important information for formulation and contracting for the work you do together. The problem list offers opportunities for normalizing strategies (i.e. the client's distress becomes more understandable). Value the list as a narrative. The problem list can lead to other interventions such as coping strategy enhancement and relapse prevention.

Source: Paul and Penson (2008).

Summary of Key Elements of the assessment:

- What is the nature of the difficulty that the client is presenting?
- In considering the client's environment, social circumstances, and mental health, what issues emerge?
- How is the practitioner positioned in this context?
- From the client and the practitioner's perspectives, is treatment/support required?
- Is the client motivated for change?
- How do the assumptions of the practitioner's preferred approach fit with the client's world-view?
- How does the presenting issue fit within the organizational context?
- Does the organization have adequate structures to enable effective work with this client?
- Is the practitioner competent to do the work?

So far we have introduced some of the challenges and complexities of the relationship between substance use and mental health. The case studies presented so far have highlighted the challenges and links between mental health, physical health, substance use and motivation to change. An understanding of the essential skills needed in risk assessment and formulation when working with individuals with dual diagnoses has been outlined through the detailed assessment template that we have presented.

The following section outlines the importance of problem formulation and conceptualization and some of the challenges of these aspects of assessment when working with dual diagnosis. It is highlighted that the process of assessment is continuous, and that assessment activities dovetail into formulation and treatment. Wills and Sanders (2013) clarified this when they stated:

> Assessment should cover not only clients' problems but also their motivation and priorities: all three elements come together in the problem list. The list aims to include all the problems that are likely to be addressed during therapy, usually in order of priority. It functions as an action template that in conjunction with the formulation template drives therapy and acts as a reference point for review. (2013: 56)

Problem formulation and conceptualization in dual diagnosis

In working on problem/case formulation (sometimes called the case conceptualization), the practitioner makes sense of the client's difficulties and presentation, from the practitioner's professional understanding informed by specific modalities (e.g. drawing from social work theories or psychological theories). In other words, we are wondering about the prac-titioner and her or his working hypotheses and how he or she professionally conceptualizes the client's presented issues or problems.

We noted above that for many clinicians this involves an initial assessment to establish the nature of the difficulties facing the client and the extent to which the psychosocial intervention to be offered is a good 'fit' for the situation. Arguably, it also enables clients to establish if the intervention is a good 'fit' for them. This formulation process is therefore a collaborative process because often clients may have tried specific interventions which may or may not have have worked for them.

'Formulations', whether implicit or explicit, will tend to be shaped by the theoretical/professional orientation of the clinician. 'Formulations' may be seen as working hypotheses which guide (or may even prescribe) interventions. They may provide causal links between aspects of the client's emotions, experience and behaviour. This is key in working with dual diagnosis; for example, understanding how depression, anxiety or psychosis may be linked to the client's behaviour and substance use. As Persons (1989) notes:

> The case formulation is the therapist's compass; it guides the treatment. The most important role of the formulation is to provide the basis for the treatment plan, which follows directly from the hypothesis about the nature of the underlying deficit producing the patient's problems. (1989:14)

It is important here, however, to note that all therapeutic approaches carry implicit hypotheses. For some theories/professions/settings, the explicit use of assessment and formulation is contentious territory, for others it is seen as an essential skill and an important first step in the therapy process.

Dudley and Kukyen (2006) suggest that in cognitive behavioural approaches, formulation involves five *Ps* which can be adapted with our assessment guidance above and other models in mind. These *Ps* are:

1. Presenting issues – a clear statement of the client's problems;
2. Precipitating factors – triggers to the presenting issues. These can be external (e.g. life events) or internal (e.g. memories);
3. Perpetuating factors – factors that sustain the current presenting issues or problems;
4. Predisposing factors – those things that may make a person more vulnerable to certain problems, such as family upbringing and history;
5. Protective factors – those things that are competencies, sources of strength and resilience.

A sound formulation would take account of all these areas and see the descriptive potency of the formulation to make links, make meaning and sense and suggest the direction of intervention. We come back to CB-based work in the next chapter when we begin to look at specific psychological models for working.

Formulations, as a shared working model can also be very simple. It is very important to help clients interested and enquiring about their own difficulties, and so a key principle of using formulation is to get the client to think within it. For instance, the formulation below (Figure 4.5) is very simple but captures a crucial relationship for the client.

Figure 4.5 A simple functional formulation, drawing links and cycles

So far in this book we have highlighted the complexities and challenges that individuals with dual diagnoses face. These often include:

- having to manage the effects of psychological distress/mental ill health, e.g. depression, serious anxiety and psychosis, when they stop using substances;
- environmental factors such as living in circumstances where there are many individuals who use substances, isolation and relational difficulties that result in interpersonal problems, etc.;
- for others the effect of withdrawal symptoms often mean that they continually use to stop themselves going onto withdrawal.

We have given many examples relating to these challenges; however, we have not explored the challenges of working with client cravings, managing relapse patterns or harm reduction, which some services (e.g. needle exchange programmes) are set up to do. In the following section we briefly outline some areas of consideration around relapse prevention.

Relapse prevention

Key terms

Exercise 4.1

What do you think the following terms mean?

Craving
Lapse
Relapse
Relapse prevention
Harm reduction

> ❏ **Case study 4.9 Challenges of working with relapse and harm reduction**
>
> A referral is made to you asking you to assess John. He has a diagnosis of depression, and it is noted that previously he used to inject heroin on a daily basis. Recently, his partner died of a drug overdose, and John is anxious that he will now not be able to have the usual supervised access to his children. John has previously been diagnosed with bipolar depression. Since his partner died, John has started drinking and using heroin in addition to his prescribed methadone of 75 ml.
>
> What may be some of the issues and challenges you will have to consider in working with John?
>
> What interventions will you use in supporting him with relapse prevention?

The main task of the practitioner in relapse prevention work is encouraging clients to accept themselves and the reality that relapse is often a part of the treatment process, and therefore can be dealt with when it happens. Relapse prevention work helps clients to understand and learn from factors that led to their relapse. It also encourages clients to work actively in the 'maintenance stage' of change when they reach it (Dryden 2012). In practice, the issue of relapse prevention is worked through in sessions as a process rather than a last session action. This enables and empowers clients to identify their triggers and plan ways of managing any lapses should they occur.

McHugh et al. (2010) in their research highlighted the importance of relapse prevention in substance use disorders (SUDs) stating that as an intervention, relapse prevention focuses on the identification and prevention of high-risk situations in which a client may be more likely to engage in substance use. They further noted that techniques of relapse prevention include challenging the patient's expectation of perceived positive effects of substance use and providing education/information to help the patient make a more informed choice in trigger situations.

In order to effectively support clients through relapse prevention work, negotiating homework tasks with clients seems to strengthen their coping strategies. Homework is therefore an essential part of relapse prevention work because clients often face triggers or psychological distress in their own environment. The following section explores the benefits and challenges of homework.

Homework in relapse prevention

Branch (2012) suggests that in order to maximize therapeutic impact, and to promote continued progress between weekly sessions, practitioners should collaborate with their clients to devise pertinent homework. Homework supports change through application of work in session to their lives outside. This translates cognitive change into emotional change (Branch 2012). From our experience of supervising practitioners who work with clients who have dual diagnoses, many state that they face challenges of clients not completing homework. When clients do not complete agreed homework, it is worth investigating what gets in the way of them doing so. This can unearth other environmental, behavioural and secondary emotional factors previously unknown to the practitioner. Therefore, homework in itself also serves as a further initial assessment (Branch 2012). Completion of homework, or failure of completion, can also inform the practitioner of the client's motivation or level of psychological distress. Substance use may also be a contributory factor as to why clients do not complete their homework. Padesky (2014) suggests that a way to increase engagement with homework tasks is to spend time in client meetings going over the task and practising. This enables the client to see its value, work through the technical requirement and troubleshoot any barriers.

Examples of relapse prevention associated homework include:

- drink/substance use diaries, to record client's levels of use/drinking;
- thought/mood diaries which can help clients to correlate their substance use with their mood;
- trialling positive self-talk and cue cards developed in session.

We acknowledge that in some cases clients do not like the term 'homework' because it may remind them of school, and therefore we suggest choosing different terms. Branch (2012) stated that for those who reject the homework label, alternative terms such as 'between session tasks', weekly targets, positive change exercises, therapeutic objectives, goals oriented practice, 'treatment tasks', etc. can be used. Although, from our experience, some clients are resistant to homework and do not do it for numerous reasons, some do complete it and state they find it helpful. From experience, we have also noted that such clients tend to work towards abstinence successfully. The following quote highlights the importance of homework in contributing to therapeutic and relapse prevention success:

> [P]atients who work diligently on overcoming their problems between sessions tend to experience mood lift, gain confidence in their ability to employ useful strategies, recover readily from lapses, improve more quickly in general and experience a greater sense of self-accomplishment. (Branch 2012:253)

We would also suggest that where clients are not agreeing to undertake homework tasks, the practitioner reflects on:

- the therapeutic alliance discussed earlier and rechecks the goals for the work together; often problems of this kind can be accounted for by ambivalence to the goals;
- the possibility of 'meta-emotions' getting in the way, such as anxiety about doing the work at all or hopelessness. Such feelings will probably need addressing before someone can make use of your further support.

Negotiating homework involves a balance that must be struck because too much homework can put the client off engaging in psychosocial interventions, and not enough work can result in treatment not being helpful for the client (Wills & Sanders 2013). Research by Gonzalez et al. (2006) evidenced a positive relationship between homework and treatment outcome through a reduction in cocaine use for those in treatment, and this research lends empirical support to the use of homework in CBT for SUDs.

Effective Relapse prevention aims to cover the following:

- restructuring daily activities to reduce boredom and increase engagement in fulfilling activities;

- when triggers have been identified, rehearsing coping strategies to resist using substances;
- having the knowledge on how to complete mood diaries or thought records;
- working with the client to recognize personal signs of mental health and the factors that influence deterioration;
- having a collaboratively formulated care plan in the event of substance use or mental health relapse, as well as following hospital discharge;
- meaningful activities and social support networks, which can include self-help peer groups (Davis & O'Neill 2005), are also important for relapse prevention.

(Adapted from Cleary et al. (2008))

Relapse prevention in mental health

While there are some similarities between the relapse preventions strategies in the mental health field and substance use, there may also be some differences and further detail we can draw upon. Such work may also sit alongside *coping strategy enhancement* and resilience work that generally makes the client more self-reliant. Much relapse prevention work has been done in the area of psychosis and there are some 'off the shelf' relapse prevention packages available. We will outline here some of the main principles.

Firstly, relapse prevention works on a hopeful and recovery-based perspective and holds the belief that relapse can be avoided in many cases. A clear rationale for the work is offered to the client so that they can choose to 'buy in' (good practice within the therapeutic alliance). Some time is then spent working out the client's 'relapse signature', based on the last and previous relapses, or in the case of first episodes, early indicators of distress or change. This is often first indicated by mood changes. Signs, and the possible triggers of the signs and the relapse, are placed in sequence and at each point in the relapse timeline a coping strategy or intervention is identified. The principle should be that the most self-reliant strategies come first, and so the client engages their self-efficacy. This can be positive self-talk, self-soothing, cue cards or activities. For some people it will also involve reducing activity and taking time to rest. This forms the basis of a 'relapse drill', which is a detailed plan and it is a drill because it is rehearsed. The earlier self-reliant strategies can often keep someone sufficiently on top of the triggers and stresses, which makes service access unnecessary. However, if these are not working, the later strategies may well include re-referral to a service or professional help. Each relapse, of whatever magnitude, should be a point of fine tuning for the relapse drill.

Harm reduction

Harm reduction is a principle that has been informing practice in dependency services and work with self-harm for some time, but it can still appear controversial. This is because to detractors it looks like it is validating antisocial or harmful ways of behaving, or even encouraging them. Even so, the evidence and views of service users is that it is the most respectful and effective. In fact:

> Current guidelines encourage harm-reduction techniques in preference to purely abstinence-based programmes ... However, this does not mean if abstinence is the

service user's aim it should not be considered, but done so using a step-by-step approach, and by setting realistic, attainable goals. (Hahn 2006:142)

The principle is that where a client is unwilling, or unable, to make a complete change towards health, such as abstinence, then the practitioner works towards reducing harm. This may be done in a variety of ways:

- Where the client self-harms through cutting, it may involve education about more or less dangerous places to cut (to avoid accidental death, or serious injury, or unnecessary scarring) and ways of doing good wound care.
- Where someone has problematic drinking, they may switch from stronger to weaker drinks, for instance from wine to beer.

Harm reduction requires that practitioners fully mobilize their empathy and see the bigger picture: that less harm is worth supporting, and perhaps whole recovery becomes an option later. Practitioners need to be cognizant of local risk management policy, of getting good supervisory support, having explicit support from case managers and colleagues and working collaboratively with clients. Harm reduction can be part of a greater positive risk-taking strategy which grades the risks that a service can tolerate with a client to support the client's experimentation and growth. Clearly, this is challenging to more custodial and paternalistic approaches to service delivery.

Key messages:

- Therapeutic relationships and the alliance are a must for any of the work you and the client do together.
- There already exist structures and processes for the organizing of client care and support, including case management and the CPA.
- As a case management task, psychosocial assessment underpins good planning and formulation.
- Having a working model with a client, such as that provided through formulation, can aid collaboration and mutual understanding.

REFERENCES

Arria, A.M., Garnier-Dykstra, L.M., Caldeira, K.M., Vincent, K.B., O'Grady K.E., & Wish, E.D. (2011). Persistent nonmedical use of prescription stimulants among college students: Possible association with ADHD symptoms. *Journal of Attention Disorders*, 15, 347–356.

Aubuchon, P.G., & Malatesta, V.J. (1998). Managing the therapeutic relationship in behaviour therapy: The need for a case formulation. In Bruch, M., & Bond, F.W. (Eds) *Beyond Diagnosis: Case Formulation Approaches in CBT*. Chichester: Wiley.

Australian Drug Foundation (2013). *Drug Info Fact Sheet: Alcohol and Other Drug Prevention in the Family*. Victoria, Australia.

Azevedo, R.C.S.D., Botega, N.J., & Guimaraes, L.A.M. (2007). Crack users, sexual behaviour and risk of HIV infection. *Revista Brasileira De Psiquiatria*, 29, 26–30.

Bellack, A.S., & DiClemente, C.C. (1999). Treating substance abuse among patients with schizophrenia. *Psychiatric Services*, 50, 75–80.

Biswas-Diener, R., Vitterso, J., & Diener, E. (2010). The Danish effect: Beginning to explore high well-being in Denmark. *Social Indicators Research*, 97, 229–246.

Boffetta, P., & Hashibe, M. (2006). Alcohol and cancer. *Lancet Oncology*, 7, 149–156.

Branch, R. (2012). Challenges with homework in CBT. In Dryden, W., & Branch, R. (Eds) *The CBT Handbook*. London: Sage.

Challis, D. (1994). Case management. In Malin, N. (Ed.) *Implementing Community Care*. Buckingham: Open University Press.

Charura, D., & Paul, S. (Eds) (2014). *The Therapeutic Relationship Handbook: Theory and Practice*. Maidenhead: Open University Press.

Cleary, M., Walter, G., Hunt, G., Clancy, R., & Horsfall, J. (2008). Promoting dual diagnosis awareness in everyday clinical practice. *Journal of Psychosocial Nursing & Mental Health Services*, 46(12), 43–49.

da Silveira Nunes Dinis, M. (2012). Social work approaches for substance-use treatment. *International Journal of Health, Wellness & Society*, 2(2), 23–35.

Davis, K.E., & O'Neill, S.J. (2005). A focus group analysis of relapse prevention strategies for persons with substance use and mental disorders. *Psychiatric Services*, 56, 1288–1291.

Department of Health (1996). *Building Bridges*. London: HMSO.

Department of Health (2002). *Mental Health Policy and Implementation Guide – Dual Diagnosis Good Practice Guide*. London: DoH.

Dryden, W. (2012). Adapting CBT to a broad range of clientele. In Dryden, W., & Branch, R. (Eds) *The CBT Handbook*. London: Sage.

Duckworth, A.L., Steen, T.A., & Seligman, M.E.P. (2005). Positive psychology in clinical practice. *Annual Review of Clinical Psychology*, 1, 629–651.

Dudley, R., & Kuyken, W. (2006). Formulation in cognitive-behavioural therapy: There is nothing either good or bad, but thinking makes it so. In Johnstone, L., & Dallos, R. (Eds) *Formulation in Psychology and Psychotherapy: Making Sense of People's Problems*. Hove: Routledge.

Echterling, L.G., Presbury, J.H., & McKee, J.E. (2005). *Crisis Intervention: Promoting Resilience and Resolution in Troubled Times*. Upper Saddle River, NJ: Pearson/Merrill Prentice Hall.

Glasgow Centre for Population Health (2011). *Briefing Paper 9 Concept Series: Asset Based Approaches for Health Improvement: Redressing the Balance*. <www.gcph.co.uk> [Accessed June 2014].

Gonzalez, V.M., Schmitz, J.M., & DeLaune, K.A. (2006). The role of homework in cognitive-behavioral therapy for cocaine dependence. *Journal of Consulting and Clinical Psychology*, 74(3), 633–637.

Hahn, S. (2006). Dual diagnosis: Substance misuse and mental health problems. In Peate, I., & Chelvanayagam, S. (Eds) *Caring for Adults with Mental Health Problems*. Chichester: Wiley.

Harris, N., Brazeau, J.N., Clarkson, A., Brownlee, K., & Rawana, E.P. (2012). Adolescents' experiences of a strengths-based treatment program for substance abuse. *Journal of Psychoactive Drugs*, 44(5), 390–397.

Haugh, S., & Paul, S. (Eds) (2008). *The Therapeutic Relationship*. Ross-on-Wye: PCCS Books.

Improvement and Development Agency (2010). *A Glass Half-full: How an Asset Approach Can Improve Community Health and Well-being*. <www.idea.gov.uk> [Accessed June 2014].

Karoll, B.R. (2010). Applying social work approaches, harm reduction, and practice wisdom to better serve those with alcohol and drug use disorders. *Journal of Social Work*, 10(3), 263–281.

Kontos, M.C., Jesse, R.L., Tatum, J.L., & Ornato, J.P. (2003). Coronary angiographic findings in patients with cocaine-associated chest pain. *Journal of Emergency Medicine*, 24, 9–13.

Kuyken, W., Padesky, C.A., & Dudley, R. (2009). *Collaborative Case Conceptualization: Working effectively with Clients in Cognitive Behavioural Therapy* (pp. 54–55). London: The Guilford Press.

Lambert, M.J., Bergin, A.E., & Garfield, S.J., (2004). Introduction and historical overview. In Lambert, M.J., (Ed.) *Handbook of Psychotherapy and Behavior Change* (5th Ed.). New York: Wiley.

Law, H., Morrison, A., Byrne, R., & Hodson, E. (2012). Recovery from psychosis: A user informed review of self-report instruments for measuring recovery. *Journal of Mental Health*, 21(2), 193–208.

McHugh, R.K, Hearon, B.A., & Otto, M.W. (2010). Cognitive behavioral therapy for substance use disorders. *Psychiatric Clinics of North America*, 33, 511–525.

Marshall, M., & Lockwood, A. (2002). Assertive community treatment for people with severe mental disorders. *The Cochrane Library*. Issue 2.

Marshall, M. (2002). Randomised controlled trials – Misunderstanding, fraud and spin. In Preibe, S., & Slade, M. (Eds) *Evidence in Mental Health Care*. Hove: Brunner-Routledge.

Moodley, R. (2005). Diversity matrix revisited: Criss-crossing multiple identities in clinical practice. Keynote paper at 'Multicultural and Counseling' Symposium. Ithaca, NY: Cornell University.

Morgan, S. (1996). *Helping Relationships in Mental Health*. London: Chapman & Hall.

Moxley, D.P., & Washington, O.G.M. (2001). Strengths-based recovery practice in chemical dependency: A transpersonal perspective. *Families in Society*, 82(3), 251–262.

National Institute for Clinical Excellence (2007). Drug misuse – Psychosocial interventions. <http://www.nice.org.uk/Guidance/CG51/chapter/related-nice-guidance> [Accessed July 2014].

National Institute for Mental Health England (2009). [DVD] *ESC Learning Materials 2009*. University of Lincoln/Centre for Clinical and Academic Workforce Innovation.

Norcross, J.C., & Lambert, M.J. (2011). Evidence-based therapy relationships. In Norcross, J.C. (Ed.) *Psychotherapy Relationships that Work*. New York: Oxford University Press.

Nutt, D. (2014). A brave new world for psychology? *The Psychologist*, 27(9), 658–660.

Onyett, S.R. (1998). *Case Management in Mental Health*. Cheltenham: Stanley Thornes.

Oregon State Board of Nursing (2010). Professional boundaries: A guide to the importance of appropriate professional boundaries. *Sentinel*, June, 12–14.

Padesky, C.A. (2014). *Best Practices: CBT for Depression and Suicide*. Workbook from workshop. Cognitive Workshops.

Paul S., and Charura, D. (2015). *An Introduction to the Therapeutic Relationship in Counselling and Psychotherapy*. London: Sage.

Payne, M. (2005). *Modern Social Work Theory* (3rd Ed.). Basingstoke: Palgrave Macmillan.

Persons, J.B. (1989). *Cognitive Therapy in Practice: A Case Formulation Approach*. London: W.W. Norton.

Prins, H. (2005). *Offenders, Deviants or Patients?* Hove: Routledge.

Prochaska, J.O., & DiClemente, C.C. (1983). Stages and processes of self-change of smoking: Toward an integrative model of change. *Journal of Consulting and Clinical Psychology*, 51(3), 390–395.

Ryan, P., & Morgan, S. (2004). *Assertive Outreach: A Strengths Approach to Policy and Practice*. London: Churchill Livingstone.

Safran, J.D., & Muran, J.C. (2000). *Negotiating the Therapeutic Alliance: A Relational Treatment Guide*. London: The Guilford Press.

Saleebey, D. (1997). Introduction: Power in the people. In Saleebey, D. (Ed.) *The Strengths Perspective in Social Work Practice*. New York: Longman Press.

Saleebey, D. (2008). *The Strengths Perspective in Social Work Practice* (5th Ed.). New York: Allyson & Bacon.

Schulte, M.T., & Yih-Ing, H. (2014). Substance use and associated health conditions throughout the lifespan. *Public Health Reviews*, 35(2), 1–27.

Tummey, R., & Tummey, F. (2008). Iatrogenic abuse. In Tummey, R., & Turner, T. (Eds) *Critical Issues in Mental Health*. Basingstoke: Palgrave Macmillan.

Turner, T., & Colombo, A. (2008). Risk. In Tummey, R., & Turner, T. (Eds) *Critical Issues in Mental Health*. Basingstoke: Palgrave Macmillan.

Welsh Government (2011). *Implementing the Mental Health Measure (Wales) 2010: Guidance for Local Health Boards and Local Authorities*. Cardiff: Mental Health legislation team, Welsh Assembly Government.

Whitaker, R. (2004). The case against antipsychotic drugs: A 50-year record of doing more harm than good. *Medical Hypotheses*, 62, 5–11.

Wilke, D.J. (2001). Reconceptualizing recovery: Adding self-esteem to the mix. *Dissertation Abstracts International*, 61(12), 4950.

Wills, F., & Sanders, D. (2013). *Cognitive Behaviour Therapy: Foundations for Practice*. London: Sage.

Ziguras, S.J., & Stuart, G.W. (2000). A meta-analysis of the effectiveness of mental health case management over 20 years. *Psychiatric Services*, 51, 1410–1421.

5 | Psychosocial Interventions

Chapter Summary

The aims of this chapter are to outline and explore:

- the different evidence-based and recommended psychosocial interventions employed in working with dual diagnoses (these include motivational interviewing, brief interventions and self-help, contingency management, cognitive behavioural therapy, psychodynamic therapy);
- the basic principles of psychosocial interventions;
- the varied and complex nature of psychosocial interventions;
- the facilitative interventions required in creating a therapeutic environment;
- the generic recommendations for inpatient settings and the criminal justice system;
- the contemporary mindfulness and technology-based interventions.

Within the UK, the National Treatment Agency is a special health authority established by the government to increase the availability, capacity, access and effectiveness of interventions. Given the recognition of drug and alcohol misuse as complex problems, there are models of care which have been formulated within contemporary substance misuse and mental health services. Another regulatory body which has been influential in formulating guidelines for psychosocial interventions has been the National institute for Health and Care Excellence (NICE). Throughout the following section we will draw on some of the NICE guidelines for working with substance use and consider them in the context of dual diagnosis.

In 2007, NICE published two guidelines on psychosocial interventions for substance misuse:

1. 'Drug misuse: psychosocial interventions' (NICE clinical guideline 51 (2007)). This guideline makes recommendations for the use of psychosocial interventions in the treatment of people who misuse opioids, stimulants and cannabis in the healthcare and criminal justice systems.
2. 'Drug misuse: opioid detoxification' (NICE clinical guideline 52 (2007)). This guideline makes recommendations for the treatment of people who are undergoing detoxification for opioid dependence arising from the misuse of illicit drugs. It covers opioid detoxification in community, residential, inpatient and prison settings, and it refers to the misuse of other drugs such as benzodiazepines, alcohol and stimulants only insofar as they impact on opioid detoxification.

These guidelines (51 and 52) jointly outline the support and treatment clients can expect to be offered if they have a problem with or are dependent on opioids, stimulants or cannabis. They also offer some guidance on how families and carers may be able to support a person with a drug problem, as well as get help for themselves.

As we have seen earlier in this chapter, having a dual diagnosis can present an individual with multiple challenges. In the following section we draw on the NICE (2007) guidelines in order to explain the recommended psychosocial interventions. It is important, however, for the reader to be aware that the NICE guidelines do not specifically cover working with:

- people with dual diagnoses;
- people who misuse alcohol, prescription drugs or solvents;
- diagnosis or primary prevention.

We therefore draw from our experience, different literature and research in outlining different psychosocial interventions for dual diagnosis. Furthermore, to help the reader understand how to apply theory to practice, we enhance our exploration with case studies.

This section covers the following psychosocial interventions:

- motivational interventions (MI);
- brief interventions and self-help;
- contingency management;
- cognitive behavioural therapy (CBT);

- psychodynamic therapy;
- mindfulness and technology-based approaches.

It is important that practitioners are clear what interventions are used in their service, are clear about the evidence base for these interventions and are competent in employing the interventions.

Motivational interventions (MI)

In this section we will focus on MI (Rollnick & Miller 1995). A case study we will present will help to illuminate the practice and challenges of employing MI. We consider four main complexities:

- A diagnosis of mental ill health and associated experiences (e.g. serious depressive episodes, hallucinations and serious anxiety) can affect an individual's motivation to maintain sobriety.
- The societal, familial stressors/stigma of having a psychiatric diagnosis can often contribute to feelings of worthlessness in those with dual diagnoses and hence affect them socially and psychologically.
- Substances often have positive benefits, i.e. helping temporarily alleviate negative feelings associated with mental distress, and hence individuals over time become dependent on them. It can be difficult and anxiety provoking to then see how individuals can cope without their substance of choice.
- With long-term substance use there may well be concurrent health problems. For instance, associated with long term, heavy alcohol use is Korsakoff's syndrome (also called Korsakoff's psychosis, Korsakoff's dementia). It is a neurological disorder caused by a lack of Vitamin B1 in the brain. Korsakoff's can present as psychosis and involves short-term memory loss.

The relationship between substance misuse and dual diagnosis is complex, and individuals with dual diagnosis have varied and complex needs which require high-quality, comprehensive and integrated care (Abou-Saleh 2004). In Chapter 4 we presented the transtheoretical model (also known as the cycle of change model) which was hypothesized by Prochaska and DiClemente (1983). From the five stages presented in this model, we saw that in some of the stages, for example the pre-contemplation stage, clients may not be aware of their problems, or risks associated with their behaviour, or indeed what maintains their distress. As clients become more aware, for example in the contemplation and preparation stages, and they start to accept that there is something problematic, they may begin to entertain the possibilities of change and action. Enhancing a client's motivation is an important factor in supporting the move towards a healthy change, but as most of us know, making change can be laden with doubt and anxiety, particularly if such a change has some painful experiences as part of it. Each relapse becomes a learning point and can locate the recovery journey on the cycle of change. Furthermore, we are being clear that while it is tempting to 'rescue' clients, or persuade them towards change, this tends not to be very successful (Handmaker & Walters 2004). The aim therefore of MI is to help individuals move from a position of ambivalence (not being very sure about making a change or the advantages of it) to making a decision about their substance use.

Importance of facilitative conditions

Before exploring MI and its application in working with dual diagnosis, we would like to start by highlighting the importance of practitioners creating a therapeutic environment and furthermore having the competencies to offer facilitative skills of therapeutic change. Besides the therapeutic alliance covered in the last chapter, there are some specific skills and characteristics. These have been cited as empathy, unconditional positive regard (being non-judgemental) and congruence (genuineness) (Rogers 1959). Charura and Nicholson (2013) gave an overview of the importance of the facilitative conditions and the therapeutic relationship when working with clients who use substances. The curative factor of the therapeutic relationship is found in its humanizing, relational quality. Where individuals feel judged and unaccepted, and perceive that the care and support they are receiving is tokenistic (i.e. someone just going through the motions of doing their job), they are likely to resist engagement and there is a risk they drop out of the treatment or the service. We therefore agree that the facilitative conditions for therapeutic change help clients to work through their ambivalence and promote positive outcomes. Alongside the facilitative conditions, it is important to employ micro-skills, which include open-ended questions, affirmations, reflections and summaries.

What is motivational interviewing?

Motivational interviewing has been described as a self-directed, motivation-enhancing intervention (Lussier & Richard 2007), and it is a commonly used method within the broader MI milieu. Exploring and resolving the individual's ambivalence is the focus of motivational interviewing (Miller & Rollnick 2002), and it is understood that ambivalence is a natural part of any change (Handmaker & Walters 2004). Through helping clients clarify their areas of strengths and aspirations, their motivation to change is evoked, and this in turn promotes autonomy of decision-making (Miller & Rollnick 2002). In this process the practitioner concentrates on the individual's desire to change more than her or his resistance to change.

Stages in motivational interviewing

Ambivalence is the main factor in an individual's outlook and decision to change. The practitioner's role therefore is to understand ambivalence and act upon it in order to promote and encourage positive behavioural changes. Below is a case study which helps us start to look at the complexity of a client's story and how to begin to hear ambivalence as a route towards change.

❏ Case study 5.1 Working with client ambivalence and motivation

Chris attends for an assessment session for detox and rehabilitation. He shares his view that his life has been 'destroyed by drugs and alcohol'. He has had numerous admissions in the past for detox and rehabs. Although he has had periods of abstinence, he has never been able to maintain sobriety for long enough 'to get his life back on track'. He explains that he has had a diagnosis of depression and anxiety. Following the recent death of his wife, his substance use has increased.

Chris has two daughters, aged 4 and 7, and Social Services became involved a few months ago following complaints from their school and neighbours that he is often seen very intoxicated. Sadly, his two children have just been taken into care because of his issues of neglect.

In the assessment with a practitioner he appears to shift from ambivalence to being clear that he wants to be abstinent, but then reverts back to ambivalence. He states he has 'nothing to live for and there's no point stopping because his wife is dead and kids who mean the world to him are now in care for the rest of their teenage years'. He blames his relapse on this and on other clients in his previous detox for being destructive, as well as a female staff member for being uncompassionate about his past.

Reflective questions

- *What may be happening in this process?*
- *What else may need to be considered along with the motivational interviewing techniques being employed?*

See below for some suggestions.

There are four main principles of motivational interviewing (adapted from Treasure (2004) and Charura & Parker (2013)):

1. **Express empathy by the use of reflective listening.** This shows the individual that you understand their experience and their point of view. An example, drawing from case study 5.1, could be an empathic response such as: '*Chris, I can see that it is so difficult to feel motivated when you can't see anything to change or live for.*'
2. **Identify the discrepancies between the individual's most deeply held values and current behaviours.** An example of this may be: '*Chris, on one hand you are saying that you want to stop drinking and get some counselling and then work towards getting your children back, yet on the other hand you are saying there is no point and that you will drink yourself to death. How can you achieve your goal if you are doing both?*'
3. **Roll with the resistance by responding with empathy and understanding rather than confrontation.** An example of this may be: '*Chris, through coming here today and through what you said this is hard for you but also that this is something you want to do, I am starting to ask myself how you can achieve your goal.*'
4. **Uphold self-efficacy by building the individual's confidence that change is possible –** shifting the decisional balance towards change. An example of this could be: '*How can I/we support you to change and to meet your goals?*'

At this point Charura and Parker (2013) advocate exploring with the client possible barriers and challenges to change and how they can be supported to overcome this. This then fits in with the MI concept of preparing the client for change talk, which is often defined by the client's consideration, motivation or commitment to change.

As already noted, throughout the session the facilitative conditions must be present. Additionally, Charura and Parker (2013) suggest that, in line with good practice, at the end of the session practitioners should ensure that:

a) In order to keep the client motivated, and leave at the end of the session with a clear perspective, practitioners collaborate with the client to formulate a clear plan. This may be about offering further appointments, for support with their mental health, or for their substance use in relation to engaging in a detox, rehab, etc., or further referral/another general appointment.
b) Furthermore, before the client leaves it is good practice to ask the client to reflect back to the practitioner what the client feels/thinks about how the session has gone, and the client's new-found clarity and plans for change.
c) Lastly, in line with motivational interviewing change talk, practitioners ask the client to outline or say something about the client's commitment to the plan.

While MI theory and techniques can be employed by most trained practitioners with satisfactory results, our experience is that when working with dual diagnoses, and complex cases, the motivation for change fluctuates and ruptures in therapeutic alliance can occur in a session, resulting in clients dropping out. This can often result in unsuccessful outcomes or a 'relapse/revolving door scenario' where clients return to the service time and time again with the same addiction.

Brief interventions and self-help

Given the present economic climate in which services are making limitations in their provision, and also given that at times those with dual diagnoses can live a chaotic life, the use of brief interventions has become an effective way of working with clients. This makes the most of brief contact rather than lamenting the lack of consistent engagement.

Consider, for example, the following case study.

❏ **Case study 5.2 A case for opportunistic brief interventions**

John has been registered with a service where he collects his methadone prescription. Over the last four months he has missed five appointments for supportive one-to-one meetings. He experiences psychotic episodes in which he becomes paranoid that there are drug dealers who want to kill him. He says he hardly goes out and states that he often shares needles with 'trusted friends'.

It has becomes apparent that all the appointments he has missed are motivational sessions with a key worker which are meant to get him ready for a detox. These are scheduled usually for an hour. Opportunistic brief interventions are considered by the team that is working with him.

Brief interventions can be used opportunistically in a variety of settings for clients not in contact with drug services (e.g. in mental health situations, general health and social care settings, and emergency departments). They can also be used with people in limited contact with drug services (such as at needle and syringe exchanges, and community pharmacies) (NICE 2007).

The focus of brief interventions can include:

- provision of information and advice about reducing exposure to blood-borne viruses; this should include advice on reducing sexual and injection risk behaviours;
- offering support and testing for blood-borne viruses;
- helpline numbers and advice on how to reconnect with a service.

Opportunistic brief interventions focused on motivation should be offered to clients such as John who are in limited contact with drug services (this includes, for example, those attending a needle and syringe exchange or primary care settings). These interventions should normally consist of two or three sessions, each lasting 10–45 minutes. In some settings such as the ones we work with, an appointment such as this can be offered during the time the client is waiting to see the doctor for a medication review (NICE 2007).

As with motivational interviewing, these sessions can also explore ambivalence about drug use and possible treatment, with the aim of increasing motivation to change behaviour, and provide non-judgemental feedback to the client. In relation to dual diagnosis, as we saw earlier in the chapter, the client's ambivalence relating to substance use behaviours that may be impacting on her or his mental health should also be explored. It may be, however, that the client's mental health at the time of accessing may be impacting on her or his ability to be motivated, and hence the practitioner can explore ways to support the client. A drop-in slot in services can often be a good way to ensure that clients take up brief interventions. The range of modalities that can be used in these sessions will depend on the service, but for dual diagnosis would generally include MI, to help shift the client's ambivalence, as well as cognitive behavioural interventions to help the client to explore ways of changing/managing cognitions (thoughts) and changing behaviours.

Guided self-help

As we have seen in this chapter when considering the the transtheoretical model (Prochaska & DiClemente 1983), motivation to change really requires the client to 'help themselves' by making the steps necessary to engage with services. From our experience, staff may be willing to support a client through home visits, engaging in detox preparatory work, and supporting the client through their mental health difficulties. However, if clients are in the pre-contemplation stage, or contemplation stage, or actively using substances, they may not be in a position to help themselves. Consider the following case study.

❏ **Case study 5.3 Client motivation and guided self-help**

Toni has been referred to the local addictions unit via her community psychiatric nurse. She has a diagnosis of bipolar mood disorder and is currently experiencing depression. She lost her mother two years ago and states that she was very close to her. She explains that before she uses the service she would like to help herself because she believes that 'God only helps those who help themselves'. She has previously attended Alcoholics Anonymous groups and local Self-Management And Recovery Training (SMART) groups following completion of an alcohol detox two years ago.

Reflective questions
- *At what stage in the cycle of change is Toni in?*
- *What self-help interventions would be helpful or available to her through your work?*

According to the NICE (2007) guidelines on psychosocial interventions, practitioners should routinely provide people who use drugs with information about self-help groups. These groups include those that are based on 12-step principles, for example, Narcotics Anonymous and Cocaine Anonymous. As noted in case study 5.3, they may also include Self-Management And Recovery Training (SMART) groups, which are 'science-based' programmes to help individuals manage their recovery from any type of addictive behaviour, including addictive behaviour with substances such as alcohol, nicotine or drugs, or compulsive behaviours such as gambling, sex, eating, shopping or self-harming.

Guidelines on self-help for dual diagnosis advocate support for clients who express an interest in attending self-help groups. This can include staff considering their role in facilitating the person's initial contact with the group, by making the necessary appointment, as well as ensuring that relevant information is readily available for clients who access the service (NICE 2007; Aram 2007). Brief interventions and self-help will be returned to in Chapter 6 when considering groups and community resources.

Contingency management

Contingency management is a set of techniques that focuses on changing specified behaviours (NICE 2007). In practice, incentives are offered for positive behaviours such as turning up for appointments, maintaining a period of abstinence, reduction in substance use, or participation in health-promoting/harm reduction interventions. It is important to note that within substance use services, the rate of not attending or cancellation of appointments is quite high. As we have seen, the complexity of having a dual diagnosis often impacts on motivation to engage or creates challenges such that clients find it difficult to leave their house. Some of these challenges may also be financial due to lack of employment or limited financial resources. As a result, contingency management is one way of engaging clients and ensuring that the chances of them attending are high. Consider the following case study.

❏ **Case study 5.4 Contingency management for maintaining motivation and client engagement**

Mo has found it hard to engage with the service and has missed three appointments with the psychosocial interventions team. He has a diagnosis of schizophrenia. He started using illicit drugs and drinking to help him cope with the persecutory voices he hears and the hallucinations.

He was offered a final appointment before being told that if he was not using the service he would be discharged, and he turned up to that appointment. On attending he stated that he is financially struggling, and he also stated that he has started to hear voices again. He states he has been trying hard and has not used any substances, but has had a drink before coming. However, he provides a negative urine sample. He states that he is willing to engage in groups or any one-to-one sessions that are on offer.

Reflective question

In order to help Mo continue engaging with contingency management plans, what can you as a practitioner put in place in order to reinforce his motivation and positive behaviours?

Mo's circumstances also highlight a further complexity in that while a substance use service may view his use as a main problem, his own need may well be towards getting some relief from persecutory voice hearing. Again, an empathic response is essential and in the range of work on offer, a practitioner may be able to suggest to Mo some work to help reduce the distress related to voice hearing. Some of the best techniques for this are CBT-based interventions, which have been around for some time (Kingdon & Turkington 1995) and are recommended by NICE (2009), and may also be cognitive behavioural approaches combined with mindfulness (Chadwick 2006).

An emphasis on reinforcing positive behaviours is consistent with current knowledge about the underlying neuropsychology of many clients who misuse drugs/alcohol or who have a dual diagnosis (NICE 2007; Schulte & Yih-Ing 2014). From our experience, we agree that the use of contingency management plans is more effective than penalizing negative behaviours or discharging clients from a service. There is good evidence that contingency management increases the likelihood of positive behaviours and is cost-effective (NICE 2007). For clients with a dual diagnosis, negotiation of the best contingency management plan is effective, as it can help them not only manage their substance use through continuous engagement, but also can impact on their mental health improvement.

For contingency management to be effective, practitioners need to discuss with the service user what the incentives are. Incentives need to be provided consistently and as soon as possible after the positive behaviour (such as submission of a drug-negative sample). Limited increases in the value of the incentive with successive periods of abstinence also appear to be effective. Within the services where we work or supervise practitioners and students, a variety of incentives have proved effective in contingency management programmes. These include vouchers (which can be exchanged for goods or services of the service user's choice), privileges (e.g. take-home methadone doses) and modest financial incentives.

Key principles of contingency management as a psychosocial intervention

- The service formulates clear guidelines about how clients will be engaged and what incentives will be available for clients.
- The therapeutic goal is agreed in collaboration with the client.

- Provision of incentives is in a timely, consistent and fair manner.
- There is a clear discussion and understanding between the client and practitioner about the relationship between the treatment goal and the incentive schedule.
- The incentive is perceived to be reinforcing, and it supports engagement with the treatment plan as well as a healthy/abstinent lifestyle.

Contingency management is aimed at reducing illicit drug use. In the following section we present a summary of some of the contingency management plans that are noted in the literature and from a mini survey that we collated from a local (Leeds) Dual Diagnosis Network meeting. We have presented our findings below, which also includes some contingency management guidelines from NICE (2007).

Contingency management guidelines

- Incentives can include vouchers that can be exchanged for goods or services of the client's choice.
- In some services where clients consistently provide a negative urine sample over an agreed amount time, privileges such as take-home methadone doses can be effective in reinforcing positive behaviour.
- If vouchers are used, their monetary values should increase as the client continues to maintain a period of abstinence. NICE (2007) recommends that vouchers can start in the region of £2 and increase with each additional, continuous period of abstinence. They also recommend that the frequency of screening should be set at three tests per week for the first three weeks, two tests per week for the next three weeks, and one per week thereafter until stability is achieved.
- In nearly all services we have worked in, urinalysis is the preferred method of testing. However, the NICE 2007 guidelines state oral fluid tests too may be considered as an alternative.
- Contingency management can also be used to improve physical healthcare. For example, for those people at risk of transmittable diseases resulting from drug use, incentives can be offered on completion of interventions such as hepatitis B/C and HIV testing, hepatitis B immunization, tuberculosis testing or attending other screening or counselling appointments.
- When working with clients who have a dual diagnosis, attending for psychosocial interventions sessions such as CBT, relapse prevention sessions, or completion of homework associated with helping to improve their mental health can also be positively reinforced through various contingency management rewards, e.g. vouchers or paying for the client's bus tickets.

Cognitive behavioural therapy (CBT) and formulation

CBT is an integrated therapy drawing on the traditions of behavioural psychology and therapy, cognitive therapy, and to an extent rational emotive behaviour therapy. CBT gained its recognition in the early 1980s through the text by Hawton et al. (1989) as a treatment approach for mood disorders, in particular offering practical and innovative responses to a range of anxiety problems.

CBT is predicated on the idea that we humans, through learning and memory, lay down our understanding of ourselves, others and the world in our early years in the form of core beliefs. Core beliefs are stable and global, and are also often held unconsciously (although CBT literature will rarely discuss the unconscious, and the therapy is predicated on the belief that people can actively learn and draw such knowledge into awareness). Core beliefs are like rules, statements and instructions that reflect our early learning, and so they do not have to be logical by anyone else's standards, but they do make sense within the context of a person's lived experience, and their information processing (e.g. what is and is not committed to memory). Such beliefs are operationalized on a daily basis and may drive distress if they are typified by conflict, unrealistic expectations, self-criticism, threat and pessimism (called thinking errors and distortions). While some critics have suggested CBT pays little attention to the therapeutic alliance/relationship, the review by Waddington (2002) suggests otherwise, and Wills (2008) states that 'therapy is an inherently interpersonal process and CBT is therefore subject to the same kind of interpersonal and transferential processes as have been identified more explicitly in other models of therapy' (2008: 10). Echoing much of what we have covered so far in this chapter, Jones and Mulhern (2004) suggest that where CBT and dual diagnosis is concerned, 'probably the best way to discover a client's reasons for misusing psychoactive substances is by establishing a good working relationship with them, which should create an atmosphere of trust in which a comprehensive, accurate assessment can be conducted' (2004:101).

The B in CBT refers to the essential role that behaviour plays in both the learning of core beliefs and their day-to-day rules for living, and in maintaining biased thinking. For instance, a person who is anxiously avoiding an anticipated unpleasant outcome will never get the chance to test if that belief is true, or that the prediction is inaccurate, and so never gets to update her or his personal rules. CBT works with people within a self-help ethos (involving lots of activity away from the therapy meetings) and expects that clients engage with their thinking as a critical learner, willing to weigh up the data of experience and the effect of interpretational biases, and to do things differently in line with their goals for therapy. This emphasis is reversed for depression wherein the B, as behavioural activation (raising activity levels and competence), is engaged before the C (or simultaneously). In reality, the C and the B often go in tandem with conversations and actions threaded throughout.

As already noted, there are many theories from which a formulation can be drawn. Having given a brief outline and critique of CBT, we will now give an example of CBT formulation as it is often used in dual diagnosis work. Greenberger and Padesky (1995) postulated a model for understanding five dimensions of a patient's life and of working with their subjective experience in practice in order to build a cognitive formulation (Walldron & Wilson 2012). This is commonly known as the 'hot cross bun', and the five dimensions include cognition, physiology, moods, behaviour and environment (see Figure 5.1 below, adapted from Greenberger & Padesky (1995)). The other way this is used is as what is called a maintenance formulation that focuses on the here and now, current problem, and the arrows in the diagram refer to the reciprocity of the components that sustain a problem. The client can be introduced to the idea of what might happen if triggers, physiology, thoughts or behaviour change, and this can begin the process of planning for change. As an educational intervention, the model also makes sense of the client's current problem and it is often used in a *recent incident analysis*, that is, you ask clients to describe the last occurrence of the target problem, organizing their information in the model, thus showing the interactions and the gaps in knowledge that can become investigative homework tasks. In our work with clients who present with dual diagnoses, when working from a CBT perspective, we also draw from a more comprehensive longitudinal formulation as hypothesized by Kuyken, Padesky and Dudley (2008). We present in Figure 5.1 an example of such a longitudinal formulation.

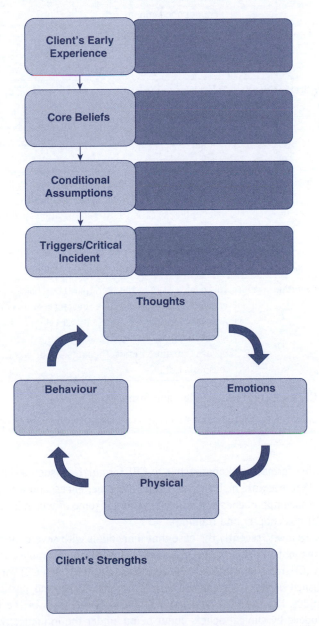

Figure 5.1 CBT longitudinal case conceptualization and formulation

Client's early experience	This part of the formulation relates to the client's early life experiences. For example, her or his primary family, relationship with parents, childhood experiences, and any other factors that impacted on early life.
Core beliefs	These are deep-seated beliefs of the client, which often go unrecognized and yet they constantly affect her or his life. For example, a client may have the core belief that 'I am unlovable', or 'I am not good enough'.
Conditional assumptions	Conditional assumptions shape the client's responses to experiences and situations. For example, the assumption that 'if people get close to me they will find out who I really am and will reject me.'
Triggers/critical incident	This relates to the specific moment a negative cycle began for the client (Wills & Sanders 2013).
Behaviour	This includes all the client's description of her or his behaviour in relation to substance use. It also includes the client's behaviour in relation to mental health.
Physical sensation	This may relate to what the client experiences physically, both in relation to mental health and physical health; for example, in anxiety, palpitations, sweating, butterflies/knotted abdominal sensations. It can also relate to physical sensations in relation to withdrawals from the substance.
Emotion/mood	This relates to the client's feelings or mood.
Thoughts/cognition	This relates to what the client may be thinking at different times; for example, just before taking a substance, during or afterwards. It is also very important to focus on motivation and triggers when asking about thoughts because this will give the practitioner an idea of the client's thought patterns. Thoughts can be words, phrases or images and visualizations.

Table 5.1 CBT case conceptualization and formulation

Source: See Kuyken, Padesky and Dudley (2008) for more on the full longitudinal formulation.

There are other formats and approaches to CBT formulation, such as classic or longitudinal approaches that integrate historical and early life experiences, and we suggest that a reader interested in such approaches seeks further reading (some of which is within the references at the end of this chapter and training).

It is only relatively recently the case that individuals with severe mental health problems have been thought to benefit from psychological or talking therapies. The growth of cognitive therapy (CT), rational emotive behaviour therapy (REBT) and CBT for psychoses followed their established work with affective disorders from the 1970s and, particularly for CBT, since the early 1980s. However, the application of talking therapies in the dual diagnosis field has been dogged by clinical beliefs about being 'under the influence' while in session, the

direction of causality (drug-induced psychosis), the influence of biomedical models in aetiology (how can a biologically based disease benefit from talking help?), notions of clinical
complexity and models of chronicity (this list is not exhaustive). In addition, psychoactive
substances may be legal, or not, prescribed or otherwise, but all of them are psychoactive. It
is arguably no easier working with a service user taking a sedating street drug than it is one
taking a prescribed major tranquilizer.

Structure in CBT

CBT makes use of a clear, coherent structure that is transparent to the client, supports
collaboration and elicits continuous feedback (Wills & Sanders 2013). We give here an
outline of what may be covered in a 12-session model of offering CBT as a psychosocial
intervention.

We have noted how the initial stage of therapy is assessment. Early on there is also the
client's first homework task, such as reading about CBT. As the sessions progress from the
second to fourth sessions, formulation is undertaken and the client is socialized to the CBT
model and working with emerging negative thoughts, and how to change them (Wills &
Sanders 2013). Such work includes homework such as thought diaries for those with depression or anxiety, or in substance use work, drink diaries and identifying triggers to cravings.
In sessions 5–9, for example, cognitive and behavioural methods are employed in therapy to
produce changes. In these middle stages of therapy the client's assumptions and rules are
elicited and tested out through behavioural experiments (Wills & Sanders 2013).

From our experience in professional practice, relapse prevention strategies and substance
refusal skills (e.g. drink refusal skills) are rehearsed in session then practised outside the session
by the client at this stage. From about session 10, if working to a 12-session model, ideas
about ending are introduced and some attention is paid to what the client is learning through
the therapeutic process and what they can do outside the sessions (Wills & Sanders 2013). The
last session is the ending session, and this session is a review of what the client has learned,
for example, managing cravings, drink/substance refusal skills, challenging negative thoughts
that may trigger using a substance. In this stage any issues around ending are also explored,
and the client is supported through these. In some services, discharge also happens at this
stage; however, in some services at around six months following treatment, sessions to review
progress and abstinence or maintenance are offered. If there is any further booster or follow-
up, they will be to deal with the final ending (Wills & Sanders 2013). Within many services
that work with clients who have dual diagnoses, CBT is offered to those clients who have
maintained 'stability' in treatment and are seeking to continue to work towards abstinence.

In CBT, behavioural experiments are planned activities, based on experimentation or
observation, which are undertaken by clients in session or between sessions. They test the
client's existing beliefs and help test more adaptive beliefs. For instance, an experiment
might test an anxious prediction or be a survey to get a range of views on an issue. In
working with dual diagnosis, often the behavioural experiment, for example, can serve to
disprove the client's belief that without the substance the client will be unable to manage.
The design of behavioural experiments is derived from the formulation, which is updated as
new knowledge is discovered.

Consider the following case study.

> ❏ Case study 5.5
>
> Kelly has been engaged in the service for the past year. She has a diagnosis of anxiety. Over the last year she has been supported through the service to gradually reduce her methadone and is stable. CBT has helped her since becoming stable on her methadone to explore:
>
> - her core beliefs and conditional beliefs (rules for everyday living and assumptions);
> - the critical incident/s that triggered her substance use;
> - the critical incident/s that triggered her anxiety;
> - understanding how her cognitions (thoughts) impact on and are interlinked with her emotions, and physical sensations that occur when she is anxious or craving;
> - what led to her injecting behaviour.
>
> As a psychosocial intervention, CBT has been key in helping Kelly work towards being stable on methadone because the behavioural experiments, which she continues to engage with, have enabled her to challenge her belief that she will not be able to cope with the anxiety if she does not 'double-up' (use another drug in addition to her methadone).
>
> The homework that Kelly has been doing has centred on keeping a mood diary and recording her dysfunctional thoughts as well as recording alternative thoughts.
>
> Lastly, the relapse prevention work that the practitioner has been collaboratively focusing on helped Kelly to identify her triggers. Furthermore, CBT work around relapse prevention has included challenging Kelly's expectation of perceived positive effects of use and providing psychoeducation to help Kelly make a more informed choice in the threatening situation.

Psychodynamic therapy

Psychodynamic therapy is one of the psychosocial interventions used in working with clients who have dual diagnoses. The psychodynamic school is an overarching paradigm in which there are theoretical ideas that assert there exists a conscious and unconscious, and that there are dynamics between the conscious and the unconscious parts of the self and the relations with the outer/social world (Howard 2008). Its initial development dates back to when Sigmund Freud developed psychoanalysis. He theorized that psychological problems can be traced back to primary relationships, childhood experiences and the unconscious mind (Howard 2008).

Our aim is not to go into diverse psychodynamic ideologies, but rather to offer a brief outline and enhance the reader's understanding of the basic assumptions of psychodynamic theory in relation to interventions for substance use and dual diagnosis.

Psychodynamic understanding of addiction

The psychodynamic literature offers many theories and ideas regarding the aetiology and treatment of substance use and dual diagnosis (Glover 1932a, 1932b; Goodman 1993; Hagman 1995; Kohut 1977; von Braun, Larsson & Sjöblom (2013); Matusow & Rosenblum

(2013); Potik, Adelson & Schreiber 2007). In this section, rather than outlining psychody-namic interventions as psychosocial interventions, we will briefly explore substance use and dual diagnosis in relation to psychodynamic ideas of object relations, attachment and diffi-culties in self-regulation.

Addiction as *transitional phase fixation*

One way of understanding dual diagnosis (which can be seen as psychopathological) is through psychodynamic *object-relations theory*. Object-relations theory is primarily concerned with love, especially the need for parental love. The psychoanalytic 'object' refers both to the infant's external relationships as well as internal representations of those relationships (Klein 1957). Objects refer to people, parts of people, or physical objects that symbolically represent either a person or part of a person (Klein 1952). From an object-relations perspec-tive, what a person internalizes from early childhood sets the foundation for establishing and maintaining relationships. It is therefore argued that psychopathology (diagnosed mental ill-health) is an expression of traumatic self-object internalizations from childhood acted out in lifelong relationships (Greenberg & Mitchell 1983). Jerry (1997) postulated an object-relations approach to working with substance use and dual diagnosis based on Malan's (1979) and Winnicott's (1971, 1974, 1965, 1968, 1986, 1988) work and demonstrated the relevance of object-relations theory through a case study of a young woman using cocaine (Potik et al. 2007).

Potik et al. (2007) believed that the psychodynamic idea of the 'transitional object' and Winnicott's theory of child development can be an additional explanation (to the so many existing ones) and may be very helpful in the treatment of substance use disorder. The term 'transitional object' describes 'the infant's journey from the purely subjective to objectivity' (Winnicott 1971). Winnicott (1953, 1971) viewed addictions to drugs, alcohol and food, and to sexual promiscuity, as attempts to re-find the lost object through direct physical gratifi-cation. Addiction to substances therefore is similar to transitional phenomena because the substance of choice in psychodynamic work is seen as representing the mother and yet is recognized as not being the mother (Summers 1994; Winnicott 1971). Potik et al. (2007) argued that unlike the child's transitional possessions, addictions are not given up naturally because they are a regressive response to deprivation, and an effort to regain an earlier rela-tionship with the mother before deprivation. Consequently, rather than moving the devel-opmental process forward, clients who present with substance use disorder tend to remain fixated (Summers 1994; Winnicott 1971).

Medication as transitional objects

In relation to dual diagnosis, different psychoanalytic writers have also noted how various medications (sedative-hypnotics, antidepressants and even some antipsychotics) can serve as transitional objects (Adelman 1985; Gutheil 1982; Hausner 1985) because they are readily available, reduce anxiety, provide relaxation and can be used before sleep, like children's usage of transitional objects (Winnicott 1953, 1971; Potik et al. 2007). Such links to medica-tion as transitional objects can be related further to the concept that often clients do present with a wish to stop psychological pain. In such a case, methadone, for example, can serve as a transitional object because it reduces pain and stops withdrawal symptoms.

Self-regulation difficulties

Another way of understanding substance use and psychological distress is through self-regulation ideas. Khantzian (2012) hypothesized a psychodynamic perspective which suggests that addiction is fundamentally a disorder of self-regulation. Clients who depend on substances cannot or do not regulate their emotions, self-esteem, relationships and behaviour. Regulating emotions, self-esteem, relationships and self-care are among the main functions upon which our survival as humans depends, and using substances, therefore, is a way of self-medicating in order to manage distress (Khantzian 2012).

Difficulties with self-regulation

Difficulties with self-regulation relate to an inability to establish:

- and maintain adequate, comforting and comfortable relationships;
- and maintain adequate control/regulation of behaviour, especially self-care;
- recognize and regulate feelings;
- and maintain a coherent, comfortable sense of self and self-esteem.

From a psychodynamic perspective this inability to self-regulate can be traced back to primary relationships and childhood experiences which would have resulted in psychological difficulties. The client may then use substances to help themselves to contain distressful experiences or pain.

Substance use as self-medication

Khantzian (1985, 1997) hypothesized a 'self-medication hypothesis' (SMH) which offers an adaptive, evidence-based perspective. This is in contrast to early psychoanalytic theories of addiction and, not insignificantly, contemporary neuroscientific theory, that identify pleasure and reward as motivating addictions. There are different aspects of the SMH:

- Addictive substances become compelling because they relieve or change a range of painful experiences.
- Addictive substances help clients to cope with a troubled inner emotional terrain.
- Clients with dual diagnoses often use substances to help them deal with their troublesome interpersonal terrain and difficulties in relating to others.

Khantzian and Weegmann (2009) cut to the heart of the matter when they stated that:

> For individuals flooded with rage, for example, such affect is fragmenting within and threatening from without, making relationships unlikely or impossible; such individuals have the discovery that opiates re-hinge within and make connections to others less threatening and thus more possible. The enfeebled and de-energized find the activating properties of stimulants to be agents that mobilize them and make the negotiation of human relationships more likely and even enjoyable, otherwise they feel unattainable. Those who suffer with anxiety are deterred from the company of others either because their apprehension immobilizes them, or defensive restraint removes them from the company of others. (2009:366)

As we have seen throughout this book, clients may use substances to mask or to cope with their psychological distress. They may also become psychologically distressed due to using substances. Whatever the case may be, Khantzian and Weegmann's (2009) statement above argues their perspective well, that is, that the use of substances in those with a dual diagnosis can be noted to be a way of self-medication. Any psychodynamic psychosocial interventions will therefore explore in depth the source of the pain that the client is trying to self-medicate against.

Understanding substance use from an attachment theory perspective

It has been suggested that addiction is an attachment disorder based on childhood insecure attachment patterns (Flores 2004). Attachment research evidences how attachment patterns throughout life influence emotional and psychological well-being. Relationally, patterns formed in childhood also influence how individuals respond when faced with trauma or challenges later in life. Bowlby (1969) hypothesized what he termed 'the internal working model'. It is a cognitive conceptual framework for making sense of the world, the self and others (Paul & Charura 2014). The model of the self reflects the messages communicated by primary caregiver(s) by word and action. This internal model governs how children feel towards their parents and towards themselves, how children expect to be treated, and how children plan for their own behaviour towards others. The internal working model is:

- based on early relationships (attachments);
- the source of transference patterns the individual operates in life.

According to Bowlby (1969), the primary caregiver acts as a prototype for future relationships via the internal working model. Adults' interactions with others are guided by memories from their internal model, which influence and help evaluate their contact with others (Bretherton & Munholland 1999). An infant who experiences frequent abuse, neglect and adversity may develop a negative internal working model that tells them: 'No one cares about me', 'I am unlovable', 'people whom I hope will love me will only hurt or reject me', 'it doesn't matter what I do or say', or 'I am not good enough'.

If this 'model' of self, others and the world and how things work is not changed as the child grows, they may develop low self-esteem, be overly dependent or overly independent, sabotage jobs, friendships or relationships, and never get what they want in life (Paul & Charura 2014). An infant who receives consistent, positive attention from their caregiver is most likely to develop a positive internal working model. Those with secure attachment styles often fare better in the face of psychologically distressing circumstances. From this perspective, therefore, it is clear how the attachment model can be applied to dual diagnosis work. Firstly, through exploration of clients' internal working models and vulnerabilities to stress and inabilities to cope with life's experiences which often consequently lead to substance use and dependence. Director (2005) added another perspective to it and considered how clients are often in fact attached to the substance itself. From this second perspective, it is noted that just as children develop internal working models in which expectancies of care and response are envisaged, so too the drug user has an internal working model of the substance – what it can do, what is desired and so on (Flores 2004; Director 2005).

The last psychodynamic perspective we will now outline relates to our experience of working with clients with dual diagnoses and supervising practitioners who work with complex cases. Often clients present to services, reduce their substance use, and some become abstinent and experience improvement in their mental health, only to return to the service a few days, weeks or months later having relapsed. Working from a psychodynamic understanding of this 'repetition compulsion' often enables practitioners to work with clients to break this cycle.

Repetition compulsion

From a psychodynamic perspective, a repetition compulsion is a neurotic defence mechanism. It can be said that the repetition compulsion is an attempt to rewrite one's own history relating to the relationship one has with her or his primary caregivers (parents). The attempt to rewrite history is typically connected to a 'troubled/difficult relationship' with parents in childhood, particularly the opposite sex parent (Meshcheryakova 2012). Freud (1920) believed that humans tend to 'revive' past unwanted and painful experiences in their transference relationship with the therapist and may repeat these unpleasant experiences 'under the pressure of a compulsion' (p. 20). This repetitive compulsion concept was further conceptualized by different authors (Cohen 1980; Horowitz 1976; Loewald 1971; Meshcheryakova 2012).

Put simply, where the client's early parental relationship was fraught with emotional neglect, disappointment, fear of the parents, rejection, a perceived or actual lack of love, abandonment, neglect or abuse, then the psychodynamic hypothesis is that the child becomes psychologically distressed. In order to survive the difficult relationship with the parents, the child must 'deny' the reality of her or his reality, as well as her or his intense anger, depression and despair (Meshcheryakova 2012; Paul & Charura 2014). Instead, the child clings to hope that, if only he or she can be good, intelligent, caring, quiet, funny enough, etc., then the parent(s) will love the child unconditionally (Meshcheryakova 2012). This psychological experience is a misinterpretation of the reality, as the child mistakenly believes that the lack of acceptance, rejection, abandonment or neglect resides with the child. As a result the child thinks that he or she has the power to control and rectify it by changing into someone more acceptable. And so the child tries desperately to change continually, but always seems to fail because the reality is, the problem is not with the child, but with the parents' inability or unwillingness to provide the love, secure family structure and acceptance which are essential for a child's healthy psychological development (Meshcheryakova 2012; Paul & Charura 2014).

As the individual interprets that the relational difficulties and lack of acceptance are entirely her or his 'fault', he or she may consequently experience mental ill-health (Paul & Charura 2014). The individual may then also use substances to deal with the pain of rejection, abandonment or the dysfunctional relationship with the family/parents. This then starts a cycle in which substances become part of the conditions that a family may give to an individual which send the message that in order for them to love and accept the individual, he or she has to stop using. When the individual stops and is abstinent, he or she may find that the love and acceptance the individual requires is not given, and the cycle begins again.

There are other explanations to the psychodynamic concept of repetition compulsion. For example, Levi (2000) proposed that repetition compulsion could be conceptualized as a response to post-traumatic stress. He suggested that the compulsive repetition of defences is designed to avoid the re-encountering of the traumatic stressor. Levi further argued:

> As the compulsion to repeat is a repetitive, self-defeating, and rigid way of being in the world that causes the individual distress, this process needs to be understood as a maladaptive attempt of mastery. (2000:47)

Compulsive repetition aims to maintain a person's psychological sense of safety; however, its fixation on the past often puts the individual at the risk of revictimization, self-destructive behaviours, and victimization of others (van der Kolk 1989; Meshcheryakova 2012). The client's self-destructive behaviours may often include use of substances, and in dual diagnosis and states of psychological distress can include self-harming or suicidal tendencies. In order to understand the different aspects of psychodynamic therapy as a psychosocial intervention we consider the following case study.

❏ Case study 5.6 Applying psychodynamic concepts to practice

Jane is a 26-year-old mother of three children. She is referred to the service by a midwife who works for the child and parenting team because Jane has recently become pregnant. On reading her clinical case notes it is evident that she has a long history of bipolar mood disorder and using heroin. It is also noted that she has three children who are already in care. Social services became involved with each child separately due to child neglect. Jane states she does not know who fathered her children because she tends to compulsively have unprotected sex with strangers.

Jane grew up in care herself after being removed from an abusive family. She described how her mother left her and her brother when they were aged 4 and 2. Jane is not using any substances at present, having been in rehabilitation for nearly a year and having come off methadone. However, she stated that she recently bought zopiclone and painkillers off a street dealer to help her sleep because she can't take the pain of what has happened in her life. After finding out about the pregnancy, however, she has not used anything.

Jane is referred to the psychosocial interventions team, who book her for psychodynamic therapy.

Reflective question

In what way can you link the psychodynamic principles discussed so far in this chapter to working with Jane?

Considering case study 5.6 above, we concur with Khantzian and Weegmann (2009), who argue that older psychoanalytic views about primitive fixation, pre-oedipal problems, oral dependency and so on are not fully adequate in explaining the complex terrain of dual diagnosis. We also believe it is important for practitioners to therefore have a wider understanding of different psychodynamic perspectives that are not excessively drive-oriented, speculative and highly interpretive. We have therefore offered a way of understanding some psychodynamic principles and how they can work in practice. An example, drawing from case study 5.6, is as follows:

Psychodynamic formulation components and links to Jane's case

- Early attachments play a significant role in Jane's life. Exploring and understanding the client's 'internal working model' will help work through her attachment difficulties. For example, the impact of her mother leaving when she was under 5 years old, the abuse and neglectful relationship with her father, etc.
- Object-relations theory, which we noted is primarily concerned with love, especially the need for parental love, can help practitioners to understand and explore Jane's sexual behaviour in which she repeats an abusive dynamic with a father figure through her sexual encounters with older, abusive, strange men.
- Ideas on medication as transitional objects and substance use as self-medication can help the practitioner explore Jane's behaviour and use of medication she buys from street dealers.
- Jane stated she cannot maintain friendships and has low self-esteem – ideas can be drawn from the difficulties in self-regulating themes we explored. In particular we could attend to the client's inability to establish and maintain adequate, comforting, and comfortable relationships.
- An interpretation of the repetition compulsion dynamic in Jane's life can be made from a range of her behaviours. For example, in her relationships with men, neglect of her children and the use of substances.

Having presented some basic principles and examples of psychodynamic interpretations in understanding the case presented above, it is important to acknowledge that what we have presented in this chapter is a very small element of psychodynamic therapy. As a modality and theory it is more complex and will require years of specialist training and supervision. However, our aim is to give you, the reader, a working example of how some of the psychodynamic theory and concepts may be used in dual diagnosis work. Below we present a brief summary of the curative factors of psychodynamic therapy as a psychosocial intervention.

The curative factors of psychodynamic therapy as a psychosocial intervention

- Through the psychodynamic relationship, the therapist is able to explore the client's forbidden wishes, feelings and thoughts, which are enacted in relation to the therapist and consciously re-experienced, thereby bringing the core conflict into the frame (Gaztambide 2012).
- A secure psychodynamic therapeutic frame in working with clients who have dual diagnoses enables new emotional and historical material to become available to consciousness, consequently allowing the transition from repetition compulsion to working through recovery and consequently abstinence (Gaztambide 2012; Paul & Charura 2014).

- In working with clients like Jane, case study 5.6, drawing on repetition compulsion as an example, the therapeutic advantages come from two sources: (1) the transference, which communicates the experience of a failed relationship, and (2) the reality that the therapist is a different object from whom the transference derives. 'The therapist must negotiate to be both the person with whom the initial negotiation failed and the person with whom it might be different' (Russell 2006c:64).
- Overall, a collaborative therapeutic relationship, attuned to the client's childhood experiences and how they link to the client's present presentation is central to psychodynamic psychosocial interventions.
- It is also worth stating that psychodynamic work is often long term and requires a highly skilled and trained therapist. We are also aware that in some services they use brief dynamic psychotherapy, which can be an effective mode of psychotherapy for selected patients, e.g. those with high ego functions, single psychotherapeutic focus, recent onset of problems and no major resistance in the form of murderous rage and guilt in relation to parents, siblings and other figures from the past (Malan 2000).

Psychodynamic therapy and what it says about the practitioner in the therapeutic relationship

In line with acknowledging the importance of the therapeutic relationship, Charura and Parker (2013) argued that it is also important for practitioners to understand psychodynamic perspectives of transference, countertransference and projection. They stressed that they advocate the importance of the knowledge of these psychodynamic concepts rather than their psychotherapeutic use. They noted these concepts, which they argued are present in every relationship with a client, as follows:

> **Transference:** the projection of past experiences with a significant figure onto a current relationship with the therapist/practitioner. It can be seen as a mirror to the internal world of the client (Grant & Crawley 2002).

> **Countertransference:** a process by which the practitioner's feelings, thoughts and behaviours are stimulated by their client and result in a personal response without reference to processing the content and its meaning (Paul & Charura 2014).

> **Projection:** a psychological process which involves the attribution of unacceptable thoughts, feelings or behaviours to others. The disowned aspects of self are transferred onto another (Grant & Crawley 2002). Client projection is an unconscious process (i.e. clients are not doing it on purpose), and so the practitioner needs to be aware of the importance of treating it with sensitivity but at the same time be willing to work with the client as her or his thoughts and feelings come to awareness.

Paul and Charura (2014) noted the importance of considering transference, countertransference and projection from the following perspectives:

- The client's experience of difficult past primary relationships is likely to come to the fore in the room as the work develops (transference and projections onto the practitioner).

The practitioner must be prepared to work with and through these with their client in a non-defensive way with focused intention of helping.

• The practitioner knows that her or his own relational patterns will have an impact on her or his own internal reaction to the client, and therefore the practitioner must ensure that these patterns do not negatively affect the therapeutic process.

Supervision is helpful in managing practitioner reactions to transference and countertransference (Charura & Wallace 2012).

Having focused on specific psychosocial interventions in this section, we note here recommendations from NICE (2007) in relation to CBT and psychodynamic therapies:

• CBT and psychodynamic therapy focused on the treatment of substance use should not be offered routinely to people presenting for treatment of cannabis or stimulant misuse or those receiving opioid maintenance treatment.

• Evidence-based psychological treatments (in particular, CBT) should be considered for the treatment of comorbid depression and anxiety disorders in line with existing NICE guidance for people who misuse cannabis or stimulants, and for those who have achieved abstinence or are stabilized on opioid maintenance treatment.

From our experience, within many services that work with clients who have dual diagnoses, CBT and psychodynamic therapies are offered to clients who have maintained stability in treatment and are seeking to continue to work towards abstinence which is in line with the NICE guidelines. We also note below a summary of approaches and interventions for dual diagnoses as highlighted by Cleary et al. (2008).

Summary of approaches to working with dual diagnoses

• The psychosocial interventions employed in services must be person-centred and aim to enhance engagement.

• Assess presenting problems, recent substance use, mental state, medications, family involvement, awareness of problems, harm reduction knowledge, level of motivation to reduce drug use, and issues specific to the client's age, gender and culture.

• Practitioners should negotiate and agree on clear realistic treatment goals, and break down goals into short-term achievable targets.

• Interact in respectful, understanding ways to connect with the client and address pressing practical needs. Be patient, flexible, optimistic and persevering.

• Minimize harm from substance use and educate the client about mental illness, psychotropic medication adherence, substances being used, risks of continued use, and the roles of the health care system and other agencies.

• Explore warning signs of deteriorating mental health, and maintain or increase positive relationships.

• Identify high-risk situations that may result in the client resorting to drug use.

• Recognize signs of the client's mental health deterioration. Develop a care plan in the event of either substance use or mental health relapse.

• Improve the client's social skills, encourage participation in self-help groups, and refer the client for specific psychosocial interventions, if applicable.

Inpatient, residential settings and the criminal justice system

The range of psychosocial interventions that we have noted should also be considered for those with dual diagnosis who are in inpatient residential settings and within the criminal justice system. We acknowledge, however, that there may be specific tailoring required in these services due to organizational and setting constraints.

Generic recommendations for inpatient, residential settings and the criminal justice system

Residential treatment may be considered for people who are seeking abstinence and who have significant comorbid physical, mental health or social (e.g. housing) problems. The person should have completed a residential or inpatient detoxification programme and have not benefited from previous community-based psychosocial treatment.

For people in prison who have drug misuse problems, treatment options should be comparable to those available in the community. Healthcare professionals should take into account additional considerations specific to the prison setting, including, the idea that for people who have made an informed decision to remain abstinent after release from prison, residential treatment should be considered as part of an overall care plan. It is important that appropriate arrangements are made in order to dovetail support from prison services. Such arrangements include mental health support and prescriptions for medications approved for the treatment of opiate dependence (methadone, buprenorphine, etc.).

There are other contingency management plans that relate to working with couples and families, such as behavioural couples therapy. These will be explored in more detail in the next chapter.

Source: Adapted from NICE guidelines (2007).

Mindfulness and technology-based interventions

In recent years there has been a growth in related interventions and studies on mindfulness and acceptance-based treatment of substance use disorders (e.g. Bowen & Marlatt 2009; Brewer et al. 2009; Garland et al. 2010; Vieten et al. 2010). Particular focus has been on Mindfulness-Based Relapse Prevention (MBRP), which emerged from meditation-based research. In contrast to cognitive behaviour-based methods, where clients are encouraged to alter maladaptive cognitions, faulty thinking, moods or behaviours, the focus in mindfulness-based interventions is on altering one's relationship to cognitive-emotional processes through the strengthening of a non-evaluative, meta-cognitive awareness, or observing self (Deikman 1982).

Building on this concept, Baer (2003) postulated that unlike most CBT-based interventions, mindfulness does not involve the evaluation of cognitions as either rational or distorted, and does not attempt to change or dispute thoughts. Instead, clients are encouraged to learn to simply observe thoughts, note their impermanence and relate to them as mental events rather than as necessarily accurate reflections of the truth. In working with dual diagnosis where clients may be experiencing negative or anxiety-provoking thoughts which consequently they may treat with substances, from the acceptance-based stance of mindfulness practice, clients are taught to accept painful or aversive experiences.

Mindfulness and acceptance-based treatment sessions are as follows:

- The first phase of working with clients from this stance is on increasing awareness of physical experiences of internal and external triggers, and of the client's physical, emotional and cognitive reactions that are associated with these triggers.
- Sessions then shift to integrating into daily life the awareness and acceptance practices learned thus far, as well as learning additional practices for coping with urges and cravings that may arise in high-risk situations.
- Finally, the last phase of sessions focuses on maintaining a lifestyle that will support recovery, strengthen relapse prevention and encourage continued mindfulness practice (Bowen et al. 2010; Vieten et al. 2010; Garland et al. 2010).

Technology-based interventions

From practice and the latest research we have noted that computer-based interventions are cost-efficient methods that may are comparable to therapist-delivered interventions (Bickel et al. 2011). Consider the following.

Technology-based interventions

Marsch and Bickel (2004) conducted research with clients who were dependent on injection opioid drugs. They randomly assigned these clients to either a fluency-based computer HIV/AIDS education programme or a standard therapist-based counselling HIV/AIDS intervention. They noted in their research results that during the three monthly follow-ups, participants who experienced the computer-based stated the following:

- They learned significantly more information about HIV/AIDS.
- They enjoyed learning through computer technology.
- They requested additional information with greater frequency than in therapist-based counselling.

Marsch and Bickel (2004) suggested that the greater retention of information was due to the fluency approach and interactive nature of the computer-based programme. The efficacy of computer-delivered interventions has also been noted as effective through research which used smartphone programmes designed to help clients with their relapse prevention. For example, Quanbeck et al. (2014) researched the experience of clients using a programme called A-CHESS, which helps clients meet the challenges they often face, such as loneliness and isolation, transportation, managing the treatment regime, cravings and insufficient coping skills in high-risk situations, and getting informal support. In a randomized trial of patients discharged from residential addiction treatment, patients with A-CHESS had 57% fewer risky drinking days than patients in the control group (Gustafson et al. 2014).

In summary, Gustafson et al. (2014) stated that new technologies and computer-based methods appear to be cost-effective, efficacious and accessible. They stated that there was research that supported the conclusions that:

- clients are often more responsive to computer-based information programmes than a standard counsellor-led intervention;
- computer-based interventions have also been found to increase motivation for abstinence and have similar levels of alliance building as therapist interventions.

We have also noted as practitioners the benefits of computer-based programmes and phone apps which clients use to help them to record their thoughts and moods as part of their relapse prevention homework. In the services we work with, smart technology/programmes have been used effectively to prompt clients and remind them of their appointments with the psychosocial interventions team. This has increased attendance rates in this client group whose attendance rate to appointments is often quite low.

It needs to be noted however that computer-based and smart technology–based therapies may not be suited to all clients with a dual diagnosis. Some may prefer and respond better to face-to-face therapy, while others may not be used to computer-based technologies, which may cause them to focus on the operation and delivery of the treatment and be less engaged with the programme's content (Magura 2000). It has also been highlighted that it is important to consider whether the present circumstances of the client require an immediate intervention by the therapist, for example, when there are issues of risk or immediate danger to the client or to others. In such circumstances the physical presence of the therapist is more appropriate (Bickel et al. 2011).

In this chapter we have explored the evidence-based psychosocial interventions in working with dual diagnosis in substance use. Overall, psychosocial interventions such as MI, CBT, relapse prevention and strength-based approaches have proven to be effective in working with dual diagnosis. We also identified and outlined the challenges of working with clients with dual diagnoses. We have noted how literature and research suggest that psychosocial interventions and treatment are more effective when used in conjunction with substitute prescribing than when medication or psychological treatment is used alone.

Key messages:

To help the reader to understand elements in working with individuals, the following were discussed:

- the varied and complex nature of the relationship between substance use disorder and mental health problems when working with individuals;
- how the transtheoretical model of Prochaska and DiClemente (1983) can enable practitioners to identify clients' stages of change as well as to consider factors impacting on motivation to change when employing psychosocial interventions;
- the place and the importance of case conceptualization and formulation;
- the contemporary psychosocial interventions employed in working with dual diagnosis and their efficacy; these include motivational interviewing, brief interventions and self-help; contingency management; CBT and psychodynamic therapy; and the use of technology-based interventions.

REFERENCES

Abou-Saleh, M.T. (2004). Dual-diagnosis: Management within a psychosocial context. *Advances in Psychiatric Treatment*, 10, 352–360.

Adelman, S.A. (1985). Pills as transitional objects: A dynamic understanding of the use of medication in psychotherapy. *Psychiatry*, 48, 246–253.

Aram, L. (Ed.) (2007). *Dual Diagnosis: Good Practice Handbook*. London: Turning Point.

Baer, R.A. (2003). Mindfulness training as a clinical intervention: A conceptual and empirical review. *Clinical Psychology: Science and Practice*, 10, 125–143.

Bickel, W.K., Christensen, D.R., & Marsch, L.A. (2011). A review of computer-based interventions used in the assessment, treatment, and research of drug addiction. *Substance Use & Misuse*, 46(1), 4–9.

Bowen, S., & Marlatt, A. (2009). Surfing the urge: Brief mindfulness-based intervention for college student smokers. *Psychology of Addictive Behaviors*, 23, 666–671.

Bowen, S., Chawla, N., & Marlatt, G.A. (2010). *Mindfulness Based Relapse Prevention for Addictive Behaviors: A Clinician's Guide*. New York: The Guilford Press.

Bowlby, J. (1969). *Attachment and Loss*, Volume I: *Attachment*. New York: Basic Books.

Bretherton, I., & Munholland, K.A. (1999). Internal working models revisited. In Cassidy, J., & Shaver, P.R. (Eds) *Handbook of Attachment: Theory, Research, and Clinical Applications* (pp. 89–111). New York: The Guilford Press.

Brewer, J.A. et al. (2009). Mindfulness training and stress reactivity in substance abuse: Results from a randomized, controlled stage I pilot study. *Substance Abuse*, 30, 306–317.

Chadwick, P. (2006). *Person-Based Cognitive Therapy for Distressing Psychosis*. Chichester: Wiley.

Charura, D., & Nicholson, P. (2013). The Therapeutic relationship: Another buzz phrase or the essence of relapse prevention success in addiction work. *Addiction Today*, 22–23(140), 22–23.

Charura, D., & Parker, C.L. (2013). Motivational interviewing: Projection, transference, countertransference. *Addiction Today*, 22–23(145), 18–19, 39.

Charura, D., & Wallace, L. (2012). Group supervision when working with complex issues in addiction work. *Addiction Today*, 23(137), 25–27.

Cleary, M., Walter, G., Hunt, G., Clancy, R., & Horsfall, J. (2008). Promoting dual diagnosis awareness in everyday clinical practice. *Journal of Psychosocial Nursing & Mental Health Services*, 46(12), 43–49.

Cohen, J. (1980). Structural consequences of psychic trauma: A new look at 'Beyond the pleasure principle.' *International Journal of Psychoanalysis*, 61, 421–432.

Deikman, A.J. (1982). *The Observing Self: Mysticism and Psychotherapy*. Boston: Beacon Press.

Director, L. (2005). Encounters with omnipotence in the psychoanalysis of substance users. *Psychoanalytic Dialogues*, 15(4), 567–586.

Flores, P.J. (2004). *Addiction As An Attachment Disorder*. New York: Jason Aronson.

Freud, S. (1920). Beyond the pleasure principle. In Strachey, J. (1954) (Ed. & Trans.) *The Standard Edition of the Complete Psychological Works of Sigmund Freud* (Vol. 18, pp. 3–64). London, England: Hogarth Press.

Garland, E.L., Gaylord, S.A., Boettiger, C.A., & Howard, M.O. (2010). Mindfulness training modifies cognitive, affective, and physiological mechanisms implicated in alcohol dependence: Results of a randomized controlled pilot trial. *Journal of Psychoactive Drugs*, 42, 177–192.

Gaztambide, D.J. (2012). A psychotherapy for the people: Freud, Ferenczi, and psychoanalytic work with the underprivileged. *Contemporary Psychoanalysis*, 48(2), 141–165.

Glover, E. (1932a). Common problems in psychoanalysis and anthropology: Drug ritual and addiction. *British Journal of Medical Psychology*, 12, 109–131.

Glover, E. (1932b). On the aetiology of drug addiction. *International Journal of Psychoanalysis*, 53, 63–73.

Goodman, A. (1993). The addictive process: A psychoanalytic understanding. *Journal of the American Academy of Psychoanalysis*, 21, 89–105.

Grant, J., & Crawley, J. (2002). *Transference and Projection*. Buckingham: Open University Press.

Greenberg, J.R., & Mitchell, S.A. (1983). *Object Relations in Psychoanalytic Theory*. Cambridge, MA: Harvard University Press.

Greenberger, D., & Padesky, C.A. (1995). *Mind over Mood: Change How You Feel by Changing How You Think*. New York: The Guilford Press.

Gustafson, D.H. et al. (2014). A smartphone application to support recovery from alcoholism: A randomized controlled trial. *JAMA Psychiatry*, 71(5), 566–572.

Gutheil, T. (1982). The psychology of psychopharmacology. *Bulletin of the Menninger Clinic*, 41, 321–330.

Hagman, G. (1995). A psychoanalyst in methadonia. *Journal of Substance Abuse Treatment*, 12, 167–179.

Handmaker, N.S., & Walters, S.T. (2004). Motivational Interviewing for initiating change in problem drinking and drug use. In Hofmann, S.G., & Tompson, M.C. (Eds) *Treating Chronic and Severe Mental Disorders: A Handbook of Empirically Supported Interventions*. New York: The Guilford Press.

Hausner, R.S. (1985). Medication and transitional phenomena. *International Journal of Psychoanalytic Psychotherapy*, 11, 375–398.

Hawton, K., Salkovskis, P.M., Kirk, J., & Clark, D.M. (1989). *Cognitive Behaviour Therapy for Psychiatric Problems: A Practical Guide*. New York: Oxford University Press.

Horowitz, M. (1976). *Stress Response Syndrome*. New York: Jason Aronson.

Howard, P. (2008). Psychoanalytic psychotherapy. In Haugh, S., & Paul, S. (Eds) *The Therapeutic Relationship: Perspectives and Themes* (pp. 92–103). Ross-on-Wye: PCCS Books.

Jerry, P.A. (1997). Psychodynamic psychotherapy of the intravenous cocaine abuser. *Journal of Substance Abuse Treatment*, 14, 319–332.

Jones, D., & Mulhern, R. (2004). Working with people who have a dual diagnosis. In Grant, A., Mills, J., Mulhern, R., & Short, N. (Eds) *Cognitive Behaviour Therapy in Mental Health Care*. London. Sage.

Khantzian, E., & Weegmann, M. (2009). Questions of substance: Psychodynamic reflections on addictive vulnerability and treatment. *Psychodynamic Practice*, 15(4), 365–380.

Khantzian, E.J. (1997). The self medication hypothesis of substance use disorders: A reconsideration and recent applications. *Harvard Review of Psychiatry*, 4(5), 231–244.

Khantzian, E.J. (2012). Reflections on treating addictive disorders: A psychodynamic perspective. *American Journal on Addictions*, 21(3), 274–279.

Kingdon, D.G., & Turkington, D. (1995). *Cognitive-Behavioural Therapy of Schizophrenia*. Hove: The Guilford Press.

Klein, M. (1952). *The Mutual Influences in the Development of Ego and Id*. In Envy and Gratitude and Other Works: London: Hogarth, 1975.

Klein, M. (1957). *Envy and Gratitude: A Study of Unconscious Forces*. New York: Basic Books.

Kohut, H. (1977). Preface to psychodynamics of drug dependence. In Blaine, J.D., & Julius, D.A. (Eds) *NIDA Treatment Research Monograph # 12*. Rockville, MD: National Institute on Drug Abuse.

Kuyken, W., Padesky, C.A., & Dudley, R. (2008). The science and practice of case conceptualization. *Behavioural and Cognitive Psychotherapy*, 36, 757–768.

Levi, M.S. (2000). A conceptualization of the repetition compulsion. *Psychiatry*, 63(1), 45–53.

Loewald, H.W. (1971). Some considerations on repetition and repetition compulsion. *International Journal of Psychoanalysis*, 52, 59–66.

Lussier, M., & Richard, C. (2007). The motivational interview. *Canadian Family Physician*, 53, 2117–2118.

Magura, S. (2000). Introduction: Program quality in substance dependency treatment. *Substance Use and Misuse*, 35, 1617–1627.

Malan D. (1979). *Individual Psychotherapy and the Science of Psychodynamics.* London: Butterworths.

Malan, D., (2000). Beyond interpretation: Initial evaluation and technique in short-term dynamic psycho-therapy (Part 1). *International Journal of Short-term Dynamic Psychotherapy,*14, 59–62.

Marsch, L., & Bickel, W. (2004). Efficacy of computer-based HIV/AIDS education for injection drug users. *American Journal Of Health Behavior,* 28(4), 316–327.

Matusow, H., & Rosenblum, A. (2013). The most critical unresolved issue associated with psychoana-lytic theories of addiction: Can the talking cure tell us anything about substance use and misuse? *Substance Use & Misuse,* 48(3), 239–247.

Meshcheryakova, K. (2012). Art therapy with orphaned children: Dynamics of early relational trauma and repetition compulsion. *Art Therapy: Journal of the American Art Therapy Association,* 29(2), 50.

Miller, W.R., & Rollnick, S. (2002). *Motivational Interviewing: Preparing People for Change* (2nd Ed.). New York: Guilford Press.

National Institute for Clinical Excellence (2007). Drug misuse – opioid detoxification. <http://www.nice .org.uk/guidance/cg52> [Accessed July 2014].

National Institute for Clinical Excellence (2007). Drug misuse – psychosocial interventions. <http://www .nice.org.uk/Guidance/CG51/chapter/related-nice-guidance> [Accessed July 2014].

National Institute for Clinical Excellence (2009). Schizophrenia: Core interventions in the treatment and management of schizophrenia in primary and secondary care (update). <http://www.nice.org.uk/> [Accessed May 2014].

Paul, S., & Charura D. (2014). *An Introduction to the Therapeutic Relationship in Counselling and Psychotherapy.* London: Sage.

Potik, D., Adelson, M., & Schreiber, S. (2007). Drug addiction from a psychodynamic perspective: Methadone maintenance treatment (MMT) as transitional phenomena. *Psychology & Psychotherapy: Theory, Research & Practice,* 80(2), 311–325.

Prochaska, J.O., & DiClemente, C.C. (1983). Stages and processes of self-change of smoking: Toward an integrative model of change. *Journal of Consultant Clinical Psychology,* 51(3), 390–395.

Quanbeck, A.R. et al. (2014). Integrating addiction treatment into primary care using mobile health tech-nology: Protocol for an implementation research study. *Implementation Science,* 9(1), 1–22.

Rogers, C.R. (1959). A theory of therapy, personality and interpersonal relationships as developed in the client-centred framework. In Koch, S. (Ed.) *Psychology: A Study of Science* (Vol. 3, pp. 184–256). New York: McGraw-Hill.

Rollnick, S., & Miller, W.R. (1995). What is motivational interviewing? *Behavioural and Cognitive Psychotherapy,* 23, 325–334.

Russell, P.L. (2006c). The uses of repetition. *Smith College Studies in Social Work,* 76(1/2), 51–66.

Summers, F. (1994). The work of D.W. Winnicott. In Summers, F. (Ed.) *Object Relations Theories and Psychopathology.* London: The Analytic Press.

Treasure, J. (2004). Motivational interviewing. *Advances in Psychiatric Treatment,* 10, 331–337.

van der Kolk, B.A. (1989). The compulsion to repeat the trauma: Re-enactment, revictimization, and maso-chism. *Psychiatric Clinics of North America,* 12(2), 389–411.

Vieten, C., Astin, J.A., Buscemi, R., & Galloway, G.P. (2010). Development of an acceptance-based coping intervention for alcohol dependence relapse prevention. *Substance Abuse,* 31, 108–116.

von Braun, T., Larsson, S., & Sjöblom, Y. (2013). Chapter 10: Perspectives on treatment, alliance and narra-tives concerning substance use-related dependency. *Substance Use & Misuse,* 48(13), 1386–1403.

Waddington, L. (2002). The therapy relationship in cognitive therapy: A review. *Behavioural and Cognitive Psychotherapy,* 30, 179–191.

Walldron, G., & Wilson, R. (2012). Multidisciplinary working in CBT practice. In Dryden, W., & Branch, R. (Eds) *The CBT Handbook.* London: Sage.

Wills, F. (2008). *Skills in Cognitive Behaviour and Counselling Psychotherapy.* London: Sage.

Wills, F., & Sanders, D. (2013). *Cognitive Behaviour Therapy: Foundations for Practice.* London: Sage.

Winnicott, D.W. (1953). Transitional objects and transitional phenomena. *International Journal of Psychoanalysis,* 34, 89–97.

Winnicott, D.W. (1965; 1992). The concept of trauma in relation to the development of the individual within the family. In Winnicott, C., Shepherd, R., & Davis, M. (Eds) *Psycho-analytic Explorations* (pp. 130–148). Cambridge, MA: Harvard University Press.

Winnicott, D.W. (1968; 1992). On 'the use of an object'. In Winnicott, C., Shepherd, R., & Davis, M. (Eds), *Psycho-analytic Explorations.* Cambridge, MA: Harvard University Press.

Winnicott, D.W. (1971). *Playing and Reality.* London: Tavistock Publications.

Winnicott, D.W. (1974). Fear of breakdown. *International Review of Psycho-Analysis,* 1, 103–107.

Winnicott, D.W. (1986). *Home Is Where We Start from – Essays by a Psychoanalyst.* New York: Norton.

Winnicott, D.W. (1988). *Human Nature.* New York: Schocken Books.

6 | Working with Groups and Families

Chapter Summary

This aims of this chapter are for the reader to develop an understanding of:

- working with groups and the different group interventions for clients presenting with dual diagnoses;
- the range of group approaches, including 12-step approaches/programmes;
- the wide range of group dynamics that may emerge from working with groups;
- key protocols informing family work;
- useful family interventions when working with dual diagnosis, such as a five-step approach and basic family systemic therapy concepts;
- family work models for working with severe mental health problems;
- social behaviour and network therapy (SBNT);
- the challenges of working in different settings.

Introduction

The aim of this chapter is to introduce the reader to the different group and family interventions that are commonly used when working with dual diagnosis clients. As we have seen in the previous chapters, there is currently no standardized treatment for dual diagnosis, largely because it ranges across such a large number of problems and involves both substance misuse services and mental health services. Services that we work with and supervise practitioners in are increasingly using motivational interviewing, cognitive behavioural therapy (CBT) approaches, strength-based approaches and pharmacological interventions. Although there are many interventions which have increased the possibility of the work becoming more standardized, as seen in the previous chapters the treatment of people with dual diagnoses can be challenging because their needs are typically complex and consequently it is often long-term work. There are also social factors to take into account, such as lack of housing or difficulty in accessing benefits, which can also hinder successful treatment (Aram 2007). In effect we would recommend that practitioners and services be aware of practices with good evidence, use best practice protocols where they are available and customize interventions to clients and families on client goals/problems and the direction a formulation suggests. If we accept some of the psychological models we have reviewed so far, we are accepting the idea that problematic substance use and mental distress may be responses to intolerable circumstances including difficult memories and poverty. We also see that a sound social intervention understands the material disadvantages that people experience.

Group-based work is thought to have some benefits for people with dual diagnoses, particularly for educational interventions, although there are some limits. For groups involving emotional expression, those people who feel unable or unwilling to, or cannot, express due to treatment effects or emotional numbness, might be less able to make gains (Horsfall et al. 2009). Alongside the individual and social complexities, it is important to note that clients also have a vast range of experiences, skills, strengths and vulnerabilities and will therefore engage with services in different ways. As we have seen in previous chapters, many people with a dual diagnosis have lives that are too 'chaotic' to attend set appointments and may need services to respond in different ways which can enable them to maintain contact with services (Aram 2007). One of the principles of the strengths-based model is that clients are offered an outreach perspective. This refers to not only community services but also to the notion that services should be prepared to give 80% to the client's 20%. The rubric of being 'met halfway' is often neglectful of the kinds of problems and barriers clients experience. Having focused on working with individual clients in Chapter 5, in this chapter we focus on the importance of working with clients in groups and also on working with their families in order to ensure increased chances of continued engagement. We go beyond outlining the nature of the different kinds of groups to exploring some of the group dynamics and challenges that may emerge when working with clients through group processes.

Later in the chapter we focus on the evidence base for working with families and useful interventions when working with dual diagnosis, which include social behaviour and network therapy and five-step behaviour family therapy. Working with families presents an opportunity to include them as part of the client's helpful social network, but it also creates different challenges and complexities, including how the practitioner can manage issues of confidentiality and child safeguarding, as well as the impact of dual diagnosis on the family system.

Group work modes

Self-help groups

For many years the use of different group therapies and inclusion of family members as part of treatment models have been important for supporting clients. Common approaches to self-help groups have long been in use within community contexts, for example in the form of groups like Alcoholics Anonymous (AA), which has been in action since the late 1930s, and Narcotics Anonymous (NA), since the early 1950s. There are also more formalized therapeutic group-work interventions that are used in different professional settings, which draw more from psychological therapy modalities. These include groups which aim to support clients in managing their mental ill health/distress or to change their substance use, as well as some which aim to help clients working towards relapse prevention. In relation to dual diagnosis, we will now offer a critique of the 12-step programme which is the basis for many groups.

What is the 12-step programme?

The 12-step programme is a set of guiding principles that has been adopted in a wide range of group-based self-help groups and interventions which outline a stepped course of action for recovery from addiction or other behavioural problems associated with substance use/misuse. The principles were originally published by AA (1939). Since their original publication different services have adapted them for different clientele, and hence we suggest adaptation to suit a wide range of those experiencing different substance dependencies. We do also acknowledge that one of the major criticisms of the 12-step programme is that its religious basis puts some people off; however, some use its components to build on programmes that are non-religious. We present it in its more original form, but for some non-religious practices people will insert the notion of any powerful being or a greater existence such as 'the universe'. This is about making the 12-step programme work in principle rather than slavishly sticking with the original religious sentiment. However, a further concern is that this appeal to a greater circumstance can also be seen as passive or abdication of one's own agency.

The 12-step programme approach of AA (1939)

1. Admitting that one is powerless over their substance of choice and – that their life had become unmanageable;
2. Coming to the belief that a power greater than the self could restore one's sanity;
3. Deciding to turn one's will and life over to the care of God as one understands him;
4. Making a searching and fearless moral inventory of oneself;
5. Admitting to God, to oneself and to another human being the exact nature of one's own wrongs;
6. Admitting that one is entirely ready to have God remove all character defects;
7. Humbly asking God to remove one's shortcomings;
8. Making a list of all persons harmed and having a willingness to make amends to them all;

9. Making direct amends to all such peoples wherever possible, except where doing so would injure them or others;
10. Undergoing a process of continual personal inventory-taking and making prompt admission;
11. Through prayer and meditation, seeking improvement of conscious contact with God, as understood by the individual praying only for knowledge of his will and the power to carry that out;
12. Having had a spiritual awakening as the result of these steps, that this message is carried to all those with an addiction and that these principles are practised in all of one's affairs.

Dual diagnosis and 12-step programmes

Different researchers and practitioners have reviewed the application and uptake of 12-step programmes with clients who have dual diagnoses. It is noted, for example, that lower rates of referral may reflect an ongoing clinical debate about whether dually diagnosed patients should participate in and will benefit from 12-step groups (Bogenschutz et al. 2006; Ouimette et al. 2003; Timko et al. 2010). However, some practitioners have advocated for attendance at 12-step intervention groups as an adjunct to dual diagnosis treatment, arguing that those with a dual diagnosis who attend can also benefit (Galanter 2000; Herman et al. 2000; Chi et al. 2006; Timko et al. 2010).

Different research suggests that the majority of clients with dual diagnoses engage in self-help groups, but only a minority become closely linked to self-help groups by using them consistently over time (Noordsy et al. 1996; Timko et al. 2010). Timko et al. (2010) note that with regard to working with the 12 steps, on average, both clients with only 'substance use disorder' and dual diagnosis clients most often almost completed the first four steps. However, the association between substance use outcomes and engaging with more steps was weaker for clients with a dual diagnosis. Some researchers hypothesize that having a 'mental illness' can often mean that some dually diagnosed patients fail to endorse that they are powerless over their consumption of alcohol (Handmaker et al. 2002; Luke et al. 2002), and may deny and minimize their substance use (Jordan et al. 2002) and have difficulty accepting and trusting the idea of God or a higher power (Timko et al. 2010). It is unclear why this is attributed to an effect of 'mental illness' when in fact other models of pathology would argue greater levels of suggestibility in such clients. Mueser et al. (2003) suggest that clients may benefit from reframing some of the 12 steps, for example the fourth step, 'making amends', need not involve a formal apology but may entail an internal process of working through one's own forgiveness for factors such as guilt that may be contributing to psychological distress.

We summarize below a critique of the 12-step group approach as noted by different authors and practitioners.

- There have been concerns raised which partly involve contrasting views of which problem is primary; being in 12-step groups that emphasize the primacy of addictions may invalidate the client's own perceptions of mental ill health and distress as the primary problem and thus may increase their distress (Laudet et al. 2004, 2006).

- AA and NA, and other services that use the 12-step approach, suggest that life is manageable if abstinence from the substance is maintained, but as we outlined in Chapter 5, psychiatric symptoms may often worsen in newly-abstinent patients, thereby making their subjective experience feel less manageable.
- 12-step group interventions which encourage subscription to the pure form of the 12-step approach may be perceived as objecting to psychotropic medications to help manage symptoms of distress (Timko et al. 2010), in what has come to be known as 'pill-shaming'.
- Jordan et al. (2002) highlighted how interpersonal avoidance associated with psychiatric problems may also make membership in 12-step fellowships problematic. As we outlined in Chapter 5, clients with anxiety or social phobias may struggle to attend for group interventions. Discomfort with crowds, strangers and emotional engagement in which one tells her or his experience of mental illness in groups may be common challenges that clients with a dual diagnosis may have, thereby making it difficult to engage.
- Timko et al. (2010) also noted that some of the steps, like taking a moral inventory and making amends, may also be challenging for some. For example, from practice and supervising practitioners we are aware of clients whose mental ill health is interconnected to experiences of abuse. The suggestion of confronting their experiences in order to make amends may require confronting painful memories and revisiting distressing experiences, which may not be appropriate in groups and which also may exacerbate psychological distress and lead to relapse.

Having noted these points on the 12-step approach, we acknowledge that it has also helped many clients within services, and within the community, in managing relapse and maintaining sobriety. We encourage practitioners to be aware of the challenges that the approach presents and to explore what the best, most fitting approach may be for their clients. In the following section we outline different modalities of group therapy as an intervention that is effective in working with clients who have dual diagnoses.

Group interventions and psychotherapy

Group psychotherapy, or group therapy, interventions can be defined generally as the treatment of a group of individuals at one time. In generic group therapy, meetings are done with individuals presenting with the same psychological problem or individuals who come together for therapy with similar goals or objectives. In this case we refer to group interventions with clients presenting with a dual diagnosis or substance use history. A broad theoretical assumption is that group therapy helps an individual to relate her or his experiences to that of the others in the group (Charura 2012).

Different theorists describe the interplay of group formation, cohesion, conflict and group process (Yalom & Lescz 2005). Rather than offer a theoretical critique of these, in our experience of working with groups, we concur that each group goes through its own process which includes the above and possibly more. We summarize below some points noted by Charura (2012) which are applicable in facilitating groups with clients who have dual diagnoses.

Key points for group facilitation

- One of the major steps in any group is building trust between group members, and it is only after doing this that the members of the group therapy session are able to bond with each other.
- It is important to affirm the importance of confidentiality and to establish ground rules together for how the group will run. This should be done from the very first session and the rules can be reflected upon during the course of the group work. Establish also who is responsible for the rules and what might be a good way of addressing any rule breaking.
- It is important to inform (or negotiate with) the group what the purpose of the group is, and to establish individual goals and answer any questions.
- It is important to be clear about the practical structure of the group, for example, that a group meets weekly for 1–2 hours, depending on the size of the group, and that each group meets weekly for 12 weeks.
- Individuals are not forced to speak or say anything that they do not feel comfortable exploring or sharing with the group. Group leaders and facilitators should comprehend the difference between confrontation and invitation to participate that is enabling, and those that are not, in their own practice.
- Managing the group dynamics (or aspects of process) and group ending is crucial to successful outcomes. By dynamics and processes we are referring to the *how* of the group work, not just the *what* (content). This may involve spotting key themes, observing how members are in the group (*what is happening in the room right now?*), eliciting feedback (*how are you finding this?*), summarizing, establishing goal-oriented perspectives, and working with emotion in the group (*what are people feeling as we sit here?*).

For some individuals it is important to reflect on points in their life where they may have detoxed/rehabilitated and had periods of abstinence, and to focus on what consequently led to relapse. This may also be linked to their mental health and experience of mental ill health. Furthermore, this enables an ability to reflect and identify corrective measures and plans to aid relapse prevention strategies such as fine tuning a relapse drill. It is argued within the research that 'opening up' to other people with the same experiences proves to be more beneficial than having a one-to-one session with a therapist (Yalom & Lescz 2005).

Resistance and challenges to the curative process in group interventions

Resistance in group interventions is another challenge which needs to be acknowledged and challenged in order for group interventions to be helpful (Charura 2012). There is a range of ways that people with dual diagnoses can find group work challenging (and rewarding). So, when we mention being challenging, or confronting, as a facilitator or group leader, we are meaning a version of challenge that is gentle and respectful, and from which a person can gain new learning. Resistance from group members can be seen in individuals retreating from problems that are disclosed or minimizing the significance of problems. It may also be evidenced by denial or the minimization of the destruction that substance abuse, or addiction, is causing in one's life and the impact on their mental health. Furthermore, it can also be evidenced by avoiding meaningful interpersonal contact or responses that are closed and brief in a way which makes exploration difficult (Charura 2012). Group interventions with individuals who have dual diagnoses require a practitioner who can challenge the individuals' resistance because most individuals acknowledge a pattern of resistance and deny their addictions to substances.

We agree that it is not enough in offering group psychosocial interventions to simply teach individuals about addiction, physiological consequences of drug abuse or psychological denial. Educational interventions have their role, but there is little evidence that on their own they result in change. For change to be optimized, group interventions must provide the individual with the right conditions, including 'space' to explore difficult experiences and challenge their fears, as well as identify shared experiences with others, which may enable a realization of not being alone or peculiar in facing problems. This in turn can enable skills and the motivation to begin a new approach to life, as well as a realization that perhaps life without alcohol/drugs can be an experience in a positive direction.

Group ending, separation and focus on relapse prevention

Preparing for clients engaging in a group ending is important. This, in many ways, could be symbolic of an ending of individuals' relationships with an old life. We have heard many groups acknowledge this as a process of bereavement or the loss of a friend (friend being the substance of choice or lifestyle associated with this). It is also important to note that this process can be also symbolic of other processes or losses in the client's life which may have contributed to them using substances to cope with their experience (Charura 2012). This may include loss and bereavement on many levels, including the death of a loved one, loss of a job or relationship or other experiences such as pain. Paradoxically, substance use could have also been a result of celebration, eventually spiralling to lack of control and consequently dependence. Again we acknowledge that any change involves ambivalence, or a range of feelings, but nevertheless it is worth undertaking in terms of the cost–benefit. In the end stage of a group it is therefore important to explore the impact of endings. The group members can share, explore their feelings and anticipate what will happen after the therapy has ended. They can also reflect on the impact of the group interventions or programme sessions which they had over the weeks and share their thoughts, reflections or fears. An important aspect in this stage is to affirm relapse prevention plans/drills and for group members to challenge or affirm each other's plans in order to ensure that each individual is fully aware of their options and possibilities.

There are some criticisms to group interventions. Firstly, we acknowledge the challenges that having a dual diagnosis can have and note that group interventions do not work for everyone and are not for everyone. Roback (2000) cites a study that showed that the condition of 10% of group members worsened as a result of group therapy (however, that 90% did not is worthy of some optimism). Indeed, in practice, practitioners will also be aware of times when individuals decline an opportunity to engage in group therapeutic interventions.

Charura (2012) noted the following in attempting to identify the curative factor of group therapy as an intervention:

It is through the pure activity of meeting and being in a group which provides the right conditions by giving the opportunity to explore one's life scripts; be challenged on resistance and denial; be listened to and be accepted; reflect on past failures/relapses and effects of one's lifestyle and impact it had on social networks. It is also through being in relationship with others and hearing their similar or different experiences and having one's maintenance of abstinence affirmed which is freeing. This allows a psychological re-adjusting process consequently enabling the individual to go into 'the real world' and be more free and abstinent. (2012:23)

Having referred generically to group interventions, we stress here the difference between group psychotherapy, which is facilitated by a qualified psychotherapist offering a specific therapeutic modality, and group interventions, which different practitioners can facilitate. In Table 6.1 below we summarize specific group psychotherapy practices/modalities and provide brief descriptions.

Modality	Underlying assumptions of the model
Psychoanalytic Group	People always seek to behave in ways which reduce the anxieties they feel in relation to themselves and others. This can be related to their experience of their primary family. As a result, they take up roles in groups to manage their internal responses in relation to 'group tension' which is a result of the conflicting needs of each individual and the group as a whole. This 'classical' approach to psychoanalysis in the group setting places emphasis on group dynamics in relation to the individuals' intrapersonal and interpersonal processes. In dual diagnosis work, individual *intrapsychic* (internal psychological) dynamics and their interconnectedness to substance use remain the central focus.
Existential	From a traditionally existential perspective, the focus of an existential group is on the subjective experience of group members working with how to respond to life's limitations, and the intersubjectivity of living, temporality, acceptance of the givens of life and the focus on authenticity are all central tenets (Paul 2012). The existential therapist works through exploring alternative ways (other than substance use) and healthier ways of managing psychological distress. The aim is to foster meaningful and authentic relationships between members of the group as well as working with members in confronting and working through existential, universal life issues.
Person-Centred	The group facilitator's role is to communicate, and thus model, empathy, congruence (genuineness) and unconditional positive regard for group members. Where the 'original group', i.e. the client's family, may have contributed to psychological distress, and consequently the client turning to substances, the person-centred group contributes a template for relating. Typically, the focus is on intrapsychic and interpersonal dynamics and not on interpretation or the dynamics of the group.

Table 6.1 Different group practices offered in working with dual diagnoses

Table 6.1 (Continued)

Modality	Underlying assumptions of the model
Gestalt	The group aims to overcome the blocks and unfinished issues that prevent the individual from being fully alive and fulfilled in the here and now, and to enable the individual to take personal responsibility. Group members are actively encouraged to 'make contact' with others in the group to work towards full contact with self and others. The group is the medium for therapy; it is the 'therapeutic field' all members are located in.
Cognitive Behavioural Therapy (CBT)	The therapist's task is to assess and treat group members using therapeutic programmes. While CBT programmes are often psychoeducational and didactic in nature, research indicates the therapeutic relationship is pivotal in relation to successful outcome.

Source: Adapted from Paul and Charura (2014).

So far we have outlined and explored the 12-step programme approach and different group interventions. In the next section we focus on family and systemic interventions in working with clients. We draw from research, from literature and from our experience of working and supervising practitioners in substance use services.

Key protocols informing family work perspectives

In our writing on key points to consider in working with families, we draw from the *Dual Diagnosis: Good Practice Handbook* published by Turning Point, which outlined good practice in dual diagnosis in different health services and partnerships throughout the UK (Aram 2007). We also draw from the Leeds joint safeguarding protocol (2010) termed *Think Family, Work Family*, which has been developed by the Leeds Safeguarding Children Board, the Leeds Safeguarding Adults Partnership, and the Safer Leeds Executive. This partnership is by organizations who have recognized a need to work better together and to find new ways of working with children, adults and families. It is noted that:

> A different approach is needed because we know that to improve the lives of those children facing the biggest challenges, we need to identify, understand and resolve the problems of the adult parents. A small minority of families struggle with a long, intergenerational history of linked complex problems, such as mental illness, abuse, learning disabilities, domestic violence or substance misuse and the evidence shows that traditional approaches cannot make the difference – a joined up approach that helps both children and adults is needed. (Leeds Safeguarding Children Board 2010:2)

As noted in Figure 6.1, there are different factors which can impact on individuals and their families. It is also noted that the presence of a dual diagnosis and additional vulnerabilities for adults as parents/carers does not automatically preclude the possibility of good parenting or being a good partner in a relationship. It is therefore important that when a practitioner is working with an individual client, they take a holistic approach which considers the client

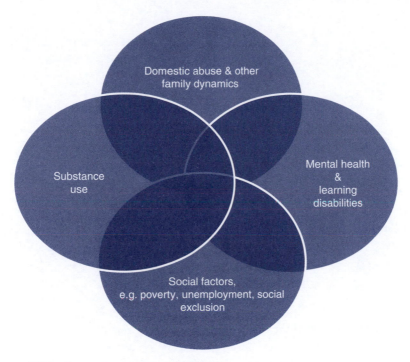

Figure 6.1 Wider factors impacting on individuals

they are working with as a member of a family who will be affected by her or his substance use or deterioration in mental health, which in turn will impact on each family member.

> **Reflective question**
> • *What may be possible impacts of a dual diagnosis on the family system?*
>   *Figure 6.2 below outlines the importance of having a holistic view of the client, incorporating and positioning them at the centre of her or his family and also of service provision.*

The importance of placing the family at the centre of practice is increasingly being acknowledged. It has, however, been noted that the needs of families of those with a dual diagnosis have been largely ignored in service provision. This neglect is attributed to consequences of the lack of a family orientation in professional training and practice, as well as different models of family functioning, which often means some families have negative experience of services and stigma, and therefore they do not engage (Copello et al. 2005). This is by no means a new phenomenon; Fadden (1997) established that despite some of the best available evidence being in favour of family interventions for psychosis, and a range of training programmes for staff, implementation was still patchy – and it is our experience that this remains so. In order to show some of the areas of risk and impact for families and communities, we have noted certain points in Table 6.2 below.

Aram (2007) noted, as highlighted by the Social Exclusion Unit's report *Mental Health and Social Exclusion* (2004), that services need to reach beyond their own boundaries and

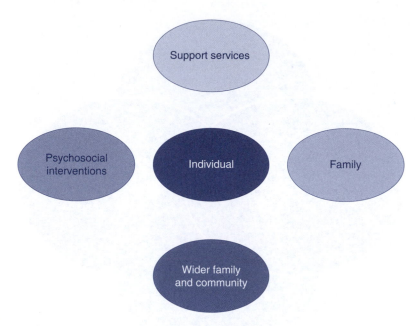

Figure 6.2 A holistic view of the client, considering family

Family factors/effects associated with dual diagnosis include:

- the stress of supporting an individual family member;
- financial strain and a family living in poverty;
- the impact on children of having a parent that uses alcohol or other drugs and/or that has positive attitudes towards drug use;
- the impact of stress in the family affecting a child's academic achievement and lack of attachment or commitment to school with early and persistent problem behaviours, such as misbehaving in school or fighting with other children;
- in single parent families there is a risk of neglect of young children;
- there is also a risk to the individual with the dual diagnosis of abuse/exploitation where he or she may be vulnerable because of mental ill health.

Table 6.2 Possible impacts of a dual diagnosis on the family

recognize that people's difficulties are not purely health related, but are compounded and influenced by a range of other factors, including housing, employment or social isolation. Involving families and carers is therefore one way in which those with dual diagnoses can be supported.

Involving families and carers

Many families feel that professionals do not trust them with information and that, consequently, they need to be very assertive to extract it. However, it is postulated that carers have a wealth of knowledge and personal experiences through living with and/or caring for someone with a dual diagnosis, and hence working with them can often also be a good option in supporting the individual client (Aram 2007). On the other hand, however, it is also important to recognize that many people with dual diagnoses have no contact with their families and are very socially isolated. For such clients, holistic support from practitioners is pivotal (Aram 2007), especially towards supporting individuals in building a network that is of worth to them.

A five–step approach

A five-step approach model for working with families was developed by Copello et al. (2000). We have provided an adapted model for working with clients with dual diagnoses and their families in Figure 6.3 below.

Copello et al. (2000) demonstrated that the five-step approach was effective in reducing family members' signs of strain (a significant reduction in both physical and psychological symptoms). They also demonstrated that this approach enabled positive altering and enhancement of families' coping mechanisms. Although this approach has been used mainly in primary care, Copello et al. (2005) noted that this approach has also been tested with a small sample in the specialist secondary care setting, showing positive results and demonstrating that the intervention can lead to changes in coping, improvements in social support and reduction in physical and psychological symptoms.

A tension here would be in how the model may construe the person with a dual diagnosis as being the one with the problem and for whom others provide care and support. Other family approaches view a family as a system that is interdependent and so avoid formulating

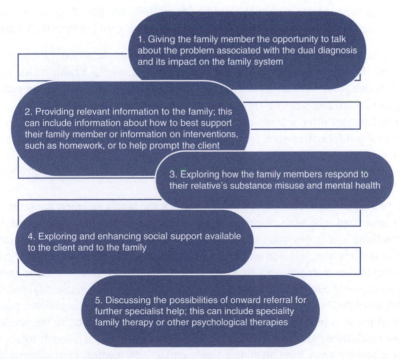

1. Giving the family member the opportunity to talk about the problem associated with the dual diagnosis and its impact on the family system

2. Providing relevant information to the family; this can include information about how to best support their family member or information on interventions, such as homework, or to help prompt the client

3. Exploring how the family members respond to their relative's substance misuse and mental health

4. Exploring and enhancing social support available to the client and to the family

5. Discussing the possibilities of onward referral for further specialist help; this can include speciality family therapy or other psychological therapies

Figure 6.3 A five-step model for working with families

ideas of who is the 'sick one', and in doing so encourage all family members to engage in strategies of change that are mutually supportive.

From our experience working in different services, non-substance using partners of individuals with a dual diagnosis can often be a positive influence in enabling motivation to change. Although we won't go into detail here, we note that couples therapy can be a therapeutic modality in which couples can be supported. In line with this, the National Institute for Clinical Excellence (NICE) (2007) guidelines for dual diagnosis noted that behavioural couple's therapy should be considered for people who are in close contact with a non-drug-misusing partner and who present for treatment of stimulant or opioid misuse (including those who continue to use illicit drugs while receiving opioid maintenance treatment or after completing opioid detoxification).

Behavioural family therapy (BFT) and cognitive behavioural (CB) interventions

There is an established body of literature that supports the use of BFT with families in which a person is experiencing psychosis. In summary, the research finds that in families where communication is critical, hostile and/or over-involved (sometimes referred to as 'expressed emotion') and there are high levels of face-to-face contact between the person with psychosis and family around them, relapse is significantly higher. In a normalizing sense, such a circumstance would be demanding of a lot of people, and, also, having someone in the family experiencing psychosis (as well as many other pressures) places great pressure on the family. CB and BFT aim to up-skill families that are feeling this demand and that may even have exhausted their coping. As mentioned above, despite this good evidence, BFT- and CB-based family work is not routinely offered. However, the principles are sound and are covered briefly in the following list:

- An early task is assessment work with individual family members to get their view of the situation. This can involve assessing their knowledge of mental health issues, unhelpful causal models, their own stress and well-being. It is understood, that in the main, these assessment discussions can be then taken into the family meetings.
- Two practitioners offer a three-phase intervention, with the first phase being that of giving health information such as information about what is distress and mental health, recovery, treatments, rights and access, stress and being healthy. Then, the family is asked to schedule a weekly family meeting with a changing chairperson to undertake homework tasks together.
- Phase two is communication skills training in which the family members are taken through highly structured rehearsals of explicit communication. It generally begins with learning and practising how to give positive remarks/feedback, and then going on to communicating negative feelings later. This is so that a family feels the benefit of positive contact first, which sets some further norms to work to. While such training can feel stilted in the early stage, the practitioner should be encouraging and often this can be an emotionally moving piece of work when family members begin to acknowledge even small but significant positives.
- The third phase is teaching problem-solving skills that aim to mobilize the whole family to their resolution. Problem definition is a key aspect to finding a relevant focus, and the family is steered away from blaming a single person and towards joint ownership of the problem. Problem-solving is active and seen as a relevant aspect of the family meetings.

In addition to working with single families, there has been some established success in delivering interventions in multi-family groups using BFT- and CB-based approaches (McFarlane 2004; Whitehurst et al. 2004). This has a number of advantages, not least of which is social contact, sharing ideas for coping and getting access, and reducing costs by seeing many families at one meeting.

Behavioural couples therapy

BCT is a structured therapy based on cognitive behavioural principles for behaviour change. Its major components include:

- cognitive behavioural strategies that will help the client to stop using and acquire the skills to respond to both substance use specific behaviours and general life problems;
- strategies that teach family members to support the individual's efforts to change, and develop better skills to cope with and communicate around substance use and mental health-related topics;
- strategies to improve communication and problem-solving skills; this also includes helping each other to recognize when mental health is deteriorating;
- behavioural contracts between the couple to support the use of medication.

We have noted positive outcomes when such behavioural couples therapy consists of at least 12 weekly sessions and focuses on:

- the client's drug misuse;
- the client's mental health;
- the impact of the client's dual diagnosis and substance use on the couple.

Basic family and systemic therapy concepts

Family and systemic therapy has been attributed to the family and systemic therapy field. If practitioners have an understanding of systemic concepts and the impact of dual diagnosis on family dynamics, they will be better equipped to achieve successful outcomes in working with their clients and clients' families. In the following section we outline some basic systemic principles.

Systemic therapists draw on a number of theoretical principles which provide a framework for working with therapeutic relationships. 'Systemic therapy' is an umbrella term for a number of distinct models of practice. These include structural family therapy, brief strategic therapy, Milan systemic therapy, solution-focused therapy, functional family therapy, collaborative-dialogical therapy, and narrative therapy, (Dallos & Draper 2005: page). Family and systemic interventions focus on attempting to understand the family system and to facilitate therapeutic change. In order for this to be achieved, systemic therapists use particular skills, including 'circular questions' to which there are three key aspects: circularity, neutrality and hypothesizing. These are understood as follows:

- **Circularity** constitutes asking questions which enable the family to make new connections and think differently and in new ways about their situation.
- **Neutrality** is the second aspect of circular questioning, and this concept protects the therapist from being forcibly drawn into a family's system and taking sides, and from

conflicting patterns, and hence this serves the purpose and implication of lack of bias (Dallos & Draper 2005; Schwartz & Nichols 2006).

- **Hypothesizing** aids the family in making connections between parts of the issues/stories the individual members bring and the actions associated with such stories. The therapist formulates a hypothesis which suggests different patterns of connections (Cecchin 1987; Jones 1993). Tomm (2006) suggested that hypothesizing refers to the therapist's/team's formulation of alternative explanations or maps regarding the problems presented by the family. He further stated that the content of a hypothesis is derived from several sources, such as information available about the family, behavioural observations, and also the therapist's and team's past clinical experience with other families.

Consider the following case study.

> ❏ **Case study 6.1 Working with a family**
>
> Tom attends for a family session with his wife, Jane, and two teenage daughters. In the session Tom starts to talk about how he is struggling to not, on occasion, use drugs in addition to his methadone, which he has been stable on for six months. He states that he finds that he tends to use when he starts to feel depressed. He also states that his wife and daughters gang up against him and don't understand him or his problems. He also states that his youngest son, Jack, has started to refuse to go to school. Tom's wife states she has thought of leaving him because she and the children feel stuck as a family.

> **Reflective questions**
>
> *As a practitioner, think about what approach you can take with this family:*
>
> - *What are the issues and conversations that may help to move things in a positive direction?*
> - *What hypothesis can you come up with about what may be going on for Tom and his family?*

In practice, it is important for practitioners to firstly ask the family about their view of what is going on within their 'system' (Dallos & Draper 2005; McGodric et al. 2005). The family's own hypothesis may be articulated in a linear format. Following their own explanation or hypothesis of what's going on, the practitioner/team should look for something else to identify or acknowledge previously unrecognized patterns in order to develop new alternatives. Circular questions that can be asked include:

- When Tom lapses, how does that impact on your relationship as a family?
- How do you relate to Tom's dual diagnosis?

In working with families, the practitioner's curiosity, coupled with a naïve standpoint of not knowing and taking a non-expert position, enables the family to work openly with the practitioner. This is in large part to make sure that alliances do not develop with particular family members, and is also about being open to the possibility that there is much not being talked about that may need to be made explicit and clarified to maximize mutual understanding. Furthermore, in formulating a hypothesis about the impact of the client's dual diagnosis on the family system, care has to be taken in understanding each family member. Dallos and Draper (2005) suggest that hypotheses which do not fit can often lead to the family dropping out of engaging with the service, or if the family remains engaged, its members may feel quite puzzled, without help and misunderstood.

So far we have outlined different group approaches and explored the importance of working with families and their presenting dynamics in relation to the impact of a client's dual diagnosis on the family system. The next section offers a summary of working with families and examples of interventions and approaches that are being used in Leeds' dual diagnosis services and have proved to be effective. Table 6.3 summarizes essential aspects of the models in use with families and also draws on the NICE guidelines (2007), which we have summarized below.

Person-centred care	For practitioners to be competent and focused on the specific client's needs, and not a 'one size fits' all approach.
Safeguarding and safety first	For practitioners to be aware of the importance of safety for all, including those within the wider community, and services working with the individual. The needs of the child are paramount, and therefore any concerns about a child's safety and welfare must be responded to by any practitioner.
	If making home visits on your own as a practitioner, always consider your own safety first and remain alert to any risks.
	Clients with dual diagnoses may also be subject to a wide range of risks including exploitation and abuse, particularly when their mental health deteriorates. Practitioners must therefore be aware of the wider impacts of a client's dual diagnosis.
Permanency	The majority of children and families want to stay together, and so where this is possible, and safe to do so, practitioners should provide the support to enable this to happen.
Valuing relationships	It is important to understand that no one exists in isolation, and so it is important to think of the wider context and the relationships with people important to clients that the practitioner may work with. This includes friends, family and their local community.
	As we have seen in Chapter 5, the therapeutic relationship is essential for increasing opportunities for better outcomes.
Competent and collaborative working	Practitioner competency is a key ingredient of successful outcomes. These competencies should include:
	• knowledge of the impact and complexity of having a dual diagnosis;
	• knowledge of substances and mental health problems – if you know what substance is being used then find out more about it;
	• the ability to work collaboratively with clients, their families and other involved agencies towards agreed therapeutic goals;
	• the ability to work with a diverse population and understand their different needs.

Table 6.3 Summary of the *Think Family, Work Family* approach

Table 6.3 (Continued)

Partnership approach	Working in partnership across agencies will help make the client and family experience better service provision. Working in partnership with families and drawing on their strengths is key to therapeutic success.
	Where consent for information sharing is given by clients, such consent helps them and their families not to tell the same narrative of their experience and history every time they see a new practitioner.
Restorative practice	Restorative practice is underpinned by values of empathy, respect, honesty, acceptance, congruence, responsibility and mutual accountability in seeking to make change.

Source: Adapted from the Leeds *Think Family, Work Family* protocol and *The Leeds Parenting Resource Kit* (2008).

Similar to CBT being an integrated therapy approach, there has for some time been a small but significant move towards integrating BFT and systemic family therapies. Innovative writings such as those by Burbach (1996) and Burbach and Stanbridge (1998) look to blend both approaches within the family work to the advantage and strengths of both models, for instance the engagement with plausible causal and explanatory models in systemic approaches with the structured skills-based communication and problem-solving training.

NICE guidelines (2007) – supporting families and carers

Staff should ask families and carers about, and discuss concerns regarding, the impact of drug misuse on themselves and other family members, including children.
Staff should also:

- offer family members and carers an assessment of their personal, social and mental health needs;
- provide verbal and written information and advice on the impact of drug misuse on service users, families and carers;
- provide information about, and facilitate contact with, support groups, such as self-help groups specifically focused on addressing families' and carers' needs;
- offer information, help to identify sources of stress and promote effective coping strategies.

Having recently gathered information at a dual diagnosis network for practitioners working in different services in and around local services in the city of Leeds, we have noted below what is already being offered as a model of good practice.

Summary of what practitioners in Leeds are already doing

1. Conducting effective dual diagnosis risk assessments;
2. Encouraging families to access services;
3. Active outreach work and liaising with treatment providers;

4. Having a dual diagnosis network with monthly meetings in which professionals come to share knowledge and discuss dual diagnosis issues;
5. Maintaining close relationship with schools;
6. Offering pre-birth assessments for pregnant women who access services;
7. Having psychosocial interventions specialist services which offer CBT, psychodynamic and family intervention therapies;
8. Engaging families in relapse prevention groups;
9. Facilitating social behaviour and network therapy groups;
10. Helping parents to access services.

Having outlined good practice relating to working with clients and engaging their families, we acknowledge that one of the major challenges of working with those with dual diagnoses is their limited social networks. We will now explore another therapeutic intervention of working with clients, namely social behaviour and network therapy.

Social behaviour and network therapy (SBNT)

Although different psychosocial interventions have strengths, integration of a coherent intervention which specifically focuses on the client's social network is also important. This will link the client and the family back to broader goals for work together or therapy – we might ask of the client and family, 'At the end of our work together, how will your life be different?' Copello et al. (2002) noted that SBNT was developed with this aim in order to produce a social intervention that could be used with the whole range of clients presenting for alcohol treatment, whether they already had social networks or not. The aim of SBNT is to maximize the client's available positive social support for a change in drinking behaviour (Copello et al. 2002). Different authors have highlighted that SBNT brings together elements of network therapy (Galanter & Kaskutas 2008), social aspects of the community reinforcement approach (e.g. Meyers & Smith 1995), relapse prevention and approaches with family and concerned others (Copello et al. 2000, 2002). SBNT integrates aspects of these approaches within a unified social treatment approach that has theoretical coherence and is based on the principle that a fundamental ingredient for successful treatment outcomes is the availability of social support for change (Copello et al. 2002). The therapist's task is to work towards this goal with the problem drinker and those members of her or his social network who are willing to support the efforts to change.

> ❏ Case study 6.2 Social behaviour and network therapy with a client
>
> James has a diagnosis of bipolar mood disorder. He says in a meeting with you that his drinking has spiralled out of control. In the past he has had moments of sobriety. At present he is motivated and willing to engage in the treatment plan. He explains that he is isolated and does not have any contact with any of his friends anymore. It is considered that SBNT will help.

In order to outline the application of SBNT in practice, we will draw on the different stages of SBNT using case study 6.2.

SBNT stages

Phase 1: Identification of the network

The first step in SBNT is to identify who is in the client's social network. Along with this it is also important to find out which network members are supportive of change in the focal person's drinking.

Copello et al. (2002) suggest that people would be ineligible for network membership if:

I. they have a drug or alcohol problem themselves or have shown in the past that they promote and support problematic drinking;
II. they have a superior or inferior relationship in terms of power to the focal person (e.g. managers at work);
III. they are under the age of 16.

We have illustrated in Figure 6.4 below a way that a practitioner can start to help a client elicit their social network.

In this first phase of therapy, time is spent identifying people in the problem substance user's social network that might be supportive of change in substance using behaviour, followed by attempts to contact potential network members and, if appropriate, invite them to take part in later sessions. The practitioner is active in supporting the client to make contact with her or his network. Figure 6.5 below shows an example of James's (case study 6.2) identified social network. Although at the start he stated he had no friends and had a limited network, through the SBNT session with his key worker they were able to draft a network map.

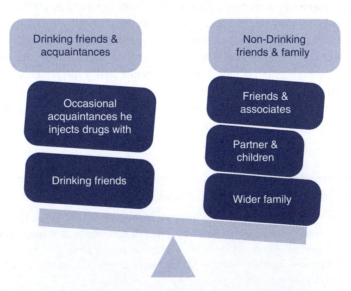

Figure 6.4 Eliciting appropriate social network members for SBNT work

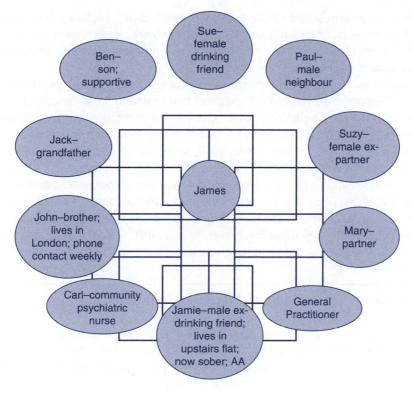

Figure 6.5 James's network map

Phase 2: Building/engaging/mobilizing the social network

This second phase of treatment is directed towards building, engaging and mobilizing a social network to support change to the substance use. Core elements of this phase include communication, exploration of how network members are coping, enhancing social support and network lapse/relapse management. For clients with dual diagnoses, this network relapse includes a plan of how the network can support the client if her or his mental health starts to deteriorate. In this phase of the SBNT, elective topics are discussed. These topics can include education about dual diagnoses, drugs, withdrawals and facilitation of alternative joint activities (Copello et al. 2002).

Phase 3: Preparing for the future

The third phase of SBNT intervention focuses on the future. The aim of this phase is to create conditions for the network to continue to provide support for change in the person's substance use post-treatment (Copello et al. 2002). This final phase is covered within the last sessions and focuses on planning for the future and maintaining the progress achieved, as well as responding to any client lapses/relapses or, for those with a dual diagnosis, creating a plan for managing and seeking support at the early onset of mental health deterioration.

Having identified the centrality of the network members, it is important to state that although they are key in helping individuals with substance use problem (e.g. alcohol dependence), the focus should remain on supporting the client as opposed to the concerned network members' own needs. It is noted that if any network members have their own needs that are brought to the fore, they are only addressed if they are relevant to the development of social support for change (Copello et al. 2002).

In Chapter 4 we noted the importance of practitioners having an awareness and valuing issues of difference and diversity. We highlighted that central to therapeutic practice are the dimensions of the client's ethnicity, gender, class, sexual orientation, disability, religion and age. We believe that these areas are also central to any work practitioners do in working with groups and families because demographic, social and other factors from these seven dimensions may impact on how clients respond to or access treatment.

So far in this chapter we have outlined the different group interventions that are used in working with clients who present with dual diagnoses. We have also presented the evidence base for working with families and useful interventions when working with dual diagnosis, which include five-step behaviour family therapy and SBNT; to end this chapter we outline below the challenges of working in different settings.

The challenges of working in different settings

- Collaboration and partnership: due to different funding streams, and professional differences, partnership working (including data sharing and cross referral between services) may be needed; however, these may yet be a challenge for practitioners because of such things as organizational policies.
- Current limitations in funding: practitioners may find themselves having to work to brief interventions, and yet are noticing that clients with dual diagnosis often need longer term support.
- Working in services that do not address dual diagnoses but only substance use, and yet encountering clients with dual diagnoses.
- Witnessing or experiencing distressing narratives or circumstances such as serious mental ill health, child neglect, violence and domestic abuse.
- Involvement in safeguarding issues which may involve removal of children from their parents' homes.
- Limited resources for adequate training and skills required to be a competent practitioner working with dual diagnoses.
- Unmanageable/ever increasing caseloads.
- A lack of family or group work ethos in service planning and design.
- Limited access to services due to different cultural and demographic challenges, e.g. certain groups may have a different belief system or support system (such as faith groups) which means they may not access services.
- Fear of stigma and shame in certain minority ethnic groups may mean family members do not engage in family-based interventions for supporting their family member who may have a dual diagnosis.
- The poor strategic use of practitioners who are trained to deliver group and family work.

In concluding this chapter and having noted evidence-based interventions as well as challenges of working in different services, we advocate for appropriate supervision for all training (qualified and non-qualified) practitioners. This enables workers to get appropriate support and training, and to develop the necessary professional competencies required for this specialist work.

Key messages

To help the reader to understand elements in working with groups and families, the following were discussed:

- Working with groups of clients presenting with a dual diagnosis requires a multi-faceted approach in which the practitioner has an awareness that although he or she may be a case/key worker for one client, inclusion and consideration of the client's wider system is important.
- There are a range of group approaches, including 12-step approaches/programmes, and a wide range of group psychotherapies, all of which aim to address the psychological and behavioural challenges that having a dual diagnosis presents.
- The range of group processes and dynamics that may emerge from working with groups include resistance and responses to group endings and separation. The awareness of these dynamics is important for practitioners working with clients who have dual diagnoses to understand.
- Key protocols informing family work focus on the centrality of family inclusion in treatment models as an important aspect of dual diagnosis work, as families help to go beyond working with the individual and encourage practitioners to consider the wider systemic challenges, implications or benefits that different treatments or interventions have.
- Some useful family interventions when working with dual diagnosis which practitioners should consider are a five-step approach, behavioural family therapy, behavioural couples therapy, basic family systemic therapy concepts and social behaviour and network therapy. It is important for practitioners to always consider the role of contextual, cultural and demographic factors which may impact on service delivery, client engagement and recovery.
- Consideration of the challenges of working in different settings and limitations in funding which impact on service provision are also important for practitioners to constantly consider in order to ensure continual development of evidence-based interventions.

REFERENCES

Alcoholics Anonymous (AA) (1939). *Alcoholics Anonymous.* New York: Alcoholics Anonymous World Services, Inc.

Aram, L. (Ed.) (2007). *Dual Diagnosis: Good Practice Handbook.* London: Turning Point.

Bogenschutz, M.P., Geppert, C.M., & George, J. (2006). The role of twelve-step approaches in dual diagnosis treatment and recovery. *American Journal on Addictions*, 15, 50–60.

Burbach, F.R. (1996). Family based interventions in psychosis – An overview of, and comparison between, family therapy and family management approaches. *Journal of Mental Health*, 5(2), 111–134.

Burbach, F.R., & Stanbridge, R.I. (1998). A family intervention in psychosis service integrating the systemic and family management approaches. *Journal of Family Therapy*, 20, 311–325.

Cecchin, G. (1987). Hypothesising, circularity and neutrality revisited: An invitation to curiosity. *Family Process*, 26, 405–413.

Charura, D. (2012). Demystifying the curative factor of group psychotherapy in rehab. *Addiction Today*, 23(135), 22–23.

Chi, F.W., Satre, D.D., & Weisner, C. (2006). Chemical dependency patients with co-occurring psychiatric diagnoses: Service patterns and 1-year outcomes. *Alcoholism: Clinical and Experimental Research*, 30, 851–859.

Copello, A., Orford, J., Hodgson, R., Tober, G., & Barrett, C. (2002). Social behaviour and network therapy: Basic principles and early experiences. *Addictive Behaviors*, 27, 345–366.

Copello, A., Orford, J., Velleman, R., Templeton, L., & Krishnan M. (2000). Methods for reducing alcohol and drug related family harm in non-specialist settings. *Journal of Mental Health*, 9, 319–333.

Copello, A., Velleman, R., & Templeton, L. (2005). Family interventions in the treatment of alcohol and drug problems. *Drug & Alcohol Review*, 24(4), 369–385.

Dallos, R., & Draper, R. (2005). *An Introduction to Family Therapy: Systemic Theory and Practice* (2nd Ed.). Buckingham: Open University Press.

Fadden, G. (1997). Implementation of family interventions in routine clinical practice following staff training programmes: A cause for major concern. *Journal of Mental Health*, 6, 599–612.

Galanter, M. (2000). Self-help treatment for combined addiction and mental illness. *Psychiatric Service*, 51, 977–979.

Handmaker, N., Packard, M., & Comforti, K. (2002). Motivational interviewing in the treatment of dual disorders. In Miller, W.R., & Rollnick, S. (Eds) *Motivational Interviewing: Preparing People for Change*. New York: The Guilford Press.

Herman, S.E. et al. (2000). Longitudinal effects of integrated treatment on alcohol use for persons with serious mental illness and substance use disorders. *Journal of Behavioral Health Services & Research*, 27, 286–302.

Horsfall, J., Cleary, M., Hunt, G.E., & Walter, G. (2009). Psychosocial treatments for people with co-occurring severe mental illness and substance use disorders (dual diagnosis): A review of empirical evidence. *Harvard Review of Psychiatry*, 17(1), 24–34.

Jones, E. (1993). *Family Systems: Developments in the Milan-Systemic Therapies*. Chichester: Wiley.

Jordan, L.C., Davidson, W.S., Herman, S.E., & Bootsmiller, B.J. (2002). Involvement in 12-step programs among persons with dual diagnoses. *Psychiatric Services*, 53, 894–896.

Laudet, A.B., Magura, S., Cleland, C.M., Vogel, H.S., Knight, E.L., & Rosenblum, A. (2004). The effect of 12-step-based fellowship participation on abstinence among dually diagnosed persons: A two-year longitudinal study. *Journal of Psychoactive Drugs*, 36, 207–216.

Laudet, A.B., Morgen, K., & White, W.L. (2006). The role of social supports, spirituality, religiousness, life meaning and affiliation with 12-step fellowships in quality of life satisfaction among individuals in recovery from alcohol and drug problems. *Alcoholism Treatment Quarterly*, 24, 33–73.

Leeds Parenting Unit (2008). *Leeds Parenting Unit Resource Kit: Working with Families Affected by Substance Misuse*. Leeds: Children Leeds.

Leeds Safeguarding Children Board (2010). *Think Family, Work Family: A Joint Safeguarding Protocol for Coordinating the Support Families Receive from Services Working with Children and Adults, Where Parenting Capacity is Impacted.* Leeds: Leeds Safeguarding Children Board, the Leeds Safeguarding Adults Board, and the Safer Leeds Executive.

Luke, D.A., Ribisl, K.M., Walton, M.A., & Davidson, W.S. (2002). Assessing the diversity of personal beliefs about addiction: Development of the addiction belief inventory. *Substance Use & Misuse,* 37, 89–120.

McFarlane, W.R. (Ed.) (2004). *Multifamily Groups in the Treatment of Severe Psychiatric Disorders.* New York: The Guilford Press.

McGoldrick, M., Giordano, J., & Garcia-Preto, N. (2005). *Ethnicity & Family Therapy* (3rd Ed.). New York: The Guilford Press.

Mueser, K., Noordsy, D., Drake, R., & Fox, L. (2003). *Integrated Treatment for Dual Disorders.* New York: Guilford Press.

National Institute for Clinical Excellence (2007). Drug misuse – Psychosocial interventions. <http://www.nice.org.uk/Guidance/CG51/chapter/related-nice-guidance> [Accessed July 2014].

Noordsy, D.L., Schwab, B., Fox, L., & Drake, R.E. (1996). The role of self-help programs in the rehabilitation of persons with severe mental illness and substance use disorders. *Community Mental Health Journal,* 32, 71–81.

Ouimette, P.C., Moos, R.H., & Finney, J.W. (2003). PTSD treatment and 5-year remission among patients with substance use and posttraumatic stress disorders. *Journal of Consulting and Clinical Psychology,* 71, 410–414.

Paul, S. (2012). Group counselling and therapy. In Feltham, C., & Horton, I. (Eds) *The Sage Handbook of Counselling and Psychotherapy* (3rd Ed.). London: Sage.

Roback, H.B. (2000). Adverse outcomes in group psychotherapy. *Journal of Psychotherapy Practice and Research,* 9(3), 113–122.

Schwartz, R.B., & Nichols, M.P. (2006). *Family Therapy: Concepts and Methods* (7th Ed.). Boston, MA: Pearson/Allyn and Bacon.

Timko, C., Sutkowi, A., & Moos, R. (2010). Patients with dual diagnoses or substance use disorders only: 12-step group participation and 1-year outcomes. *Substance Use & Misuse,* 45(4), 613–627.

Tomm, K., (2006). *Evaluation Family Therapy.* New York: Brunner & Mazel.

Whitehurst, T., Ridolfi, M.E., & Gunderson, J. (2004). Multiple family group treatment for borderline personality disorder. In Hofmann, S.G., & Tompson, M.C. (Eds) *Treating Chronic and Severe Mental Disorders: A Handbook of Empirically Supported Interventions.* New York: The Guilford Press.

Yalom, I.D., & Lescz, M. (2005). *The Theory and Practice of Group Psychotherapy.* New York: Basic Books.

7 Working in Community Settings: Dual Diagnosis and the Recovery Movement in a Community Context

Chapter Summary

This aims of this chapter are for the reader to develop an understanding of:

- the lived experience of challenges faced by professionals working in the community with clients who have a dual diagnosis;
- the recovery movement within the community;
- the importance of the integration of harm reduction and recovery-oriented practices;
- the social model of disability as a route towards access.

Mental illness is never greeted with open arms but if there is a drug or alcohol as well it's even worse.

(Coombes & Wratten 2007:387)

The quote above is from a community mental health nurse who worked with clients who have dual diagnoses, and it is a befitting start of this chapter. In Chapters 5 and 6, the focus was on working with individual clients, their families and their networks. However, working with communities is equally important because clients often spend the majority of their lives in and amongst communities. Working with communities is sometimes a difficult prospect for seconding mental health and for dependency services because often it is viewed as the preserve of community development and public health areas of practice, and the individualized model of care most services work to is threatened by the prospect of involving non-family members in care and support. There is a sense of the above quote referring to a lack of warmth and the stigma that having a dual diagnosis can attract within communities. The focus of this chapter is to outline and explore community development and community action in dealing with systemic causation underlying both mental health and substance use. It also aims to highlight some community-led recovery approaches in securing long-term independence from substance use and mental health services. As practitioners become more aware of the systemic influence of communities in dual diagnosis and recovery, they become more competent in making informed choices of appropriate interventions for the clients they work with.

We would strongly advocate the use of Day's (2013) *Routes to Recovery via the Community: Mapping User Manual* to support a range of activities towards successful community living for people with dual diagnoses. Many of the practices it advocates are ones we also discuss in this book such as network mapping with clients. The manual gives practical methods for the worker and a clear process to follow. We understand that in working with clients with dual diagnosis there are multiple problems the clients face, and by extension, these can become challenges to the practitioner. Persistence and patience become as important as technical skill in such circumstances, and it is also important to believe that clients with dual diagnoses have the same right to a good life within a community as anyone else.

We start this chapter by identifying some of the challenges of community contexts that have emerged from research and from our work with different organizations that work with clients who have a dual diagnosis.

The lived experience of challenges faced by professionals working in the community

Coombes and Wratten (2007) conducted a key study on the lived experience of community mental health nurses working with people who have dual diagnosis. From their study we note the following:

- Working with clients who have dual diagnoses was experienced as hard and challenging, not often rewarding and often seeming like an impossible challenge. It was found that within the community, clients were hard to engage and often appeared helpless and lacking hope.
- The experience of practitioners was that many clients were reluctant to accept help.

- Practitioners noted that there was a need for specialist knowledge, skills and support for work with clients with dual diagnoses. The increased need for information and training about dual diagnosis was noted as paramount.
- Practitioners noted difficulties with the process of assessing clients with a dual diagnosis, acknowledging that a comprehensive assessment of the person who has a dual diagnosis is an important initial component of care. However, there are several barriers to achieving this.

In Chapter 4 we discussed the importance of the relationship and of assessment as a basis for both care planning activities and also working towards a shared formulation of a client's problems. Coombes and Wratten (2007) also found difficulties in undertaking assessments, including the following:

- When conducting assessment in the community, often the client's mental state and level of intoxication makes obtaining accurate information difficult.
- Information gathered during assessment is on an ad hoc basis because of the chaotic nature of some of the clients' lives. Agencies and organizations that are involved in their care do not always have a coherent record nor do they communicate it across services.

These reported experiences highlight that community practitioners found the work challenging, and they stated the importance of training and that many dually diagnosed clients required long-term commitment in order to build trusting relationships. Coombes and Wratten (2007) discussed the difficulties with the process of change regarding clients who have a dual diagnosis. They stated many of the professionals they interviewed were deeply concerned about the destructive behaviour of clients, but the professionals reported that many clients appeared unmotivated to change. This lack of motivation, and absence of change for long periods of time, was one of the most difficult aspects of providing care and support. In Chapters 5 and 6 we outlined how experiencing mental ill-health and using substances impacts on motivation. As we have noted, practitioner training in motivational interventions and a diverse range of psychosocial interventions may more readily equip practitioners. It may also be the case that acknowledging and seeking supervision in order to accept that some clients may be unwilling to change at present or are in pre-contemplation stages will be helpful. This latter point is a challenge for many practitioners who state that there are external pressures for practitioners to deal with the ever-increasing numbers of dually diagnosed clients. Some community psychiatric nurses who responded to Coombes and Wratten (2007) noted that there is pressure from the general public for health and social services 'to do something' about people with such problems as those found in dual diagnosis. It seems there are limited numbers of agencies that can support individuals with 'substance use disorders' and mental health problems, and consequently community mental health professionals take the case. This is often without regard for existing caseloads, or experience, or expertise of working with dual diagnosis or psychosocial intervention.

A final point noted, as a challenge by community practitioners, is the inappropriateness and inadequacy of the medical model of care for clients who have a dual diagnosis (Coombes & Wratten 2007). As has been noted throughout this book, social and economic problems are inextricably linked to physical and mental health problems that many clients present with. Given this argument, it is therefore clear that a community-based recovery approach which can contribute to dealing with these interlinking problems is likely to be more successful. We briefly discussed ASSET-based outlooks in Chapter 4, but these do rely on mobilizing upwards from within communities even where there is service support. It needs to be understood that given that services often divide clients up by the nature of individual clinical case management approaches, as well as clients' own lack of resources to mobilize, this means that some community approaches seem too far beyond reach.

As noted in the section on challenges faced by professionals working in the community, it is clear that practitioners also need to focus on client-empowering, community-based recovery approaches. These can contribute to dealing with the interlinking social and economic dynamics, and they are likely to be more successful. We present in the following section an outline of some community recovery perspectives. Furthermore, there is a paradox in broad mental health practice where community perspectives are concerned. On the one hand, there is widespread acknowledgement that people with mental health problems are excluded in large part due to the stigma attached to notions of 'madness'. By definition, 'exclusion' means that irrespective of the willingness of a person to participate in their community, there are pressures around them to keep the person on the margins. Intuitively, it would seem that if we took a value-based approach to such a circumstance, then the intervention would be towards those people doing the excluding – it is not the fault of the excluded, and they are likely to be in a position of lower influence. Conversely, mental health services deal, on the whole, with exclusion through interventions on the person who is excluded. We take the view that this is an approach that sustains stigma rather than reduces it, and if we consider mental health as an issue of civil rights, it is tantamount to victim blaming.

Recovery movement within the community

This section looks at the recovery movement firstly from within substance use circles, then looking at a slightly different iteration of recovery as it has come to be understood in the mental health field.

Within the field of substance use, the recovery movement is a multifaceted grassroots effort led by clients who are themselves in recovery from substance use disorders. It began in the mid-1990s, but gained momentum in the mid-2000s (Krentzman 2013). The movement is built on a recovery-oriented, rather than a medical or pathology-oriented, framework from which dual diagnoses are understood. These clients work from an established set of values and goals. They also work collectively to remove obstacles to treatment, support multiple paths to recovery and make larger social systems more supportive of recovery lifestyles (White 2007; Krentzman 2013). Different examples of recover groups include Alcoholics Anonymous (AA); Narcotics Anonymous (NA); Women for Sobriety; and a wide range of recovery community centres, recovery homes, recovery schools, recovery ministries and recovery industries (White et al. 2012). Below we note some of the community recovery groups and brief outlines of their ethos.

Community-led recovery and support programmes

In Chapter 6 we noted a wide range of community-led recovery 12-step approaches in securing long-term independence from substance use and mental health services. These include AA and other services which place the 12 steps at their core. In addition:

Al-Anon family groups provide support to anyone whose life is, or has been, affected by someone else's drinking, regardless of whether that person is still drinking or not (http://www.al-anonuk.org.uk/).

Alateen is for teenage relatives and friends of alcoholics. Alateen is part of Al-Anon and believes that alcoholism is a 'family disease' that affects everyone in the family. Alateen meetings are attended by 12–17 year olds. They meet to share their experiences of having, or having had, a problem drinker in their lives. They help and support each other, and by attending meetings young people gain an understanding of the illness and feel the benefits of realizing they are not alone. They learn that they did not cause this problem and that they are not responsible for their relative's or friend's drinking or behaviour. By sharing their experiences, they find solutions to their problems and hope for the future (http://www.al-anonuk.org.uk/alateen).

Self-Management and Recovery Training (SMART) is one of the new recovery community science-based programmes which are designed to help people manage their recovery from any type of addictive behaviour. SMART helps participants decide whether they have a problem and has a four-point recovery programme:

1. Building and maintaining motivation;
2. Coping with urges;
3. Managing thoughts, feelings and behaviours;
4. Living a balanced life.

Within SMART, labels are thought to not help with recovery and are avoided. People are not called 'addicts', 'alcoholics', 'druggies', 'overeaters', 'sex addicts' or other disparaging labels during meetings (http://www.smartrecovery.org.uk/).

As can be seen, many of these groups are not specific to individuals with dual diagnosis. Aram (2007) noted, however, that there are some limited recovery groups supported by specific services to offer a mix of community skills, nutrition and dietary information, crisis and risk management planning, including access to Mental Health Act assessment. In Chapter 6 we offered a critique to the challenges and benefits that these recovery groups present for clients with a dual diagnosis. However, the strength of the recovery movement is that of being based in the community and being client led. In addition, the recovery movement has organized itself into advocacy groups which actively work to support treatment-friendly legislation, fight stigma and change public opinion (Krentzman 2013). Valentine (2011) argued that as a result of such advocacy, recovering individuals increasingly have a place at the table when policies and legislation are written and reformed, thereby empowering clients and ensuring tailor-made services (Krentzman 2013).

It is suggested that the evidence of the effectiveness of the recovery movement takes three forms:

- evidence for its core ideas;
- evidence of the impact of new recovery institutions; and
- outcome research on interventions that follow a continuity-of-care, versus an acute-care, model (Krentzman 2013).

A further strength of the recovery-focused approach is the use of *peer support* (Campbell 2005). Utilizing dual diagnosis recovery and support groups, as well as developing interagency collaborations with peer-run programmes, offers clients with dual diagnosis an opportunity to gain a sense of hope and belonging as they mutually share knowledge, experiences and self-help strategies regarding mental ill-health, addiction and recovery (Campbell 2005).

Recovery in mental health circles has some similarities to that in dependency circles, but there are some differences too. Recovery in mental health has increasingly come to mean social recovery, not clinical recovery. This means that individuals can come to live a life they value that integrates their 'mad' experiences rather than cures or removes them. In effect, someone could still be coping with the experience of hearing voices but work towards a job, being in education and having a family and a social life. The recovery movement began as a user-led form of activism that questioned the pessimistic models of chronicity that were advanced in medically dominated psychiatric services. Stories emerged that people can be in severe distress without that typifying their lifelong trajectory, and often such recovery stories were in spite of the help that was on offer from services. In fact, for many ex-service users, they refer to themselves as survivors, not beneficiaries, of mental health services. Pilgrim (2014) notes some problems of the notion of recovery in mental health:

1. There is no agreed, final and consensual definition of recovery shared by all the stakeholders whom it affects.
2. Therefore, it is a 'polyvalent' concept meaning different things to different people (although we also note that different meanings do not simply correspond to different levels of influence in advancing certain meanings) and can be said to be a 'working misunderstanding' (2014:234).
3. Different notions of recovery have emphasis at different points, although there is a consistent affiliation between the user movement and social movements in the disability activism field.
4. Mental health problems vary, hence the difficulties in definition and operationalizing practices.
5. If a client does not value the notion of recovery or does not recover by the locally understood definition, what is to be done?
6. The notion of recovery still tends towards an individualized conception locating the process in self-responsibility, functional improvement and self-management, which fails to account for socio-political influences on well-being.

Given that there is little firm agreement on what recovery is, how best to describe or define it (Davidson & Roe 2007), there is little agreement on how to assess if it is happening (Law et al. 2012). It is probably best understood, for the time being, in a few ways:

- an ethos that informs the intentions and activities of services and practitioners;
- a model that understands why stigma, iatrogenic risk and domineering models act counter to recovery;
- a civil rights movement that promotes the ideas that madness is part of human experience and need not preclude a valued life to be lived. To do otherwise is a form of 'racism' (Foucault 2003) that permits the mistreatment and marginalization of a social subgroup based on the presumption of some form of inferiority or pathology.

Therapeutic communities

There are numerous residential rehabilitation programmes (sometimes called 'therapeutic communities'), which are usually long-term programmes where clients voluntarily live and work in a community of other substance users, ex-users and professional staff (Jhanjee 2014). Such programmes can last up to 24 months.

The aim of residential rehabilitation programmes is to help clients develop the skills and attitudes to make long-term changes towards a substance-free lifestyle. From our experience of working in different therapeutic communities, we have noted that while they can be beneficial to those with dual diagnosis, at times being substance abstinent can trigger psychological distress because subjective experiences are no longer 'masked'. Although the literature for the effectiveness of therapeutic communities is sparse, clients we have worked with who engage with these communities highlight their positive benefits in psychoeducation and maintaining sobriety. However, sometimes, after spending a long time in such communities, on returning to ordinary life some clients can find it difficult to readjust and consequently relapse.

We have noted some research outcomes that compared clients with a dual diagnosis in community to those in hospital care: one-year outcomes and health care utilization and costs (Timko et al. 2006). Below, the results of this research highlight some benefits and challenges of community treatment approaches.

- Dually diagnosed patients who were followed up for one year had better substance use outcomes when they were initially assigned to community rather than to hospital acute care.
- Patients assigned to hospital care had shorter index stays, but these index stays were more costly than were the longer index stays of patients assigned to community care.
- Patients assigned to hospital care also had more mental health visits, and more costly mental health follow-up stays, over the study year.
- Moderate-severity dual diagnosis patients were treated more effectively in community-based programmes.
- Compared to hospital-based programmes, community programmes may have had treatment environments emphasizing personal responsibility such that moderately ill patients responded by decreasing their substance misuse.
- Moderately ill patients in hospital programmes also had more costly mental health follow-up stays over the study year than for treatment in community.

The findings in Timko et al.'s (2006) research, which evidence that hospital care was more expensive and did not yield better outcomes, agrees with the reports on a randomized trial and cost and cost-effectiveness study of hospital versus residential crisis care for patients who have serious mental illness by Fenton et al. (1998, 2002) and also sits alongside the research presented on case management in Chapter 4. These results extend previous work with dual diagnosis patients by demonstrating the effectiveness of community care in the substance use domain, and that it is as effective in the psychiatric domain as hospital care for this population, when service intensity is the same in both locations (Timko et al. 2006). Mancini et al. (2008) suggest that even while knowing the advantages of community residential care over hospital inpatient care (i.e. that outcomes are better for most clients receiving residential care), policymakers may shun community residential treatment because its costs are typically higher than those for outpatient services.

Having cited the different community approaches and their strengths, it is clear that for some clients, engagement with services is not about abstinence but harm reduction, and for some it's a way of practitioners empowering them to self-manage. The following section explores components of harm reduction in the context of the community. Harm reduction was mentioned briefly in Chapter 4 as a perspective within wider delivery of care and support.

Integration of harm reduction and recovery-oriented practices

Harm reduction intersects with mental health recovery in the areas of empowerment, supportive relationships, pragmatic risk management and access to resources within the community. Interventions that help clients to identify goals while cultivating their ability to target resources and skills to manage psychiatric symptoms and substance use are tenets of both mental health recovery and harm reduction (Mancini et al. 2008).

As we have noted throughout this book, clients with dual diagnoses need to be equipped and empowered to help themselves when they face severe challenges. This can be done through treatment and lapse/relapse plans, which include targeting and addressing harmful behaviours such as higher-risk drug using behaviours (needle sharing, inhaling or 'huffing' solvents), trading unprotected sex for drugs/money, or using bill-paying or grocery money to purchase drugs (Mancini et al. 2008). Practitioners working with clients with dual disorders can tailor treatment and psychosocial interventions to include psychoeducational sessions on the intersections of psychiatric symptoms, substance use and medications. This will empower clients by enabling them to make more informed choices about their substance use and impact on mental health or vice versa.

Assertive intensive community treatment and recovery approaches enable the integration of the principles of harm reduction and recovery, although this may not be consistent with the aspirations of service user activists. These recovery approaches offer an alternative to inpatient services, and through 'empowering clients' to be their own self-managers in their recovery and mental well-being, practitioners can focus on being supportive rather than prescriptive. A client's level of community engagement/non-engagement can also be a tool that practitioners use to gauge the client's level of commitment to change or indeed deterioration in her or his motivation. It should be noted that clients who are highly dependent on drugs, and express no intention to change, and who are currently engaging in behaviours that pose an imminent risk of serious harm to self or others, may benefit from interventions that are more focused on abstinence and safety, such as hospitalization or admission to inpatient professionally supported treatment services (Mancini et al. 2008).

Critics of such approaches would see that self-management is another form of self-control as advocated by the state. In Foucault's (1975) *Discipline and Punish* there is a description of a panopticon which was viewed as the idea form of physical structure for prisons. The panoptic notion was that cells were in direct view at all times by a central tower, but that view was not reciprocated. Prisoners could see that they might be observed at any moment of their day, but could not know for sure because they could not see inside the tower. Foucault suggests that this had the effect of inducing prisoners towards internalizing the prison guard observer by imagining their surveillance throughout the day. The upshot was that prisoners learned to self-censure and so the intervention ran into the prisoner's psyche, altering their conduct, their motivation and their behaviour through this process of internalizing the guard (also referred to in some ways as subjectivization, wherein the person becomes a subject). Critics of the self-management movement in service provision see a similar process at play – the aim is to increase compliance within the norms of acceptable social conduct through self-limiting internal discourse. Foucault takes this up further throughout his oeuvre as he develops ideas of what he comes to call 'governmentality'.

The social model of disability: rights of access

The social model of disability (SMD), as described in Chapter 3, is one predicated on gaining access to ordinary community resources. It is apparent that the SMD is rarely applied in understanding issues of dependency (despite the codification of addiction within psychiatry and medicine, and the use of disease model thinking in movements such as AA) because it is conveyed in terms of deviant consumerist substance use and antisocial non-participation. However, mental health and dual diagnosis, because of its inclusion in psychiatric diagnosis, is increasingly being seen in disability terms. To recap, the SMD perceives that impairment, physical, sensory or psychological, is poorly treated in social context, and also in processes, such as access to a job market. The SMD expects that attitudes and environments accommodate and adapt to the range of people who may be present, and to not do so continues the disabling exclusion. Even though the SMD has been around in the UK since the 1970s, Beresford (2005) writes that at that point of publication, there was no comparable model applied in mental health.

For practitioners, students and scholars considering dual diagnosis, the SMD can be a useful point for thinking about improving the lives of people we see. As we noted in Chapter 3, there are some critiques that question the underlying mechanisms of a disease or illness model in understanding mental ill-health and distress. That might look like a problem for the SMD because there is no clear impairment that underpins the social exclusion that follows. However, practitioners can work on exclusion predicated on the presumption of an underlying impairment, and so they can advocate on behalf of their clients; get access to independent access; support and encourage self-mobilization, self-advocacy and activism; and acknowledge the importance of political action. Clearly, as a professional and an employee, some of these activities would be at odds to the employing organization's activities or priorities, which may feel like a difficult place to be for the supportive worker. However, at the minimum, the ethical practitioner should not obstruct the activism of clients who are attempting to embrace their agency, and to exercise their power, and they should not pathologize resistance and conflict as being commensurable with psychological dysfunction. If we can learn one thing from service user activism it is that when services and local bodies do not respect the priorities and concerns of the service user, the service users may use a number of strategies to discredit them (Friedman & Beckwith 2014).

We conclude here with a box which summarizes some good practice points.

Key practice points

- Dual diagnosis is a community issue, even if many services still operate with the individual as their main focus.
- In order to effectively support clients within the community, staff need to have a strong commitment to developing knowledge and skills in relation to mental health, substance misuse and dual diagnosis.
- Dual diagnosis teams should be proactive rather than reactive, and engage service providers and service users assertively, e.g. through liaison clinics, home visits (or seeing people in a place of their choice), spending time on inpatient units and collaborating with community teams.
- It is important to develop a specialist team which has clearly defined responsibilities, otherwise highly skilled staff end up getting pulled into doing routine tasks.
- Where possible, client involvement in training and group work should be included because this reaps enormous benefits for other clients in terms of peer support and modelling.
- As a team, identify opportunities for maximizing and supporting community and recovery approaches, then offer a wide range of interventions including harm reduction and clear pathways for inpatient/residential service for those that need intensive support (detox or rehabilitation).
- Ensure that you access continued professional development and training.
- Engage in ongoing supervision for the dual diagnosis caseload you work with.
- Update and use evidence-based evaluation data and tools from assessment to evaluating interventions.
- Consider the benefits of concurrent models such as the social model of disability.

Key messages:

It is important for the practitioner to be aware of the following:

- There is a diverse range of lived experiences documented by practitioners and by professionals working in the community with clients who have dual diagnoses. These include challenges that professionals face with clients' lack of motivation and the complexity of conducting assessments with clients who have dual diagnoses. Awareness of these lived experiences and challenges could help practitioners identify areas that they need to work on in order to be competent practitioners.
- Awareness of the components of recovery, and of the recovery movement within the community and the diverse groups and programmes available in different settings, is important because this empowers clients on their recovery journey.
- The importance of the integration of harm reduction and recovery-oriented practices is highlighted in this chapter because these help clients be self-empowered and access resources within the community.

REFERENCES

Aram, L. (Ed.) (2007). *Dual Diagnosis: Good Practice Handbook*. London: Turning Point.

Beresford, P. (2005). Social approaches to madness and distress. In Tew, J. (Ed.) *Social Perspectives in Mental Health: Developing Social Models to Understand and Work with Mental Distress*. London: Jessica Kingsley Publishers.

Campbell, J. (2005). The historical and philosophical development of peer-run support programs. In Clay, S., Schell, B., Corrigan, P., & Ralph, R.O. (Eds) *On Our Own, Together: Peer Programs for People with Mental Illness*. Nashville, TN: Vanderbilt University Press.

Coombes, L., & Wratten, A. (2007). The lived experience of community mental health nurses working with people who have dual diagnosis: A phenomenological study. *Journal of Psychiatric & Mental Health Nursing*, 14(4), 382–392.

Davidson, L., & Roe, D. (2007). Recovery from versus recovery in serious mental illness: One strategy for lessening confusion plaguing recovery. *Journal of Mental Health*, 16(4), 459–470.

Day, E. (Ed.) (2013). *Routes to Recovery via the Community: Mapping User Manual*. London: Public Health England. <http://www.scie-socialcareonline.org.uk/routes-to-recovery-via-the-community-mapping-user-manual/r/a11G0000003225tIAA>.

Fenton, W.S., Hoch, J.S., Herrell, J.M., Mosher, L., & Dixon, L. (2002). Cost and cost-effectiveness of hospital vs. residential crisis care for patients who have serious mental illness. *Archives of General Psychiatry*, 59, 357–364.

Fenton, W.S., Mosher, L.R., Herrell, J.M., & Blyler, C.R. (1998). Randomized trial of general hospital and residential alternative care for patients with severe and persistent mental illness. *American Journal of Psychiatry*, 155, 516–522.

Foucault, M (1975). *Discipline and Punish*: The Birth of the Prison. London: Penguin.

Foucault, M. (2003). *Abnormal: Lectures at the Collège De France 1974–1975*. New York: Picador.

Friedman, M., & Beckwith, R. (2014). Self-advocacy: The emancipation movement led by people with intellectual and developmental disabilities. In Ben-Moshe, L., Chapman, C., & Carey, A.C. (Eds) *Disability Incarcerated: Imprisonment and Disability in the United States and Canada*. New York: Palgrave Macmillan.

Jhanjee, S. (2014). Evidence based psychosocial interventions in substance use. *Indian Journal of Psychological Medicine*, 36(2), 112–118.

Krentzman, A.R. (2013). Review of the application of positive psychology to substance use, addiction, and recovery research. *Psychology of Addictive Behaviors*, 27(1), 151–165.

Law, H., Morrison, A., Byrne, R., & Hodson, E. (2012). Recovery from psychosis: A user informed review of self-report for measuring recovery. *Journal of Mental Health*, 21(2), 193–208.

Mancini, M.A., Hardiman, E.R., & Eversman, M.H. (2008). A review of the compatibility of harm-reduction and recovery-oriented best practices for dual disorders. *Best Practice in Mental Health*, 4(2), 99–113.

Pilgrim, D. (2014). Recovery and mental health policy. In Taylor, P., Corteen, K., & Morley, S. (Eds) *A Companion to Criminal Justice, Mental Health & Risk*. Bristol: Policy Press.

Timko, C., Chen, S., Sempel, J., & Barnett, P. (2006). Dual diagnosis patients in community or hospital care: One-year outcomes and health care utilization and costs. *Journal of Mental Health*, 15(2), 163–177.

Valentine, P. (2011). Peer-based recovery support services within a recovery community organization: The CCAR experience. In Kelly, J.F., & White, W.L. (Eds) *Addiction Recovery Management: Theory, Research and Practice*. New York: Springer.

White, W.L., Kelly, J.F., & Roth, J.D. (2012). New addiction recovery support institutions: Mobilizing support beyond professional addiction treatment and recovery mutual aid. *Journal of Groups in Addiction & Recovery*, 7, 297–317.

Conclusion

The aim of this book is to orientate the practitioner working in health and social care, statutory or third sector, to the most helpful ways of thinking and doing work with people with problems that arise out of the label *dual diagnosis*. We are also hoping that this book contributes to the critical discourse and learning in the field, and so it may well be appealing to scholars and learners alike. In this final chapter we will summarise where we have travelled and leave the reader with some further points for thought. Figure C.1 below summarises the ground we have covered.

Figure C.1 The stratification of intervention in dual diagnosis, mental health and substance use

Why is this stratification important? As we set out from the start we are hopeful about the interventions that practitioners can offer in reducing distress and helping people to reconnect with lives that they value. However, we are questioning about the extent to which this is likely to result in the wide and lasting changes necessary for people to be less in distress and therefore to be less likely to combine their distress with unhelpful substance use (although in the short term the substance user often offers alleviation through numbing or an altered state).

Wilkinson and Pickett (2009) caused a stir with their book *The Spirit Level: Why Equality is Better for Everyone* because of how it correlated a number of measures and arrived at a picture of ill-health that runs counter to conceptions of the wellness of post-industrial capitalist democracy that we have at present. They consistently found, on a number of measures of health, two things: firstly, they established a link between poverty and ill-health. Secondly, they established that health outcomes were consistently poorer in societies with greater levels of inequality, of which the UK is one. Using World Health Organisation criteria they found that 'anxiety disorders, impulse-control disorders and severe illness are all strongly correlated with inequality' (2009:68).

This seems to underpin to a large extent our stratification, that the socio-political conditions for well-being are commensurate with a drive towards equality, which in turn will involve reducing the gap between the top 'haves' and the bottom 'have-nots'. The DoH (2002) states that

> substance use is usual rather than exceptional amongst people with severe mental health problems and the relationship between the two is complex. Individuals with these dual problems deserve high quality, patient focused and integrated care. This should be delivered within mental health services. This policy is referred to as 'mainstreaming'. (2002:4)

So we have a tension in our stratification – there is a possibility that dual diagnoses have little to do with individual pathologies, but as much, or, if not, more, to do with the social conditions of the time. However, we fail to see any clinical guidance that recommends political or economic reform other than that which calls for more resources for treatment approaches. Evidence-based practice should demand reform given the findings of *The Spirit Level*. The process of locating ills within individuals on the basis of presumed psychopathology has been called *subjectivisation, psychologising* or *psychiatrisation* and it is an established response to behaviours that are not valued, or that bring into question the powerful, current norms of a given developed society. We have a further conundrum; while the DoH (2002) guidance does in fact note the frequency of dual diagnosis issues, it, and other guidance texts, comes to treat dual diagnosis as a specialism within service areas rather than the stuff of routine practice. This is not unique to dual diagnosis; Neria et al. (2002) found high numbers of service users reported traumatic experience, and in our experience, trauma is often seen as an issue requiring specialist input and therapy. Similar to the issues seen in dual diagnosis, the 'symptoms' of trauma are confused with psychosis, and are misdiagnosed and the relationship between trauma and mental health is complex and 'chicken and egg' (Mollon 1996). It is the case that some of the most common experiences met in the mental health field are paradoxically seen as some of the most specialist.

If we take all this together, what we have is a sense that socio-economic and political factors have a strong, it seems, causal or maintenance relationship with distress, substance use and general ill-health; however, interventions are located at the level of the individual. If this is correct, then we are treating at the wrong end of the stratification. Part I of this book describes and critiques what we believe to be the necessary conditions to arrive at the idea that someone in 2014 has a dual diagnosis which is treated through ameliorating their distress and training them out of their maladaptive habits. We suggest therefore that, taking Foucault's lead, some of the best ways to understand dual diagnosis are to see it in terms of an archaeology of discourse which

> refers to an account not so much of the truth of the claims of psychiatry [or any dominant discourse] and its earlier iterations, but to the conditions and

contingencies that allowed psychiatry and psychology to position themselves
as disciplines, and be able to make certain statements about madness that can
only be made if certain social, legal, practical and political conditions are such'
(Penson 2014:130)

It may feel that the practitioner in mental health services, facing the mainstreaming of a
client with complex substance use and mental health issues, is distant from such mechanisms; but they are not. The terms of a *psychiatrising* discourse require multiple points of
action and so can involve multiple points of resistance. It is not as simple as promulgating an
authoritative, stated point of view; that is, that dual diagnosis is something to be treated in
the individual. It is also necessary to get services and practitioners to undertake the activities
commensurate with that statement position. Understandably, all practitioners will want to
do the best they can for their clients and so the socio-politics of dual diagnosis may feel a
world apart from everyday practice. But we have seen clearly outlined in Chapter 4, in regard
to the Care Programme Approach and similar administrative systems, that despite a number
of government directives, practitioners and service areas, intentionally or not, did not 'play
ball'. It is also the case that there was a misinterpretation of the US data on intensive case
management. We believe that this fosters a hope that in a political system that seems to be
at odds with the needs of the citizens it is there to serve, and in services, clients they see and
serve, doing something different is an option, and working with the most ethical interests in
mind is also possible.

One final thought on the socio-politics of dual diagnosis and the associated areas is that
in the UK almost all practitioners will also be voters. They will all be represented at a local
level by a member of parliament and by local councillors; many will also be members of
trade unions and professional bodies which consult their members. To be a good employee
is important in making sure one secures lasting employment, and there are avenues of
communication that mean that the issues that are dear to us, law and social policy that
are going through parliament, can also be influenced by your view not as a clinician but
as a citizen.

The second half of the book accepts the premise that most service provision is at the level
of the individual and sometimes with their families. We have set out a rubric for how this
should begin:

1. Workers supporting someone with problems around a dual diagnosis should invest in
   building a sound therapeutic alliance, within current care arrangements like CPA, with
   reference to sound risk management, which, where possible, works to the aspirations and
   goals of the client.
2. Workers and clients benefit from collaborating on their work together, which makes
   therapy more of an adult learning model; in many ways more so than a treatment
   approach (Chadwick 2006). Clients can benefit by clear dialogue about how the clinician/
   practitioner views their problems and having that articulated as a joint formulation to
   work together on and within.
3. Specific models conceive dual diagnosis issues in different ways which may variably
   appeal, or not, to the practitioner and client both. All models require the involvement of
   the client and do benefit from finding ways to activate motivation towards change.

4. Many of these models are delivered in one-to-one work meetings but they seem to be advantageous in other modalities such as group and family work too.
5. While service delivery has over decades become mostly community based, this may not be with community development in mind. Irrespective of the level of the intervention (individual through to community) the practitioner contends with issues of access, and the social model of disability can be enabling in addressing this.

What we have not covered are some allied areas that would take a significant further contribution. For instance, we have mentioned briefly criminal justice issues in practice and there is considerable concern for offender and prison populations in terms of mental health and substance use. This dovetails with another population, those of forensic psychiatric patients. It seems that it can be arbitrary as to whether a given person ends up being seen in one service context, or another, but when distress is combined with substance use issues, by dint of their illicit status, we start to see criminal justice involvement. Ben-Moshe et al. (2014) illustrate extensively how, in the US, there is a carceral system predicated on the inter-relationship of the disciplines with institutions including education, health and criminal justice. This is a long-standing relationship dating back to the seventeenth century (Foucault 1978) and has since become further entwined with the interests of industry.

So, this leaves us at the point of really considering what is of most importance in dual diagnosis practice. Without a doubt we believe that practitioners should:

1. Have a sound value base that promotes an optimistic and recovery-based outlook
2. That they take the time to conference and consult with those who are like-minded to form effective and supportive communities of practice
3. Take opportunities to influence service development and direction with the client's needs, hopes and health in mind, which is likely to involve taking some positive risks
4. Make the most of contacts with students and new staff to influence their thinking along progressive lines and to support them away from models of chronicity and pessimism
5. To take the opportunities for mature reflection that good supervision offers and continuing professional development (CPD) to see sharpening skills as an on-going process.

And finally, to hold their clients in esteem as fellow people with all the flaws and possibilities that any of us have, and understand that some life experience, some social and material conditions, are likely to severely reduce the effectiveness of even the most enduring efforts to 'get on'. People do not like being in such pain and distress, the like of which we see in services, and so they may take actions to alleviate it.

Glossary of Key Terms

Contingency management: A set of techniques that focus on changing specified client behaviours.

Dual diagnosis: Commonly understood to be when a person has a diagnosable mental health problem and concurrent substance use problem. This term has also been used to denote a mental health problem with a coexisting learning difficulty.

Formulation: A working hypothesis which guides (or may even prescribe) interventions. The formulation may provide causal links between aspects of the client's emotions, experience and behaviour, enabling the practitioner/team to come up with possible treatment plans.

Governmentality: A term coined by Foucault to describe the 'conduct of conduct', which denotes the systems and methods by which people are induced to self-manage.

Harm reduction: A model of treatment particularly used when clients are not ready for abstinence. In this model of working, focus is on the client reducing negative effects of substance abuse, without necessarily having to abstain from using entirely.

Medical model: The presumption that certain forms of deviant behaviour and distress are expressions of an underlying medical complaint that can be treated.

Neo liberalism: Can be described as a political and economic model within capitalism that promotes free market economics within all areas of society.

Objects: A psychoanalytic concept in which the word 'objects' refers to people, parts of people, or physical objects that symbolically represent either a person or part of a person.

Psychiatrization: The process by which a steadily growing emphasis is placed on a wide range of experiences as psychopathological, with psychiatric disciplines being key to assessing and ameliorating this.

Psychoactive substance: Also called 'psychoactive drug' and is any chemical substance that when taken alters the mood, perception or mental state of the user. These substances can either be legal or prohibited by government.

Psychological model: Presumes that distress and problems arise out of problems in thinking and feeling, for instance the meaning we give to events and troubling memories.

Psychosocial: The idea that there is an integrated way of viewing a service user's experience that draws on psychological and social perspectives and often within an implied, if not stated, 'bio' component.

Recovery: In dual diagnosis, recovery has come increasingly to mean social recovery, not clinical recovery. This means that individuals can come to live a meaningful and satisfying life, as defined by themselves, in the presence or absence of symptoms.

Repetition compulsion: A psychodynamic concept which refers to the way individuals repeat unpleasant experiences which they would have experienced in past primary relationships.

Social model of disability: The shift to understanding that impairment does not preclude full participation but rather attitudes and environments do.

Strengths–based approach: A case management approach where the focus is on clients' strengths and their capacity to learn, grow and change rather than on their problems.

Therapeutic community: Refers to a community of individuals working a structured therapeutic intervention to address or explore issues relating to substance use or mental health.

Index